Implementing the ESL Standards for Pre-K–12 Students Through Teacher Education

Marguerite Ann Snow, Editor

TESOL

Founded 1966

Teachers of English to Speakers of Other Languages, Inc.

Typeset in Cochin and Helvetica Condensed
by Capitol Communication Systems, Inc., Crofton, Maryland USA
and printed by
Pantagraph Printing, Bloomington, Illinois USA

Teachers of English to Speakers of Other Languages, Inc.
700 South Washington Street, Suite 200
Alexandria, Virginia 22314 USA
Tel. 703-836-0774 • Fax 703-836-7864 • E-mail tesol@tesol.edu •
http://www.tesol.edu/

Director of Communications and Marketing: Helen Kornblum
Managing Editor: Marilyn Kupetz
Copy Editor: Ellen Garshick
Cover Design: Ann Kammerer

ISBN 0-939791-82-X
Library of Congress Catalogue No. 99-076451

Contents

Introduction

■ The ESL Standards: A Brief Background

The publication of *ESL Standards for Pre-K–12 Students* (TESOL, 1997) cast the educational spotlight on the historically marginalized but fastest growing population of school-age children in the United States—those who come from non-English home backgrounds. The demographics are staggering. The number of limited English proficient students in the United States increased 109% from 1985 to 1995, and estimates were that by the year 2000 the majority of the school-age population in 50 or more U.S. cities would come from language minority backgrounds.

Despite these changing demographics, ESL was not included in the 1994 educational reform legislation authorizing the development of standards for major areas of the K–12 curriculum. As drafts of the standards from the other subject areas began to circulate, it became clear that the standards being developed, including those for English, did not address the special needs of second language (L2) learners. Thus, in 1994, the professional organization Teachers of English to Speakers of Other Languages (TESOL) created a task force to develop a conceptual framework upon which ESL standards could be based and, ultimately, to prepare standards appropriate for English language learners. After a 3-year, largely volunteer effort by TESOL professionals from across the United States, *ESL Standards for Pre-K–12 Students* was published in 1997.

ESL Standards specifies three goals for L2 learners: (a) to use English to communicate in social settings; (b) to use English to achieve academically in all content areas; and (c) to use English in socially and culturally appropriate ways. *ESL Standards* addresses beginning, intermediate, and advanced proficiency levels in English as well as the needs of students with limited formal schooling. The three goals and nine standards are presented in chart form on p. x.

■ Implementing the ESL Standards Through Teacher Education

The education of L2 students is one of the most compelling challenges currently facing U.S. schools. Initiatives that ban instruction in students' primary language make the effective implementation of the ESL standards even more critical. Moreover, the content standards developed in the disciplines, though important and useful, do not provide educators with the strategies they need to assist ESOL learners because these standards assume students can understand English and use it to engage content material. In fact, many of the content standards developed in the disciplines do not even acknowledge the central role of language in understanding content.

ESL Standards for Pre-K–12 Students provides the first national guidelines aimed at assisting educators in addressing the specific instructional needs of ESOL students, who must acquire a new language and at the same time learn academic content. This volume carries this important work one step further by focusing on teacher education.

The volume has been designed with teachers-in-training, hereafter referred to as teacher learners, and practicing teachers in mind, both in ESL and in the content areas, who are enrolled in credential/licensure/certification programs and MA programs in U.S. colleges and universities. Faculty and providers of technical assistance to school districts will also find the volume useful for in-service teacher development. Written by experienced ESL teachers and teacher educators who played key roles in TESOL's Standards and Assessment Project, the volume also attempts to link the various materials produced in the project, with particular emphasis on integrating instruction and assessment.

■ To the Teacher Educator

The book has multiple purposes; the organization of the volume is, therefore, somewhat unusual. In an attempt to create a useful resource for both teacher educators and teacher learners, the book begins with a prologue, "Incorporating *ESL Standards* Into Teacher Education: Ideas for Teacher Educators," which speaks specifically to the teacher educator. It describes the role of the teacher educator in standards-based educational reform and suggests a variety of activities that can be undertaken using resources developed in the ESL standards project. The prologue is replete with practical ideas and activities for using *ESL Standards* in various courses within teacher education programs, including theoretical or foundational courses, instructional and assessment methods courses, field experiences such as student teaching, and culminating experiences like final projects and examinations. To take advantage of the suggested activities, users of the volume will need access to TESOL's various standards publications, in particular *ESL Standards for Pre-K–12 Students*.

As mentioned, the writing team created this volume with several different audiences in mind. Teacher educators can adopt it as a course text in both credential/licensure courses and graduate-level MA programs in a variety of disciplines. It is particularly suitable for courses in MA programs in ESL/TESOL, English, language arts, and reading. As it is our deep conviction that teachers across all content areas must understand the special instructional needs of L2 students, we encourage teacher educators in disciplines such as mathematics, science, and social studies to incorporate readings from this volume into their courses as well.

■ To the Preservice or In-Service Teacher

To meet the needs of prospective teachers and teachers already in the field, chapters 1–8 provide necessary reading for all teachers working with linguistically and culturally diverse students in U.S. schools. These chapters present the theory and research on which the ESL standards are based and applications to curriculum development and assessment. Specifically, they treat the following topics in order to prepare teachers well for effective standards-based instruction and assessment:

- diversity in ESL student populations and the different educational programs in which these students are typically placed (chapter 1)

- the standards reform movement as backdrop to the development of the ESL standards (chapter 2)

- relevant research in first and second language acquisition that supports a view of language as a cognitive, social, cultural, and academic activity (chapter 3)

- application of the ESL standards to curriculum development, with examples of the different paths districts and states have taken in curriculum development and standards implementation (chapter 4)

- historical and current trends in testing and measurement and a conceptual model for standards-based assessment (chapter 5)

- implications of standards-based instruction for large-scale assessment of ESOL students using standardized tests (chapter 6)

- approaches to assessment of ESOL students by teachers at the classroom level (chapter 7)

- a framework for dissemination of the ESL standards and suggestions for ways teachers can advocate for standards implementation (chapter 8)

Each chapter of the book contains tasks designed to assist readers in delving deeper into the topics and applying the concepts to actual instructional settings. To undertake many of the tasks, readers will need to refer to sections of *ESL Standards for Pre-K–12 Students*. The volume also includes a glossary of terms and a comprehensive list of references in an attempt to be a rich resource to teachers. Taken together, the information in this volume gives teachers the necessary background to work effectively with linguistically and culturally diverse populations in U.S. public schools.

Acknowledgments

I am particularly grateful to Dona Mitoma, librarian at Pasadena City College and recent TESOL MA graduate of California State University, Los Angeles. She applied a librarian's eye for detail to the book's many citations and provided valuable feedback on chapter drafts from a student's perspective. I applaud the foresight of the TESOL Board of Directors and Helen Kornblum in recognizing the role of teacher education in standards implementation and give thanks to Marilyn Kupetz and Ellen Garshick for their expert editorial assistance. Special thanks go to the talented writing team. Their skill in applying their extensive experience in developing the ESL standards to a volume committed to training teachers for standards-based instruction and assessment is impressive.

Marguerite Ann Snow, Editor
California State University, Los Angeles

ESL STANDARDS FOR PRE-K–12 STUDENTS

Goal 1: To Use English to Communicate in Social Settings

Standard 1: Students will use English to participate in social interaction.

Standard 2: Students will interact in, through, and with spoken and written English for personal expression and enjoyment.

Standard 3: Students will use learning strategies to extend their communicative competence.

Goal 2: To Use English to Achieve Academically in All Content Areas

Standard 1: Students will use English to interact in the classroom.

Standard 2: Students will use English to obtain, process, construct, and provide subject matter information in spoken and written form.

Standard 3: Students will use appropriate learning strategies to construct and apply academic knowledge.

Goal 3: To Use English in Socially and Culturally Appropriate Ways

Standard 1: Students will use the appropriate language variety, register, and genre according to audience, purpose, and setting.

Standard 2: Students will use nonverbal communication appropriate to audience, purpose, and setting.

Standard 3: Students will use appropriate learning strategies to extend their sociolinguistic and sociocultural competence.

Source: TESOL (1997, pp. 9–10).

Incorporating *ESL Standards* Into Teacher Education Programs: Ideas for Teacher Educators

Nancy Cloud

The recent educational reform efforts in the United States, of which the development of *ESL Standards for Pre-K–12 Students* (TESOL, 1997) is clearly a part, focus on improving curriculum and instruction and the assessment of students. By identifying the characteristics of high-quality pre-K–12 ESL programs, *ESL Standards* makes an important contribution to the field. But the contribution of teacher educators to ensuring the delivery of high-quality programs to ESOL learners is equally important, for without knowledgeable and competent teachers, the attainment of the goals in *ESL Standards* is unlikely. The fundamental interdependence of the standards set for students and those set for their teachers has been acknowledged by key reform groups, most notably the National Commission on Teaching and America's Future (NCTAF, 1996), which concludes, "the single most important strategy for achieving America's educational goals is to recruit, prepare, and retain excellent teachers for every school" (as cited in Bradley, 1996, n.p.).

This prologue describes how teacher educators can use *ESL Standards* in their work with teacher learners throughout the professional education program and beyond, whether in comprehensive teacher preparation programs or in continuing education. It provides teacher educators with practical ideas and identifies resources to support their work with current and future teachers. These ideas and resources include ways to use technology to foster awareness and ways to implement the standards competently and apply them to diverse populations, two mandates emphasized by teacher education accreditation agencies.

To frame the discussion, I begin with some general considerations for teacher educators who want to link their work to current educational reform efforts using standards specifically designed for this purpose. I then offer suggestions and resources for applying the ESL standards in theoretical courses; in instructional methodology and assessment courses; during field experiences; and in qualifying examinations, final projects, and research.

■ General Considerations in Incorporating Standards Into Professional Development Programs

On Standards and Teacher Preparedness

According to the NCTAF (1996), standards are a tool that students and teachers can use to improve the outcomes of schooling in the United States. Among the commission's major recommendations is that teacher education and professional development programs be organized around standards for students and teachers. Macdonald (1997) has captured the interrelationship among the quality of professional development provided to teachers, its effect on instructional programs provided to students, and ultimately the effects these two forces exert on the educational outcomes obtained (see Figure 1). The performance of a hypothetical student, Ana, depends on the quality of the instructional program provided to her, and that quality can be ensured only if her teachers know what second language (L2) learners should know and be able to do as a result of high-quality ESL instruction (of course, taking into account Ana's learning history and learning characteristics). In turn, Ana's teachers can create high-quality instructional programs only if they have received high-quality professional preparation that gives them the knowledge and skills necessary to teach and assess well. Thus, Ana's performance is only the tip of an iceberg, the base of which rests on high-quality and ongoing professional development for teachers.

Two sets of standards, those of the National Council for Accreditation of Teacher Education (NCATE, 1995) and of the National Board for Professional Teaching Standards (NBPTS, 1998), are both aimed at reforming the quality of preparation received by teachers like Ana's.

The NCATE standards (1995) ask that teacher education pro-

INTERRELATIONSHIP BETWEEN STANDARDS FOR STUDENTS AND STANDARDS FOR TEACHERS

Ana's performance (as shown in a work sample evaluated with a teacher-made rubric) . . .

Assessment standards

. . . depends on the quality of the instructional program provided to Ana (based on what Ana knows and can do in relation to the content standards), . . .

Content standards

. . . which depends on the quality of professional development provided to Ana's teacher.

Professional teaching standards

Source: Adapted from a figure by Maritza B. Macdonald, Community School District 10, Bronx, New York, summer 1997.

grams be derived from conceptual frameworks that are "knowledge based, articulated, shared, and coherent" (p. 17). In this regard, *ESL Standards for Pre-K–12 Students* is an important contribution to those constructing or implementing teacher preparation programs because it articulates the knowledge base that undergirds high-quality ESL programs (see TESOL, 1997; chapters 3, 4 in this volume).

NCATE (1995) further requires that "teacher candidates acquire and learn to apply the professional and pedagogical knowledge and skills to become competent to work with all students" and create meaningful learning experiences for them (Standards ID and E, pp.

17–18). The ESL standards were designed with diverse ESOL learners in mind, integrating references to students with limited formal schooling and special education needs throughout the document, not as an afterthought or prefatory statement. *ESL Standards* defines high-quality ESL instruction; the vignettes and discussion sections that follow each of the standards, presented by grade-level clusters, portray meaningful learning experiences in classrooms. In short, the standards represent best practices for teaching all ESOL learners.

The NBPTS's *English as a New Language Standards for National Board Certification* (1998) outlines 12 standards for teachers seeking NBPTS certification in English as a new language. With regard to the knowledge base needed by ESL teachers, the document mentions four areas: (a) knowledge of students, (b) knowledge of language development, (c) knowledge of culture, and (d) knowledge of their subject matter. In terms of advancing students' learning, the standards specify that teachers should be able to provide meaningful learning experiences, understand that there are multiple paths to knowledge, use instructional resources effectively, create positive learning environments, and employ a variety of assessment methods to understand students' needs. Finally, the NBPTS wants teachers to reflect on their practice, establish strong linkages with families, and provide professional leadership in their schools.

Successful implementation of the ESL standards depends upon these very abilities in teachers. At the same time, the ESL standards directly contribute to the field's understanding of highly accomplished teaching practice by articulating a shared and coherent set of goals and standards for student learning, establishing a vision of effective education for ESOL students, listing principles on which to build high-quality instructional programs, challenging erroneous teacher beliefs and negative attitudes that undermine the effectiveness of programs, and portraying effective teaching practice in diverse classroom settings. Thus, teacher educators who seek to reform educational practice for ESOL learners in the nation's schools must understand and capitalize on the dynamic relationship between standards for teaching and standards for students.

A pyramid similar to the one in Figure 1 can be used to portray this dynamic interaction. At the base would be standards such as those articulated by NCATE (1995) and NBPTS (1998); in the center would be *ESL Standards for Pre-K–12 Students*, standards in other content disciplines, or both; and at the pinnacle would be the resultant student performance: the degree to which individual students attain the standards as measured by valid assessments.

Information on the student and teacher standards noted in this section is available on the World Wide Web (see Table 1). Although the standards documents can be obtained through traditional means, I encourage teacher educators to make use of these Web sites. Doing so will expand the competence of teacher learners in using technology for professional purposes, a competence promoted by accreditation agencies such as NCATE.

The Teacher Educator as a Model

To maximize their impact on current and future teachers, teacher educators must model the best teaching and assessment practices in their own instruction. Thus, if prospective and current teachers are to understand what it means to respond to the culture of their students, make learning meaningful, provide multiple paths to knowledge, use varied learning resources, create positive learning environments, and employ a variety of valid assessment methods, teacher educators must model these competencies in the courses they teach. Likewise, if teacher educators want current and future teachers to reflect on their practice,

TABLE 1

STANDARDS ON THE WORLD WIDE WEB

Organization	Home page	Follow these links:
TESOL	http://www.tesol.edu/	The ESL Standards for Pre-K–12 Students Publications, then Standards
NCATE	http://www.ncate.org/	About NCATE, then NCATE Standards, then Major Themes of the NCATE Standards About NCATE, then Publications Order Form
NBPTS	http://www.nbpts.org/	The Standards Seeking National Board Certification About the National Board, then Publications

have strong and growing knowledge bases, and provide professional leadership, they must demonstrate these qualities.

Teacher educators are not exempt from the process of reflection and self-evaluation that the standards are designed to engender. As they become familiar with the teaching standards, teacher educators will want to engage in self-reflection to determine if they meet the standards they intend to apply to teacher learners.

Program Review and Development

The standards are a useful vehicle for analyzing program strengths and weaknesses on a course-by-course level as well as in the program as a whole. By holding the program accountable to the standards—that is, by assessing whether program graduates can meet the teaching standards and create learning environments where students attain the content and performance standards set for them in English language learning—teacher educators can evaluate the effectiveness of their own efforts and make improvements when necessary.

When used in this way, the standards are a means of reforming education for all teachers of ESOL learners. The result will be professional education programs of the highest caliber that produce teachers who, in turn, help improve student achievement in the schools.

Continuing Education

The student and teaching standards also have a place in continuing education efforts, whether they consist of course offerings, participation in professional development schools, teacher study groups, or university-sponsored conferences and institutes. For teachers who must retool and for those who continue to advance their practice in relation to the standards, the standards serve as a guide to uncovering unmet areas of need in individual teachers and in teams of teachers.

The developers of the Concerns-Based Adoption Model (CBAM) (Hall & Loucks, 1978; Loucks & Pratt, 1979) demonstrated that an important step in supporting teachers' individual development as professionals is to understand where they are in the change process. According to the CBAM, teacher educators would identify individual teachers' Stage of Concern (SoC) regarding the *innovation* (e.g., the ESL standards), from their awareness and need for information through collaborative delivery of standards-based education, as well as their current level of use (LoU) of the innovation in their classrooms, from no use of the ESL standards to routine and expert use. By so doing, teacher educators can engage teachers in activities that support their growth and development and advance their creative and effective use of the innovation. (For more information on this model, see Bailey & Palsha, 1992.)

Extending the understanding of the teacher development process, constructivists (who believe that knowledge is temporary, developmental, and socially and culturally mediated and that learning is a self-regulated process of resolving cognitive conflict through concrete experience, collaborative discourse, and reflection; see Fosnot, 1993) emphasize the cycle of inquiry that is crucial to reflective decision making and professional growth. Here the use of methods such as personal histories, self-assessment using video- or audiotape, journal writing, cognitive coaching, case studies for discussion and written reflection, problem framing, and action research can develop teachers' reflective decision-making abilities. For a brief overview of these techniques and the theoretical model that supports them, see Langer and Colton (1994) and Kaufman and Brooks (1996).

■ Integrating the ESL Standards Into Specific Program Components

Types of Courses Offered in Typical Credential and Licensure Programs

In discussing the integration of *ESL Standards for Pre-K–12 Students* and companion documents (Short et al., 2000; TESOL, 1998, in press) into professional education programs, I address separately each type of experience typically offered to preservice and in-service teachers: theoretical or foundational courses; courses on instructional methods and assessment; field experiences (those that accompany courses and those that stand alone, such as practica, internships, and student teaching); and final projects (including original research, examinations, and professional portfolios). Because these types of experiences frequently occur in the same professional development offering, teacher educators should refer to all the sections that follow to consider ways to best integrate *ESL Standards* into specific courses or offerings.

The suggestions below cover the full range of techniques used by teacher educators:

- readings

- reflection (through logs, journals, and autobiographical writing)

- position and other scholarly papers

- interviews and observation (directed and open ended)

- small- and large-group discussion

- group projects and cooperative learning activities

- panel presentations

- lesson planning

- analysis of teaching (e.g., microteaching, videotape analysis)

- application activities (e.g., assessment of teacher learners)

- case studies (written and media based)

- primary and secondary research

- exhibits and demonstrations (professional portfolios)

- program visits

For additional ideas on techniques used by L2 teacher educators in their professional development efforts, see Freeman (1993) and Richards (1998). Though not directed toward standards per se, these volumes offer many types of activities for teacher educators to use in promoting the professional development of their teacher learners. Also of interest to teacher educators are Boswood (1997), Brinton and Master (1997), J. D. Brown (1998), Fantini (1997), Hanson-Smith (1997), and Schinke-Llano and Rauff (1996).

Integrating *ESL Standards* Into Theoretical Courses

Most credential or licensure programs include theoretical or foundational courses such as second language acquisition (SLA)/applied linguistics courses, bilingual/multicultural education courses, and courses on the sociocultural context of schooling in the United States for language minority students. Several important components of *ESL Standards* can be integrated into these offerings, among them the "Access Brochure" (pp. 159–161); four sections of the introduction, "Promising Futures" (pp. 1–10: "Why ESL Standards Are Needed," "Myths About Second Language Learning," "TESOL's Vision of Effective Education for All Students," and "General Principles of Language Acquisition"); "References for Further Reading" (pp. 11–14); and the glossary (pp. 153–158). Companion documents, such as those related to the assessment of attainment of the standards, can also be incorporated, most notably *Managing the Assessment Process: A Framework for Measuring Student Attainment of the ESL Standards* (*MAP*; TESOL, 1998).

All the activities described in this section are appropriate for elementary and secondary school preservice and in-service teachers as well as ESL and bilingual specialists. For the former, the activities might be used in foundational classes other than those mentioned above.

Using the "Access Brochure"

Bilingual/multicultural education courses and courses on the sociocultural context of schooling are ideal places to include the "Access Brochure" (TESOL, 1997, pp. 159–161). The "opportunity-to-learn" standards detailed there highlight the importance of full access to services and positive learning environments in student achievement. By asking themselves the 15 questions in the "Access Brochure," schools can identify and remove barriers to ESOL student achievement.

Suggestions for Using the "Access Brochure" in Theoretical Courses

- Have teacher learners interview administrators, teachers, and students in various schools to determine each group's perspectives on ESOL students' current opportunities to learn.

- Have teacher learners observe schools and classrooms using a rubric or survey constructed around the 15 standards of access in the "Access Brochure." For one survey, see the Conceptual Framework section of *Training Others to Use the ESL Standards: A Professional Development Manual* (Short et al., 2000).

- Have teacher learners read research articles and summaries of research citing evidence that the 15 aspects of access influence student achievement. Assign follow-up presentations or discussions in class.

- In relation to the preceding activity, divide the teacher learners into teams based on the four areas named in the brochure. Have each team construct a chart listing that section's points, the names of researchers or authors who support each point, those who challenge the points, and any additional information that expands on the points in question. Compile the work of the four teams, and distribute the document to the class.

- Ask teacher learners to interview one another on their own experiences as students in relation to the 15 standards of access. Ask them to describe how the situation they encountered helped or hindered their learning.

- Ask teacher learners to select the 5 most critical standards of access from among the 15 listed and to justify their selection.

- Present an actual or fictitious case of a school in which several of the features named in the "Access Brochure" are getting in the way of students' success. Ask teacher learners to identify the problematic areas using the 15 standards listed in the brochure and to recommend ways to overcome these barriers.

- Show a video illustrating some of the 15 standards of access. For example, the Center for Applied Linguistics' video series, Meeting the Challenge of Teaching Linguistically Diverse Students, consists of case studies of bilingual and multilingual classrooms in which ESOL students are enrolled. Possible areas of focus in these videos include (a) access to a positive learning environment, (b) access to appropriate curriculum, (c) access to full delivery of services, and (d) access to equitable assessment. Although not all videos in the series bring out all the points listed in the "Access Brochure," they stimulate discussion of many of the standards of access. (Order the videos from the Center for Applied Linguistics, 4646 40th St. NW, Washington, DC 20016-1859; telephone 202-362-0700; http://www.cal.org/.)

- In autobiographical poetry and prose written by ESOL students on their experiences in schools, have teacher learners identify the aspects named in the "Access Brochure" that contributed to these students' positive or negative experiences. Two sources of such writing are *Cool*

Salsa: Bilingual Poems on Growing Up Latino in the United States (Carlson, 1994) and *Crossing the Schoolhouse Border: Immigrant Students in the California Public Schools* (Olsen, 1988). Many local and statewide collections of ESOL student writings also include appropriate material.

Related to the subject of standards of access for schools, the National Study of School Evaluation (NSSE) relies on *ESL Standards* in its K–12 school accreditation process. In 1995, the NSSE began a comprehensive retooling of its evaluative criteria for public and private schools and worked with TESOL to identify school characteristics shown by research to ensure the academic achievement of ESOL students. The NSSE then incorporated these characteristics into its evaluative criteria for schools, *Indicators of Schools of Quality, Volume 1: Schoolwide Indicators of Quality* (NSSE, 1997; see "New K–12 Accreditation Process Features TESOL Standards," 1998).

Using "Promising Futures"

This document, embedded in *ESL Standards* (TESOL, 1997, pp. 1–10), is the conceptual framework for the standards. It orients the reader to the purpose of the standards, lays out TESOL's vision for the effective education of ESOL students, and presents a framework for using *ESL Standards* in educational programs designed for ESOL students. Described below are several sections of the document that would work particularly well in theoretical or foundational courses.

"Why ESL Standards Are Needed." This brief overview and justification for ESL standards development (TESOL, 1997, p. 1), which places the ESL standards in the context of the larger national standards movement (see also chapter 2 in this volume), is useful for teacher educators offering foundational courses on the sociocultural context of schooling or on bilingual/multicultural education.

Suggestions for Using "Why ESL Standards Are Needed" in Theoretical Courses

- Introduce the standards movement to teacher learners, if necessary.

- Show the interrelationship between the ESL standards and the standards for other curricular areas.

- Referring to the Audience section of "Promising Futures" (TESOL, 1997, pp. 5–6), identify ways in which *ESL Standards* can be useful to all educators.

An additional resource is the standards-related material on TESOL's Web site (http://www.tesol.edu/). In addition, *Struggling for Standards*, Education Week's (1995) special report on standards, may be a useful source of readings to spark discussion on the standards movement.

"Myths About Second Language Learning." Though very brief, this section of "Promising Futures" (TESOL, 1997, p. 3) is critically important to educators of ESOL students, as the myths persist in the wider culture and restrict program effectiveness. To investigate any tacit assumptions held by students, teachers of courses in applied linguistics or SLA theory, for example, might make the myths about L2 learning into a true-false quiz and ask their teacher learners to justify their responses.

Another useful resource on the examination of teachers' assumptions is "Exploring Teachers' Beliefs" (Richards & Lockhart, 1994, chapter 2). The chapter contains information about this topic and sample inventories for investigating teachers' beliefs related to L2 learning.

Suggestions for Using "Myths About Second Language Learning" in Theoretical Courses

Have teacher learners

- survey administrators, teachers, and parents in the schools to which they have access to determine the percentage of each group that subscribes to the myths. If certain myths are prevalent, have teacher learners devise strategies for educating the constituent group or groups.

- investigate the source of each myth and the research that refutes the myth and write short papers on the topic or make presentations in class. If possible, have in-service teachers make presentations at their school sites.

- make lists of the potential consequences for ESOL students if educators subscribed to each myth, and draw connections between these myths and the points listed in the "Access Brochure."

- read the book *How the Other Half Lives* (Riis, 1890/1971) or view documentaries concerning the daily life of early immigrants in the United States to gain factual information with which to refute Myth 3 when it is presented as fact.

"TESOL's Vision of Effective Education for All Students." Transformative educators seek to challenge existing notions of schooling rather than blindly reproduce the status quo. To confront these notions, educators must critique existing practice and envision the alternatives. Following the model provided in this section of "Promising Futures" (TESOL, 1997, pp. 3–5), teacher educators might ask their teacher learners to outline their vision of an exemplary school for ESOL students (e.g., by writing an essay called "An Ideal School for Language Minority Students," which could be refined over the course of their program and placed into a professional development portfolio). This vision would incorporate the best of what the field knows and create new structures and practices for attaining the loftiest goals in educating language minority students.

Suggestions for Using "TESOL's Vision of Effective Education for All Students" in Theoretical Courses

- Have teacher learners rate the schools with which they are familiar on how well those schools are fulfilling each of the five components of the vision statement. If teacher learners visit or work in the same schools, have them form discussion groups and discuss how that school is or is not achieving each part of the vision statement and what actions the school might take to reach TESOL's vision.

- Ask teacher learners to state their agreement or disagreement with each component of the vision statement (e.g., by indicating their level of agreement or disagreement on the following scale: *strongly agree, agree, neither agree nor disagree at this time, disagree, strongly disagree*). Use the results of this survey to better understand teacher learners' attitudes and shape instruction accordingly.

- Find out whether or not the schools with which teacher learners are familiar have constructed vision statements for their schools. If so, tell the teacher learners to investigate whether any of TESOL's points have been mentioned in those documents. Likewise, have teacher learners examine vision statements constructed by state education departments for any convergence of opinion between the views expressed in TESOL's vision statement and that of the state departments of education.

- Have teacher learners compare policy documents constructed by other professional organizations (e.g., National Association for the Education of Young Children, 1996) with TESOL's vision statement and identify points of agreement and disagreement.

"General Principles of Language Acquisition." This section (TESOL, 1997, pp. 6–8), by far one of the most useful in "Promising Futures," lays out the knowledge base from which the student standards were constructed. Seven in number, the principles are derived from "current research and theory about the nature of language, language learning, human development, and pedagogy that underlie the *ESL Standards*" (TESOL, 1997, p. 6).

Suggestions for Using "General Principles of Language Acquisition" in Theoretical Courses

- Evaluate applied linguistics and SLA theory courses to determine whether they emphasize the principles, thus giving future and current teachers the knowledge base they need to appreciate and support the standards. If the courses do not do so, revise them accordingly.

- Ask teacher learners to give examples from their own language learning histories of times when these principles were respected and times they were not, and to explain the effects on their learning.

- Have teacher learners rank the principles according to a given criterion (e.g., those most widely accepted and understood by teachers).

- Have teacher learners write implications for each principle as "The Seven Commandments of Effective Language Teaching."

For more information on the principles of SLA and other tasks for teacher learners, see chapter 3 in this volume.

In its work on educational reform, TESOL has been mindful that the standards for instruction and assessment must stem from a recognized knowledge base that is "articulated, shared and coherent" (NCATE, 1995, p. 15). Therefore, just as the components of "General Principles of Language Acquisition" guide the instructional standards, TESOL has articulated principles of assessment to guide the assessment standards (see *Managing the Assessment Process*, TESOL, 1998, pp. 6–10). *MAP* presents the conceptual model for assessment along with 19 guiding principles in the areas of planning assessments, collecting and recording information, analyzing and interpreting assessment information, and using information in reporting and decision making. In courses relating to the "Principles of Assessment" in *MAP*, teachers could plan activities parallel to those used in theoretical courses, for example.

Suggestions for Using "Principles of Assessment" in Theoretical Courses

Have teacher learners

- explain key terms used in *MAP* in learning logs or reflective journals in order to gauge their understanding of important theoretical constructs (e.g., reliability, validity, bias, fairness, formal vs. informal assessment, assessment vs. evaluation)

- review assessment practices in programs with which they have contact and evaluate those practices against the principles outlined in *MAP*

For additional information and helpful references for teachers of assessment courses, see chapters 5, 6, and 7 in this volume and *Training Others to Use the ESL Standards* (Short et al., 2000).

Another resource for teachers of assessment courses is *Scenarios for ESL Standards-Based Assessment* (TESOL, in press), which, in addition to reprinting *MAP,* provides concrete examples of best practices in performance assessment, a reference list, and a glossary of terms.

Finally, related to the standards presented in "Promising Futures" (TESOL, 1997, pp. 8–10), teacher educators should make certain that current and future teachers understand the three main areas named as goals for ESL instruction: the development of social language, academic language, and sociolinguistic competence. Useful resources for teacher learners include

- *Conceptualizing Academic Language* (Solomon & Rhodes, 1995)

- relevant publications of the National Clearinghouse for Bilingual Education (e.g., Collier, 1995)

- ERIC Digests (e.g., Adger, 1996; Beebe & Leonard, 1994; Crandall, 1994; Galloway, 1993; Hancock, 1994; McLaughlin, 1992)

Various in-class activities, individual projects, or group projects could accompany these readings.

"References for Further Reading." This section of *ESL Standards* (pp. 11–14) gives the primary sources for the general principles of language acquisition.

Suggestions for Using "References for Further Reading" in Theoretical Courses

- Have teacher learners generate traditional research summaries on particular topics.

- Assign comparisons and contrasts of articles on the same topic (with a Venn diagram or in narrative form).

- Use the sources to inspire reaction or reflection papers by teacher learners.

- After the completion of assigned readings on a topic, assign learning logs that demonstrate what teacher learners have learned from these readings.

- After the completion of assigned readings, have teacher learners generate research questions for future investigation of the topic. These topics might be pursued in research courses later in the program.

Glossary. Teacher educators might use the glossary in *ESL Standards* (pp. 153–158) or in this volume to create classroom tools and activities.

Suggestions for Using the Glossary in Theoretical Courses

- Use the glossary to generate pre- and posttests for particular courses.

- Use the glossary as a basis for cooperative learning activities. For example, ask teams of teacher learners to create categories for the terms in the glossary and explain their reasoning for the categories produced. Have the teams present their categories, and have the class vote on the most appropriate set produced.

- Make a list of terms and concepts in the glossary not generally understood by mainstream teachers, parents, and community members. This list would give ESL specialists practice in providing comprehensible explanations when using these terms with nonspecialists.

- Use the glossary to generate a list of competencies that should be included in preservice and in-service professional education programs (e.g., cross-cultural competence, competence in the use of such methods such as content-based ESL and sheltered instruction, the ability to deliver high-quality instruction to ESOL learners through such program models as two-way immersion programs and self-contained ESL classes).

Integrating *ESL Standards* Into Instructional Methodology and Assessment Courses

Most professional education and continuing education programs include courses that teach methodology for ESL, reading and writing, and content areas as well as methods of assessing students. To integrate *ESL Standards* into these widely offered methodology courses, teacher educators should investigate with their teacher learners how the principles they have learned in their theoretical courses are enacted in practice. The following activities make use of "Promising Futures" (TESOL, 1997, pp. 1–10); and *MAP* (TESOL, 1998).

Suggestions for Using "General Principles of Language Acquisition" in Instructional Methodology and Assessment Courses

Have teacher learners

- conduct classroom observations in which they determine if the principles are being respected in the lessons offered to ESOL students

- in the vignettes that follow each standard in *ESL Standards*, look for evidence of the points in "General Principles of Language Acquisition," identify where they find each principle, and explain how the principle is enacted in the vignette

- explain how several of the principles would be enacted in developing particular language skills (e.g., reading and writing)

Suggestions for Using "Principles of Assessment" in Instructional Methodology and Assessment Courses

- Have teacher learners interview assessment personnel to identify aspects of their assessments of ESOL students that are going well and those that require further development. Ask teacher learners to inquire what the practitioners perceive as barriers to implementing particular principles and practices outlined in *MAP*, and have the teacher learners generate strategies for overcoming these barriers.

- Have teacher learners find recent newspaper articles about statewide or district assessment plans and controversies.

- Ask teacher learners to interview language minority students and their parents on their views of assessment practices they have experienced.

- Have in-service teachers evaluate their own classroom-based assessment practices against the principles and practices outlined in *MAP*, identify areas of strength and weakness, and create action plans to overcome any weaknesses uncovered.

Besides focusing on how the principles are enacted in the standards themselves (presented by grade-level clusters in *ESL Standards*, pp. 31–151), teacher educators can engage in activities aimed directly at improving teachers' use of curricula and materials so that they support standards implementation.

Suggestions for Teachers of Curriculum and Materials Development Courses

Have teacher learners

- evaluate curriculum in relation to the three broad goals of ESL instruction

- when necessary, develop and revise curriculum

- compare the English language arts and ESL standards to make sure teachers are familiar with both as they work with students of varied proficiency levels

- compare state- or district-developed standards with the ESL standards, and make sure teachers align their curriculum with both

- make certain that all reading and language arts methods classes taken by elementary and secondary teachers—not just ESL methods classes—introduce the ESL standards

- use the ESL standards for textbook evaluation assignments or for textbook selection and adoption

- plan lessons and units with the ESL standards in mind (See the lesson plan formats in the Instructional Practices section of Short et al., 2000.)

- try the lessons out in the classroom and reflect on their effectiveness with learners of diverse backgrounds

- use the vignettes to locate methods they are learning about and get an idea of how they would be used in implementing the ESL standards

- visit classrooms and write instructional vignettes that parallel those they have reviewed in *ESL Standards*

- conduct observations in classrooms, and write up reports of their experiences

- view videotaped lesson segments in class, and describe in writing how the lessons viewed would lead to standards attainment and how they represent best practices in the field

- interview teachers and students about their experiences in implementing or meeting the ESL standards

For additional ideas, see the section Internet-Based Research and Research Using *ERIC* and Other Databases in this Prologue.

Suggestions for Activities to Develop or Practice Assessment Techniques

Have teacher learners

- investigate placement and assessment procedures used in programs to which they have access; evaluate those practices in relation to the principles and procedures recommended in *MAP* (TESOL, 1998)

- try out alternative assessment procedures, such as those suggested in *MAP* and in *Scenarios for ESL Standards-Based Assessment* (TESOL, in press)

- construct tests, rubrics, and observation and interview protocols for use with ESOL learners

- evaluate the procedures they construct against the principles of assessment outlined in *MAP*

- test individual ESOL students to understand their learning needs in relation to standards attainment

- read case studies of assessment procedures or actual assessments of students and determine their adequacy in relation to the principles of assessment in *MAP*

Applying the ESL Standards During Field Experiences

NCATE and other accreditation agencies emphasize that field experiences provided in professional education programs should be well planned, sequenced, and of high quality. Typically, teacher learners engage in activities in the field beginning with their first courses and culminating in student teaching, practica, or internships. The purpose of field experiences, according to NCATE (1995), is to "relate principles and theories from the conceptual framework(s) of a program to actual practices in classrooms and school, as well as create meaningful learning experiences for all students, and study and practice in a variety of communities with students of different ages and needs" (p. 20). These experiences are meant to engender reflection by candidates and provide the opportunity for feedback from others.

In this section, I discuss in turn early participation in classrooms, student teaching and practicum experiences, and postgraduate fieldwork.

Early Participation in Classrooms

Early experiences in classrooms could include visits; school and classroom observations (guided and open-ended); interviews with administrators, teachers, students, and parents; and directed participation in classrooms. In these experiences teacher learners might focus on understanding themselves in relation to the decision to teach linguistically diverse populations of students, understanding the educational reform movement and the role of teachers in promoting needed reforms, and observing current teaching and testing practices.

Many of the ideas given in the sections above are ideal for early field experiences for teacher learners; I mention some additional ideas below.

Suggestions for Applying the Standards During Early Field Experiences

- Have teacher learners discuss occasions when standards were implemented in their own schooling experience and the effect of standards on their educational experience (including the ways their attainment of standards was measured and their reaction to this assessment process).

- Have teacher learners visit school districts that have made a commitment to standards-based reform, and ask administrators and teachers about their experiences in redirecting their teaching efforts toward standards set by state education departments or professional organizations.

- Ask teacher learners to interview several teachers and find out (a) how knowledgeable they are about the ESL standards, (b) how they view their own roles and responsibilities in implementing the standards, and (c) what experiences (positive and negative) they have had in implementing standards; have them write a brief report on their findings.

- Have teacher learners produce exhibits of documents collected on site visits (e.g., student work samples, lesson plans, policy documents) that give evidence of standards-based reform in the site in question.

- Ask teacher learners to visit advocacy agencies and interview personnel about their perspectives on standards-based reform.

- Have teacher learners interview librarians, guidance counselors, coordinators of special programs, and after-school program directors in relation to the areas named in the "Access Brochure" (TESOL, 1997, pp. 159–161).

- Have teacher learners participate in planning a lesson for a particular group of ESOL students integrating the ESL standards.

- Have teacher learners observe one or two young ESOL learners at work and determine how well they meet a particular ESL standard.

Student Teaching or Practicum

During the student teaching or practicum experience, candidates develop and deliver many units of instruction for learners of diverse ages and abilities.

Suggestions for Applying the Standards
During Student Teaching or the Practicum

Have teacher learners

- develop all lesson and unit plans with standards in mind by directly referring to goals and standards in their plans

- try out the full range of assessment approaches suggested in *MAP* (TESOL, 1998, pp. 11–18)

- reflect on how their students are progressing in attaining the ESL standards

- educate parents, community members, and other educators with whom they come in contact and who subscribe to the myths detailed in "Promising Futures" (TESOL, 1997, pp. 1–10)

- adapt published curriculum materials so that they address the standards more successfully

- participate in faculty meetings in which standards implementation is discussed

- review videotapes or audiotapes of their teaching and comment on how well they are meeting the areas outlined in the "Access Brochure" (TESOL, 1997, pp. 159–161) (i.e., positive learning environment, appropriate curriculum, full delivery of services, and equitable assessment)

- either through reflective essays or oral commentary in weekly seminars, evaluate how successfully their lessons and those of others address the ESL standards

For additional ideas related to teacher development that could be applied to standards implementation, see Richards and Nunan (1990).

Suggestions for Applying the Standards During Later Field Experiences

- Ask teachers to grade their schools on the 15 points raised in the "Access Brochure" (TESOL, 1997, pp. 159–161) and to identify one or two areas for which they could provide professional leadership in their schools through in-service training, dissemination of information, faculty discussions, or person-to-person networking.

- Consult the *ESL Standards Implementation Database* (Center for Applied Linguistics, n.d.). to identify schools and programs that are implementing standards. Have experienced teachers contact or visit programs, interview administrators and teachers, and visit classrooms. Use the visits to advance in-house curriculum reform efforts (individual or collective).

- Join *ESLSTDS*, the ESL standards implementation discussion list, by sending an e-mail message to request-eslstds@ caltalk.cal.org. In the subject line, type *subscribe*. Leave the rest of the message blank.

- Develop collaborative arrangements (via e-mail or a direct working relationship) between programs or schools. Select an area of concern and work together to advance practices in this area. For example, with a partner school, develop assessment checklists or rubrics, pilot them in the respective schools, and share results of the efforts to validate the effectiveness of the assessment tools.

- Have teachers reflect on their implementation of the ESL standards by using the "ESL Standards Implementation Survey" in chapter 2, Appendix B.

- Through professional development schools, bring together the work of experienced and novice teachers on instructional improvement for specific populations of students. For example, have teachers target improved practice for students with limited formal schooling or special education needs in relation to standards attainment or assessment.

- Have experienced teachers mentor novice teachers on standards implementation in their classrooms.

- Develop curriculum for specific grade levels or programs through multiyear projects designed to ensure meaningful and lasting curriculum change.

Using *ESL Standards* in Culminating Projects and Research

Candidate Examinations

Throughout comprehensive professional preparation programs, candidates may be required to take qualifying examinations. The most frequent of these are comprehensive examinations given at the end of a degree program. These examinations focus on the totality of learning that has taken place during an individual's professional education program, and *ESL Standards* can be very useful in assessing candidates' knowledge and skill in relation to the assessment and instruction of language minority students.

Suggestions for Applying the Standards During Comprehensive Examinations

Have candidates

- define terms from the glossary in *ESL Standards*

- explain how they would assist students in meeting particular standards (e.g., list explicit techniques or strategies, give steps they would take)

- given certain principles of assessment or instruction as outlined in "Promising Futures" (TESOL, 1997, pp. 1–10) or *MAP* (TESOL, 1998), cite research for each of the principles, and describe ways they would honor the principles in their classrooms

- discuss current educational reform efforts, their role, and the role of educational standards in promoting needed educational reform for ESOL students

- using excerpts from particular vignettes, describe the standards that are being met, the instructional strategies in use, and the reasons they are effective in promoting L2 learning

- read case studies that describe instructional or assessment practices, and discuss those practices in relation to the ESL standards and current best practices

See also "Sample TESL Comprehensive Examination" in *Training Others to Use the ESL Standards* (Short et al., 2000).

Final Projects

Comprehensive teacher preparation programs sometimes require or allow culminating experiences other than examinations, most notably the production of professional portfolios or the completion of special projects.

Suggestions for Applying the Standards in Final Projects

Have candidates

- present professional portfolios into which they have placed, for example,

  - audio- or videotaped presentations related to standards

  - lesson plans and other exhibits (e.g., evaluations of students) that account for standards

  - standards-related research, reaction, and reflection papers

  - standards-specific journals and logs

  - vision statements

  - outlines of their principles of teaching and assessment, acknowledging those drawn from *ESL Standards*

- conduct research to create collections of readings on each of the four areas named in the "Access Brochure" (TESOL, 1997, pp. 159–161); publish and make those readings available to other schools in the region for school improvement purposes

- write comprehensive position papers or action plans for particular purposes (e.g., a language minority parental involvement plan for a school or district that is implementing standards, a standards-based program improvement proposal to submit to a school board)

Research Activities

It is frequently the case in theoretical courses that teacher learners expand their knowledge base by conducting research using the Internet, *ERIC*, and other databases. Likewise, research is a frequent component of methodology courses, in which teacher learners investigate various methods in use. Many programs also encourage original research projects as culminating experiences for their teacher learners so that they become contributors to the ever-expanding knowledge base in their fields of interest. Three general types of research activities can be related to *ESL Standards*: Internet-based research, research using databases such as *ERIC*, and action research in classrooms.

Internet-Based Research

Resources for Internet-Based Research on ESL Standards

- As mentioned, NBPTS (http://www.nbpts.org/), NCATE (http://www.ncate.org/), and TESOL (http://www.tesol .edu/) are good sources for standards-related material.

- *What Matters Most: Teaching for America's Future* (NCTAF, 1996) outlines what has been learned through research on the relationship between teaching standards and school improvement. This document is an excellent starting point for those who want to investigate quality-of-teaching issues.

- *Developing Educational Standards* (Putnam Valley Central Schools, 1999a) is a list of Internet sites containing standards that have been developed for L2 learners in various parts of the country. Especially of note is *Educational Standards and Curriculum Frameworks for Foreign Language/ESL* (Putnam Valley Central Schools, 1999b), which describes current state and national efforts to create and implement L2 standards. Research projects that could be initiated from this site include comparisons of standards development projects, standards policies, or standards implementation across states.

- Of interest in understanding how to use e-mail to engage in professional dialogue and collaboration are *E-Mail for English Teaching* (Warschauer, 1995; see especially chapter 2) and *The Internet Guide for English Language Teachers* (Sperling, 1997; see chapters 2, 3, 5). These books also give information on K–12 e-mail discussion lists that can be used to facilitate discussion with other practitioners on standards issues and concerns.

- The Resources section of *Training Others to Use the ESL Standards* (Short et al., 2000) lists Web sites of interest to teachers of methods and assessment courses. These sites are good sources of lesson plans and curriculum units that may have been constructed (or could be adapted) with standards in mind. As well, teacher learners could investigate assessment practices that are aligned with the principles and practices presented in *MAP* (TESOL, 1998).

- The *ERIC Clearinghouse on Assessment and Evaluation* (http://ericae.net/) is one of the best Internet sources on assessment and standards. From the home page users can search *ERIC*, use the Test Locator, read Assessment FAQs, and visit the Bookstore and the Full-Text Library. Also available are links to assessment and evaluation sites, e-mail discussion lists, the *Educational Testing Service Test Collection* database, the *Center for Equity and Excellence in Education Test Database*, and the Buros Institute's *Mental Measurements Yearbook*. Here teacher learners can investigate assessment concepts (e.g., test reliability, test bias), particular assessment methods (e.g., oral language rating scales, cloze procedure), or commonly used tests (e.g., the Language Assessment Battery). A host of valuable projects could be constructed in relation to this site. For ideas, see Checklist for Selection of Language Proficiency Instruments, Checklist for Reviewing Assessment Tools, Criteria for Evaluating a Rubric, and Portfolio Design Checklist in the Assessment section of *Training Others to Use the ESL Standards* (Short et al., 2000), which could be used in conjunction with investigations conducted via the Internet.

Research Using ERIC and Other Databases. Teacher learners often learn to conduct research using educational databases (e.g., *ERIC*, *PsychLit, Dissertation Abstracts*). By writing papers related to standards development or implementation, teacher learners develop search techniques and other important research skills, advance their writing skills, and expand their knowledge.

Resources for Database Research on ESL Standards

- *ERIC* (http://ericir.sunsite.syr.edu/) can be searched via the Internet and, like other databases, in on-campus libraries. Local librarians can advise users of the most helpful databases and often provide on-campus training programs on their use.

- *All About ERIC* (ACCESS ERIC, 1995; see especially the search worksheet and "Tips for Teachers") is a useful resource for educating teacher learners about this valuable database. Through *ERIC* searches, researchers can locate journal articles and documents related to standards development and implementation.

- Newsletter subscriptions are available through the various ERIC clearinghouses of interest.

Action Research in Classrooms. Action research attempts to link theory and practice directly. In action research, the investigator identifies issues and states problems, develops and implements plans to remedy the issues identified, and collects and evaluates data to determine the effect of the actions taken (see Bullough & Gitlin, 1995, chapter 8).

Suggestions for Action Research Related to Standards

- Have teacher learners engage in action research projects to help change assessment practices where needed and study the effects of the changes they institute.

- Ask teacher learners to establish local benchmarks for English proficiency for students of various ages and proficiency levels against which to measure all students in a district.

- Have teacher learners use the ESL standards to promote the use of effective instructional strategies (e.g., by reflecting on the strategies in use in the vignettes following each standard and those in use in particular schools or classrooms), identify under- or unused strategies and develop procedures for increasing their use (e.g., in-service courses, peer coaching), and construct action research around the process of instructional improvement.

- Have teacher learners use the standards to make decisions about the curriculum and, when necessary, take action to revise the curriculum. Ask teacher learners to study the change process and its effects on students' performance.

- Determine the characteristics of instructional environments that work for particular populations of ESOL students, and disseminate information about these characteristics.

Additional readings on action research include Freeman (1998), Johnson and Chen (1992), Noffke (1997), and Nunan (1990, 1992).

■ Conclusion

For the ESL standards to be fully implemented in classrooms, they must influence teachers' beliefs, knowledge, and skills and thus must be integrated into the experiences that make up comprehensive teacher development programs. It is hoped that current and future teachers will act as competent professionals to transform curriculum, instruction, and assessment practices in schools for the benefit of ESOL learners.

Chapter 1

Changing Populations, Changing Needs in Teacher Preparation

Natalie Kuhlman and Denise E. Murray

P*etar is an ethnic Serb who grew up in war-torn Croatia. He and his family arrived in the United States a year ago as refugees. Before then he had had no exposure to English, and his schooling had been interrupted several times by the war. As a result, his literacy in his native Serbian is at about a fourth-grade level. For a year Petar has been attending ESL pull-out classes for limited English proficient students at his school, where he is the only Serbian speaker in the 10th grade. His family and several other Serbian families who have settled in the area all attend the local Serbian Orthodox Church. His parents are learning English there in a class taught by volunteers. His father was a mechanic in Croatia, and his mother, a seamstress. Both completed high school and vocational training. Although they had little need for Serbian literacy in their jobs, they were avid readers.*

Guadalupe was born in the United States; her six siblings were all born and started school in Michoacan, Mexico. Her parents were migrant farm workers who traveled back and forth across the U.S.-Mexican border for many years. When the Immigration Reform Bill was passed in 1996, they took the opportunity to become legal residents. Her parents now pack fruit in a local cannery. Two of her brothers work; her other siblings are in school. The family primarily uses Spanish in the home because her parents have very limited English skills. Guadalupe interacts with her siblings in a mixture of English and Spanish. As a first-grade student, she is in a bilingual program for Spanish speakers. The school expects that she and her peers will become fluent in English by the time they are in Grade 3, at which time they will be put into English-only classes. Her family expects that she will do well in school and get a good education.

Han was born in Vietnam, and she and her mother immigrated a year ago to join her father and two brothers, who arrived in the United States several years ago. Her parents are highly educated. Her father was an adviser to the U.S. military during the Vietnam War, and her mother was a doctor. They speak French and Vietnamese fluently and read voraciously in both languages. Both parents were placed in reeducation camps as a result of their high positions in the South Vietnamese government. Her brothers have already earned college degrees and are working to support their extended family. Han, an eighth grader, is diligent in school but feels she will never live up to her parents' expectations that she become an accountant. She is interested in art, and her teachers tell her she has talent. She finds English a challenge. When she arrived, she knew no English and was placed immediately into a regular middle school classroom. The other Vietnamese students in the class translate the lessons for her, but she continues to struggle with English.

These three scenarios are only a few of the many we could write about the 3 million to 5 million limited English proficient (LEP) students in U.S. schools today (the numbers are approximations because not all students requiring English language services are counted). The schools these students attend are vastly different from those of the 1950s or 1960s and even of the 1980s. This chapter describes the changing demographics of U.S. schools, common instructional programs for second language (L2) learners, and the kinds of teacher preparation programs currently available to meet the needs of these students. This background information provides a context for what teachers need to know in order to teach English language learners effectively.

Throughout this chapter, we use the term *ESOL students* to describe speakers of non-English languages who are learning English, *ESL* to refer to the field, and *ESL Standards* to refer to *ESL Standards*

TASK 1

Think about your own elementary school and high school experience. How many students spoke languages other than English? How did the school organize instruction for those students? In a free-writing exercise, briefly explore your memories of the schools you attended and the languages you heard spoken. If you attended a school in which all students and school personnel spoke one language, interview a friend or colleague, and write about his or her experiences.

---

for Pre-K–12 Students (TESOL, 1997). We use the term *LEP* when quoting directly from or referring to particular studies or reports that use that term. (See the Glossary for additional terms.)

■ Changing Demographics and the Effects on Pre-K–12 Schools

Schools have changed since the late 1980s because of the large numbers of immigrants, refugees, and other students from non-English backgrounds who have entered the United States or were born there. From that time to the mid-1990s, the number of school-age children using a language other than English increased 68.6% (TESOL, 1997). These students can be found in schools across the nation, not just in the three "large immigrant states" of California, Texas, and New York. For example, speakers of 18 different languages make up the student body in the schools of Garden City in western Kansas. Their mostly Asian and Latino immigrant parents have moved to that area to work in the meat-packing industry; other parents have likewise moved to Georgia, Iowa, Nebraska, and North Carolina, where jobs in the meat-packing or poultry industry are plentiful. Other previously non-immigrant states such as West Virginia now see ESOL students in their schools as their parents come to the United States to work for Asian car manufacturers. Although the numbers of students requiring English language instruction in these areas may not be as large as in California, Texas, or New York, often the percentages are overwhelming to local schools and communities. In one elementary school in Dalton, Georgia, for example, Latino students make up 70% of the student body. The school has initiated a bilingual program by retraining its teachers and hiring bilingual Mexican teaching assistants (Stocking & García, 1998).

During the 1991–1992 academic year, more than 42,791,000 students, approximately 6% of whom were ESOL students, were enrolled in public and nonpublic schools in the United States (see Table 1-1). This number represents an increase of 9% over the previous year. However, the actual figures were probably much higher because only those states receiving federal Title VII funds were required to report these statistics (Henderson, Abbott, & Strang, 1993). During that school year, 1.68 million (72.9%) of these students were from Spanish-speaking backgrounds, and an additional 91,000 (3.9%) spoke Vietnamese. No other language group constituted more than 2% of all

TABLE 1-1

STUDENTS IN U.S. SCHOOLS SPEAKING LANGUAGES OTHER THAN ENGLISH, 1991–1992

Language spoken	% of U.S. students
Spanish	72.9
Vietnamese	3.9
Hmong	1.8
Cantonese	1.7
Cambodian	1.6
Korean	1.6
Laotian	1.3
Navajo	1.3
Tagalog	1.1

Source: Adapted from Fleischman and Hopstock (1993).

ESOL students. Additionally, 2.5% of LEP students spoke 1 of 29 different Native American languages (Fleischman & Hopstock, 1993).

Three states—California, Texas, and New York—have had the largest numbers of LEP students. State education agencies across the United States and its territories reported a 16% increase in LEP students between the 1992–1993 and 1993–1994 school years. In 1991–1992, more than 66% of these students were in Grades K–6, 18% were in Grades 7–9, and the remaining 14% were in Grades 10–12 (Fleischman & Hopstock, 1993). The average yearly increase between 1985 and 1994 was 9.6% for the nation (Donly, Henderson, & Strang, 1995). The number of identified LEP students in California, however, almost tripled between 1985 and 1998, increasing from 585,000 to 1.4 million (California State Department of Education, 1998).

Like the largest groups of school-age children, the largest groups of adults from non-English backgrounds are Hispanic (69%) and Asian (19%) (Fitzgerald, 1995). Demand for adult ESL instruction

TASK 2

Find out the demographics for your state, district, or both. What changes have occurred over the past 10 years? What effect have the changes had on program models for the schools and for teacher preparation?

increased 268% over the 12 years from 1980 to 1992 (Wrigley, 1993). Adults in ESL classes represented 51% of all adult education students and 76% of the hours of adult education. Waiting lists for adult ESL instruction are common. In San José, California, for example, more than 4,000 adults were reported to be on waiting lists, and 15,000 were identified statewide by the Massachusetts State Department of Education (National Clearinghouse for ESL Literacy Education, 1996).

■ The Diversity of ESOL Students and Program Models

National studies of LEP students have shown that they are likely to attend low-income schools, attend schools in the West and South, have parents with low levels of English language proficiency, and have mothers with limited education (Moss & Puma, 1995). Even though Moss and Puma's congressionally mandated study of language minority and LEP students indicated that such students are particularly disadvantaged, their study, like all studies based on aggregated data, merely hints at the tremendous variety within the ESOL school population. The three profiles at the beginning of this chapter provide a brief glimpse at this variety.

ESOL students in particular come from disparate educational backgrounds. Some have had their schooling disrupted because they come from war-torn or economically depressed areas. Others have had good educational opportunities. Some learned English in their country of origin; others have not had such opportunities. Some come from families with high levels of education and have parents who earned university degrees and worked in professional occupations in their homeland; others are from families that have limited literacy even in their home language. About all that these students have in common is the need to develop their English language skills in order to participate in mainstream classes in the United States.

Go to a local school of your choice. Interview two senior teachers about the ESOL students in their school. Describe the overall demographics of the school, and write profiles of two individual students. What kind of information would you want to include in the profiles?

Given the variety of ESOL students, what types of programs exist to help them succeed in U.S. schools? Although many ESOL students are in programs that facilitate their English language development, "thirty percent of LEP students in the 1st and 3rd grades do not receive ESL/bilingual assistance from any source (federal, state or local), largely because they attend schools that lack these services" (Moss & Puma, 1995, p. i-11). For example, in California, only 30% of the 1.4 million eligible children receive primary language instruction by a fully credentialed bilingual teacher.

Program models for ESOL students vary greatly across the United States, from complete English submersion with no special help to fully developed bilingual programs spanning kindergarten through high school. This section presents a composite of some of the more common models and key program characteristics drawn from four recent treatments of bilingual education (Baker, 1996; Díaz-Rico & Weed, 1995; Faltis & Hudelson, 1998; Ovando & Collier, 1998) (for another detailed description of program models, see Genesee, 1999).

Baker (1996) divides the program models into those which offer weak or strong support for the first language (L1), whereas Faltis and Hudelson (1998) look at characteristics of bilingual program models. Ovando and Collier (1998) and Díaz-Rico and Weed (1995) give critical overviews of each model. Faltis and Hudelson discuss models for elementary grades, including *enrichment, maintenance, transitional,* and *ESL.* They also identify the educational goals, the learners served, the language of instruction, the duration of the program, the delivery system, and the training and linguistic skills of teachers in the programs. Díaz-Rico and Weed divide the models they discuss into *submersion* (including pull-out ESL and structured immersion), *transition* (early and late exit), *maintenance, immersion* (enrichment and two-way), *individualized instruction,* and *newcomer centers.* For secondary programs, most researchers identify separate courses by proficiency level in ESL as the most common model, whereas some districts use sheltered

English content-area courses (called *SDAIE*—specially designed academic instruction in English—in California). (See Table 1-2.)

Instructional strategies within these programs also vary widely depending on how much time per day or week is devoted to primary language instruction, English language development, and sheltered content instruction. The following discussion of the strengths and weaknesses of each of the major program types is based on Baker (1996), Díaz-Rico and Weed (1995), Faltis and Hudelson (1998), and Ovando and Collier (1998).

Sink-or-swim programs, also known as *submersion* programs, place non-English-speaking children in mainstream English language classrooms and expect the children to learn alongside native speakers

---

TABLE 1-2

CHARACTERISTICS OF ESL PROGRAM MODELS

	Model				
Characteristic	*Enrichment*	*Maintenance*	*Transitional*	*ESL*	*Submersion*
Educational goal, societal aim, or outcome	Bilingualism	Bilingualism	Assimilation	Assimilation	Assimilation
Children served	Language majority, language minority	Language minority	Language minority	Language minority	Language minority
Language of instruction	L1, L2	L1, L2	Some L1, mostly L2	L2	L2
Duration	Unlimited	Unlimited	2–3 years	2–3 years	Unlimited
Delivery system	Immersion, dual language	Various	L1 for literacy	All English	All English
Instructor	Credentialed bilingual teacher	Credentialed bilingual teacher	Credentialed bilingual teacher, aide, or both	Certified ESL teacher	Monolingual English-speaking teacher with no special training

Sources: Baker (1996), Díaz-Rico and Weed (1995), Faltis and Hudelson (1998), Ovando and Collier (1998).

without any special support. Most researchers consider this model a completely inadequate form of instruction for English learners (Berman et al., 1992); Ramírez, 1992; Thomas & Collier, 1995).

Pull-out ESL programs are often combined with submersion programs, providing ESOL students with as little as 20 minutes a day or several periods of instruction in the English language that is not necessarily connected to instruction in the mainstream class. This format is usually considered the next weakest model of instruction.

The most common form of bilingual education in the United States is *transitional bilingual* education. In the *early-exit* transitional model, the goal is to provide primary language instruction only while children are learning English. Children are moved into mainstream classrooms as quickly as possible, usually within 2–3 years. According to Ovando and Collier (1998), the transitional model "has many problems. As with ESL pull-out, transitional classes are generally perceived as a remedial program, a lower track for slow students" (p. 57).

Late-exit transitional programs are generally preferred by the four sources cited because research shows that students enrolled in such programs at least through the fourth grade achieve academic success (Berman et al., 1992; Ovando & Collier, 1998; Ramírez, Yuen, Ramey, & Pasta, 1991; Thomas & Collier, 1995). *Maintenance* or *developmental bilingual* programs, which Faltis and Hudelson (1998) also call *late-exit bilingual* programs, develop the first language (L1) while adding English. These programs have "as a major goal the development of proficiency in both the learner's L1 and in English, and the utilization of both languages in the learning of significant content" (p. 30). Díaz-Rico and Weed (1995) characterize maintenance programs as holding an empowering view of schooling whereas other transitional models follow a deficit view.

One type of enrichment model is *immersion education*. This model is discussed here primarily because of its general misuse in discussions of bilingual education in the mass media. Immersion programs, begun in St. Lambert, Quebec, Canada, in the 1960s, immersed children from majority language and cultural backgrounds (English) in a minority language (French). The objective is to produce bilingual and biliterate individuals who would become more tolerant of their minority-culture peers (Genesee, 1987; Swain & Lapkin, 1982). In this type of program, there is no threat of replacing the home language or culture with the new one; rather, the intent is to enhance the majority language and culture. The model has been replicated in a variety of settings in the United States with success equal to that in

Canada (Bernhardt, 1992; California State Department of Education, 1984).

Enrichment models also take a variety of other forms. The most common ones combine native-English-speaking students with native speakers of another language to form *dual-language* or *two-way* immersion programs (see Christian, 1996; Christian, Montone, Lindholm, & Carranza, 1997). In two-way programs, all children maintain their L1 while developing proficiency in languages and academic subjects in their new language. This model also has many different forms, the most common of which begins with as much as 90% of the day in the nonmajority (e.g., Spanish) language, moving to 50% in each language by the third or fourth grade. In some models, the different languages are taught in the morning and the afternoon; in others they alternate by day or week. Ovando and Collier (1998) note, "In research studies on this model, in both Canada and the United States, academic achievement is very high for all groups of students participating in the program, when compared to comparable groups receiving schooling only through English" (p. 59).

Structured immersion, according to Ovando and Collier (1998), is a "misnamed program model that was promoted by English-only proponents with a political agenda in the early 1980s" (p. 56). The model, still being defined, was approved by ballot initiative in California in June 1998. A controversial aspect of this model is that LEP students receive intensive English instruction for usually no more than 1 year but have little or no L1 instruction. Children are then placed in classes with native-English-speaking students. Many analysts believe that structured immersion is a misapplication of the Canadian enrichment model, which has as its goal bilingualism and biliteracy for native English speakers (Hernandez-Chavez, 1984). Moreover, the immersion model is additive in nature, not subtractive. Lambert (1984) describes subtractive bilingualism (the deficit view) as "a consequence of social pressure sometimes present in majority-minority relations . . . . Subtractive bilinguals perform less well on many cognitive and academic measures than additive bilinguals (who acquire L2 and maintain L1)" (cited in Ovando & Collier, 1998, p. 98). Ovando and Collier report that children's achievement scores in one structured immersion program "plummeted as they reached cognitively more complex work" (p. 57). Consequently, the immersion model should not be used in implementing the ESL standards unless the intent of the program is to introduce the foreign language to language majority students.

Obtain a copy of California's Proposition 227. Evaluate it by answering the following questions:

- What type of program does this initiative propose?

- What assumptions does it make about ESOL students?

- To what extent does the proposition reflect or not reflect the ESL standards formulated by TESOL?

- How successful do you think ESOL students will be in schools where this proposition is implemented?

■ Preparing Teachers to Meet the Needs of ESOL Students

The 1996 report of the National Commission on Teaching and America's Future (NCTAF), *What Matters Most: Teaching for America's Future,* recommended five major changes to ensure quality education for all students:

- get serious about standards for students and teachers

- reinvent teacher preparation and professional development

- overhaul teacher recruitment and put qualified teachers in every classroom

- encourage and reward teaching knowledge and skill

- create schools that are organized for student and teacher success (p. vii)

These imperatives for U.S. education are even more critical for ESOL students, whose record of success has been marginal. Attention to the knowledge and skills of teachers of ESOL students is vital for the future success of ESOL learners. The NCTAF's report pointed out that large numbers of teachers lack the training required for their jobs, as nearly one fourth of all secondary teachers do not hold even a minor in the discipline they are teaching. The statistics are even worse for mathematics and science teachers. For ESOL students the situation is equally dismal: "A small proportion of LEP students have regular classroom teachers who have ESL or bilingual education certification" (Moss & Puma, 1995, p. i-11). While the number of ESOL students is increasing, the number of teachers competent to instruct them is decreasing. Pevalin Associates, Inc. (1991), for example, reported that 70% of bilingual teachers and 60% of ESL teachers have no formal training or certification. And Recruiting New Teachers (1998), a national nonprofit organization formed in 1986, claims that "only about one-third of all teachers who have LEP students in their classrooms have completed college course work in subjects such as language acquisition, methods for teaching English to non-native speakers, or cross-cultural communication" (p. 2).

What Matters Most (NCTAF, 1996) sharply criticizes current teacher standards and states that the most important determinant of students' success is access to a "caring, competent, and qualified teacher . . . in schools . . . [that] support student learning" (p. 3). However, the data show that many teachers lack the background knowledge and training to instruct these students. The study does not blame teachers but rather blames a system that does not emphasize teacher quality. Therefore, both preservice and in-service teacher education programs are crucial in developing faculty who can deliver appropriate instruction and implement the ESL standards.

Exacerbating the situation is the fact that the United States will face an acute teacher shortage in all areas in the first decade of the 21st century. Estimates are that the entire United States will need 2 million new teachers. California alone will need 200,000–300,000 teachers by 2005. These shortages will occur because half of the nation's teachers will retire, and, at the same time, student enrollment will continue to skyrocket, reaching almost 3 million students by 2006 (Recruiting New Teachers, n.d.). Shortages will be particularly acute in bilingual education, ESL, math, science, special education, and elementary education.

■ Common Teacher Preparation Models for Bilingual and ESL Certification in the United States

Several follow-up studies of teacher education (see NCTAF, 1997, for a summary) have been conducted as a result of the publication of *What Matters Most* (NCTAF, 1996). One study of exemplary preservice teacher education programs (Darling-Hammond, 1997) found several characteristics among all such programs:

- a common vision in all course work and clinical experiences

- well-defined standards of practice and performance

- the expectation that graduates will know specific content, including pedagogy, child development, learning theory, and student assessment

- rigorous theoretical content and rigorous practical content with clear articulation between the two

- extended clinical experiences that are clearly connected to specific content

- strong university-school partnerships

- extensive use of case studies, teacher research on teaching and learning, and performance-based assessment of learning

Because these characteristics are essential for the success of students in general, it is necessary to examine whether current preservice programs for ESL teachers share these features. Like ESL program models, teacher preparation models vary widely. A 1994 survey of state education agencies (Fleishman, Arterburn, & Wiens, 1995) showed that 31 U.S. states and the District of Columbia offered certification or some form of endorsement in bilingual education; 40 states and the District of Columbia granted an endorsement for ESL. Six states (Alaska, Oregon, Pennsylvania, South Carolina, South Dakota, West Virginia) offered no certification or endorsement for bilingual education or ESL. However, although the majority of states grant some kind of certification or endorsement, the way teachers achieve the credential vary considerably, as revealed by a directory developed by the Center for Research on Education, Diversity and Excellence (Walton, in press). The purpose of the directory is "to identify nationally the teacher preparation programs (preservice and in-service) that are addressing, promoting and implementing effective preparation for teachers who will teach in linguistically and culturally diverse classrooms" (p. 1). Some states give statewide tests for competencies in pedagogy, culture, and language for bilingual certification (e.g., California administers such tests for 10 languages) in addition to a statewide examination (or course work) for ESL certification. Some (e.g., Arizona) give postcredential endorsements for course work; others include core ESL methods courses within the basic credential.

Walton (in press) has developed a typology in which she has identified several key components of teacher preparation programs. Those that she identifies as bilingual education preparation programs (nos. 4–6 below) do not specify which model of preparation is being used. The components are as follows:

1. *general with a multicultural emphasis:* These programs offer general teacher education and require a course or a series of courses that address diversity. Multicultural content may be infused throughout program. Student teachers are placed in settings with diverse student populations.

2. *English as a second language:* The orientation of these programs is primarily linguistic and focuses on teaching the English language to speakers of languages other than English (e.g., teaching in an ESL pull-out program).

3. *English language development and multicultural:* These programs include ESL and ongoing English language development, the teaching of content through specially designed methods such as sheltered English. They infuse multicultural content throughout the program. Attention is given to emergent literacy in English and transitional methods. Programs also include the study of the role of bilingual education in L2 development. Student teachers are placed in diverse classroom settings to teach English and academic content.

4. *bilingual:* In these programs, an unspecified amount of the primary language is used. Programs often do not specify the various components of a full bilingual and biliteracy preparation program (e.g., course work is not clearly specified for preservice teachers of ESL and sheltered English, nor are literacy and content in the primary language required, but there is a diversity requirement). Cultural content is bicultural (ethnic studies) but not multicultural. Student teachers are generally placed with one non-English language group.

5. *bilingual/biliterate/multicultural/bicultural:* These programs fully specify courses for literacy and academic content for English and an L1. They provide training to teach literacy in the L1 and L2 and to teach content in English using sheltered methods. The goal is to prepare teachers to

provide instruction leading to bilingual, biliterate students. Student teaching provides experience in emergent literacy instruction in English and the L1 as well as content in the L1. Cultural content includes multicultural as well as bicultural material (specific to or related to the primary language) and knowledge of specific linguistic groups. Teacher candidates are placed in multilingual/multicultural classrooms and in single-language classrooms to teach literacy and content in a language other than English. Walton (in press) notes that course work for these teacher candidates includes such courses as L1 acquisition, teaching L1 language arts, methods of teaching ESL and content areas, multicultural education, curriculum development in bilingual/ESL settings, and use of instructional technology.

6. *bilingual/multicultural:* These programs do not specify the various components that are included in a full bilingual and biliteracy program. Course work is not clearly specified for ESL and sheltered instruction or for literacy and content in the primary language. Culture content is multicultural and moves beyond the study of one ethnic group. Methods courses are taught in a non-English language. Student teaching includes one non-English language group and takes place in multicultural settings.

7. *multicultural:* These programs prepare candidates to teach in socioeconomically, ethnically, racially, and culturally diverse communities. They teach an educational strategy in which students' cultural backgrounds are used to develop effective classroom instruction and school environments (Gollnick & Chinn, 1997). They also teach a curriculum that promotes social equality, affirms diversity and democracy, and includes culturally responsive pedagogy. Teacher candidates are placed in diverse teaching settings. However, these programs do not necessarily address issues of bilingualism, ESL, or sheltered instruction.

Examine the preparation that you are receiving or have received to teach ESOL students. Which of the above models best describes this preparation?

■ Conclusion

The enormous change in the U.S. population since 1970 has dramatically affected the demographics of the nation's schools. Immigrants and refugees have come to the United States in large numbers as the result of political and economic conditions in their home countries and changes in U.S. immigration policies. U.S.-born children live in homes and communities in which a language other than English is the primary language. The changing population of U.S. schools has resulted in the need for changes in the nature of instruction of children and youth and the preparation of their teachers. This chapter has described many of these changes and demonstrated the need for *ESL Standards for Pre-K–12 Students* (TESOL, 1997) to serve as a guide for teacher preparation and curriculum reform.

Chapter 2

A History of the ESL Standards for Pre-K–12 Students

Emily L. Gómez

Events leading up to the publication of TESOL's *ESL Standards for Pre-K–12 Students* (1997) began in the early 1980s, the result of a convergence of matters in the educational reform movement in the United States and the work of a great many people in the field of ESL education and in other disciplines. This progression of events created, defined, and refined the notion of what standards-based educational reform looks like and how it can be achieved. Throughout the process, TESOL as a professional organization has taken a leading role in ensuring that the needs of second language (L2) students are included in the national discussion.

■ *A Nation at Risk* Released

Following the 1983 release of *A Nation at Risk* (National Commission on Excellence in Education, 1983), educators throughout the country began to use a new rhetoric to talk about educational reform, linking the nation's financial and economic security with the quality of education students received in the public schools. Advocates of educational reform pointed to the dismal results of U.S. students on international examinations comparing the academic achievement of students from industrialized countries as signs of a decaying system (Marzano & Kendall, 1996). Educators pointed to the especially poor results of linguistically and culturally diverse students on these exams as an area of particular concern.

TIME LINE FOR THE DEVELOPMENT OF THE
ESL STANDARDS FOR PRE-K–12 STUDENTS

1983   *A Nation at Risk* released by the National Commission on Excellence in Education, leading to the beginning of the educational reform movement.

1988   National Council of Teachers of Mathematics (NCTM) begins developing mathematics standards.

1989   At National Governors' Association education summit, governors agree to six goals for education to be reached by the year 2000. Goal 3 stipulates that all students must master challenging subject matter in five subjects: English, mathematics, science, history, and geography.

          NCTM releases *Curriculum and Evaluation Standards for School Mathematics,* the first set of standards developed by a national professional organization.

1989–1993   Organizations representing other subject areas push for their inclusion in the final legislation.

1991   Bush administration launches an effort to reach goals of America 2000, providing federal monies to support the development of standards for English, mathematics, science, history, and geography.

          TESOL establishes a task force to monitor the standards-based reforms and the place of English language learners within it.

1993   TESOL task force publishes the *Access Brochure.*

          ESL Development: Language and Literacy in Schools is published by the National Languages and Literacy Institute of Australia, providing a model for the task force.

1994   Goals 2000: Educate America Act is enacted by Congress. Included in Goal 3 are four additional subject areas: civics and government, foreign languages, economics, and arts.

          TESOL Board of Directors approves the formation of a second task force, which explores the possibility of developing ESL standards and begins to develop a conceptual framework.

1995	Conceptual framework is presented at the National Association for Bilingual Education Conference in Phoenix, Arizona.
	Draft of *Promising Futures* is released at the 29th Annual TESOL Convention in Long Beach, California.
	TESOL Board of Directors approves the ESL Standards Project.
	Drafts of the English language arts and foreign language content standards are released, providing additional models for the ESL Standards Project.
1996	First draft of *ESL Standards for Pre-K–12 Students* is released at the 30th Annual TESOL Convention in Chicago; feedback is widely solicited.
	The project is renamed the ESL Standards and Assessment Project, reflecting an additional focus on assessment.
	TESOL is invited to participate in the development of the National Study of School Evaluation's *Indicators of Schools of Quality, Volume 1: Schoolwide Indicators of Quality.*
1997	Draft of *Managing the Assessment Process: A Framework for Measuring Student Attainment of the ESL Standards* is released at the 31st Annual TESOL Convention in Orlando, Florida; feedback is widely solicited.
	ESL Standards for Pre-K–12 Students is published by TESOL.
1997–present	TESOL supports standards implementation activities, including TESOL academy seminars, curriculum development workshops, and professional development sessions with state education departments and local school districts.
1998	TESOL sponsors its first training of trainers workshop, entitled *Using the ESL Standards for Curriculum, Assessment, and Professional Development.*
	Managing the Assessment Process: A Framework for Measuring Student Attainment of the ESL Standards is published by TESOL.
1999	Draft of *Scenarios for ESL Standards-Based Assessment* is released at the 33rd Annual TESOL Convention in New York City; feedback is widely solicited.
2000	*Implementing the ESL Standards for Pre-K–12 Students Through Teacher Education* and *Training Others to Use the ESL Standards: A Professional Development Manual* are published by TESOL.

■ National Education Goals Defined

Growing concern over the mediocrity of the U.S. educational system spearheaded efforts in two arenas: educational and political. In the educational arena, the National Council of Teachers of Mathematics (NCTM) began to develop the first national voluntary standards for school mathematics, which were drafted and revised in the late 1980s and published in 1989. In the political arena, the concern led to the 1989 National Governors' Association Education Summit in Charlottesville, Virginia, where the educational standards movement came to the nation's attention. Then-President George Bush and the nation's governors agreed to six broad goals for education to be reached by the year 2000. The goals and the governors' rationales for them were later published in *The National Education Goals Report: Building a Nation of Learners* (National Education Goals Panel, 1991). In 1991, the Bush administration created legislation that established comprehensive goals for U.S. schools. America 2000, reauthorized by the Clinton administration in 1994 as the Goals 2000: Educate America Act, defined goals designed to move all students, including ESOL students, in U.S. schools to achieve higher standards. Based on the premise that all students can meet high standards of learning, these goals spoke to a variety of educational purposes. Goal 3, which called for all students to master challenging subject matter in core content areas, had the greatest impact on the development of voluntary national content and performance standards. It reads as follows:

> Goal 3   Students will leave grades four, eight and twelve having demonstrated competency in challenging subject matter including English, mathematics, science, history and geography; and every school in America will ensure that all students learn to use their minds well, so they may be prepared for responsible citizenship, further learning, and productive employment in our modern economy. (sec. 102)

As a result of the development of these goals and the discussion leading up to them, the nation focused more attention on educational reform.

■ Events Leading up to Goals 2000

Shortly after the governors' summit, the NCTM released its national standards document, entitled *Curriculum and Evaluation Standards for School Mathematics* (1989). These curriculum standards for mathematics were the first standards to be published by a national professional organization. They offered not only content objectives, describing what students should know and be able to do, but also teaching principles, instructional strategies, and suggestions for integrating the subject with other disciplines. The development of the first content-area standards document and the National Education Goals Panel's 1991 report led to a more cohesive national discussion regarding the need to raise academic standards nationally, fueled in part by bipartisan support in Congress. Many educators and educational organizations rallied behind the standards-based reform movement. One notable organization, the American Federation of Teachers (AFT), became a powerful force in the educational reform movement nationally and leveraged the support of many of the nation's teachers for standards-based reform (AFT, 1997; Shanker, 1996).

By the early 1990s, many national professional organizations, including the National Council of Teachers of English (NCTE); the International Reading Association (IRA); the National Research Council, which produced the *National Science Education Standards* (1996); and the National Center for History in the Schools had begun the process of developing national content standards, following NCTM's model. In fact, the math standards development process, which involved grass-roots consensus building followed by a broad review from members in the field, has been held by many in the education field as the paradigm for other subject areas.

■ TESOL Responds

In early 1991, TESOL as an organization began to formally monitor the educational reform movement when a group of ESL experts in K–12 education (policy makers, teacher educators, administrators, and classroom teachers) began to discuss strategies for TESOL's involvement in advocating for language minority students. The TESOL Board of Directors established and approved a task force to produce guidelines for the effective education of linguistically and culturally diverse students. TESOL also held its first meeting for ESL representatives of state education agencies (SEAs) at the 25th Annual TESOL Convention in New York.

Later in 1991, the TESOL board appointed a 3-year task force to begin developing guidelines for the effective education of linguistically and culturally diverse students. This task force, headed by Denise McKeon, then of the National Clearinghouse for Bilingual Education at the George Washington University, worked with the president of TESOL in putting together a 20-member task force. Although the group did not originally set out to develop content standards for ESL, its objective was to monitor whether ESOL students were being included in other content-area standards.

A subcommittee of the task force met at the National Association for Bilingual Education's (NABE) conference in Albuquerque in 1992. This meeting was followed the same year by a second meeting of ESL representatives of SEAs at the 26th Annual TESOL Convention in Vancouver, Canada. As an outgrowth of these meetings, TESOL began an effort to secure funding for the development of materials advocating the inclusion of ESOL students in the standards-based reform movement.

When funding did not materialize outside the TESOL organization, the task force submitted a request for funds to the TESOL board. The purpose of the proposed project was to develop an "access brochure" describing the framework of services necessary for the delivery of education to language minority students. The brochure would be disseminated to the public and the membership, accompanied by a packet, called the *TESOL Resource Packet* (TESOL, n.d.), that included existing TESOL literature on helping language minority students meet the national goals. Upon its publication in late 1993, the *Access Brochure* (TESOL, 1993) became the first of several advocacy tools that could be used to encourage inclusion of ESOL students in the educational reform movement.

■ Goals 2000: Educate America Act

By the time the *Access Brochure* (TESOL, 1993) was published, the federal government had given strong bipartisan support for the development of voluntary national standards in a variety of content areas. In 1994, Congress enacted the Goals 2000: Educate America Act, which listed eight goals (see Appendix A) and defined the following disciplines as core curricular areas: English, mathematics, science, foreign language, civics and government, economics, arts, history, and geography. This legislation was intended to become a blueprint for federal K–12 policy. In the words of AFT President Albert Shanker, Goals 2000 was "the most important education legislation we've ever had" (Family Research Council, 1999, n.p.).

Goal 3 as proposed in 1989 and then modified over the years became the linchpin for the development of national standards in various subject areas, with many professional organizations actively designing and revising content-area standards. The federal government provided varying levels of funding for the subjects listed in Goal 3.

Professional and educational organizations applied for and received funding to develop voluntary national standards in science, history, English language arts, civics, geography, and other areas (e.g., the National Council for Geographic Education, in collaboration with the American Geographical Society, the Association of American Geographers, and the National Geography Society developed standards for geography; the NCTE and the IRA worked on English language arts standards). During this period, TESOL also tried to secure federal funding to begin developing standards for ESL. Unfortunately, due in no part to lack of effort, TESOL did not receive funding for the development of content standards. The denial of funding was based in part on the false premise that no separate standards were needed for ESOL students. Experts in the field of ESL disagreed.

TESOL recognized that the various content-area standards-writing teams were not taking the needs of ESOL students into account as they developed their standards; nor did the teams include ESOL students in their classroom scenarios. In fact, as late as 1996, only two of the national content standards specifically made reference to ESOL students or culturally diverse students. The English language arts standards supported the concept of first language (L1) education, stressing the importance of developing L1 literacy to aid in English language literacy. The foreign language standards emphasized the importance of teaching about culture when learning a new language.

Meanwhile, demographic changes were requiring more, not less, attention to the historically marginalized population of ESOL students. Even the objectives and data-gathering criteria established by the National Education Goals Panel, charged with monitoring national progress toward meeting the national goals, did not identify *limited English proficient* as a category needing special examination ("Goals Panel Expresses Concern," 1993). It was becoming clearer to the task force, recently restructured and now headed by Else Hamayan of the Illinois Resource Center, that content standards addressing the issues relating to ESOL students were needed.

Concurrently, at the international level, a group of experts at the National Languages and Literacy Institute in Australia published the ESL Bandscales in *ESL Development: Language and Literacy in Schools* (National Languages and Literacy Institute of Australia, 1993). The ESL Bandscales, followed by ESL Assessment Activities and a reporting format, are essentially performance standards for what students in Australian K–12 ESL and literacy programs should achieve at various stages of their education. These bandscales describe seven levels of proficiency in English in three grade-level clusters of the K–12 spectrum—junior primary, middle and upper primary, and secondary—and define how well students should be able to complete various tasks in listening, speaking, reading, and writing. This publication provided the TESOL task force with a concrete model.

The Australian initiative addressed the need for a clear definition of what students should know and be able to do as a result of ESL instruction. This need for a distinct picture of the relationship among curriculum, instruction, and assessment in the ESL field became one of the primary reasons the TESOL task force decided to develop content standards for ESOL students. The task force recognized that the development of national content standards would be a great service to the ESL profession in the United States.

Unknown to the TESOL task force, at about the same time a similar project under way in Alberta, Canada, was defining the goals for ESOL students there (Alberta Education, 1997). The goals, called *learner outcomes*, are followed by specific examples of activities, similar to the progress indicators used in TESOL's *ESL Standards for Pre-K–12 Students*, that students at five levels of English proficiency can perform to demonstrate mastery of the general outcome. According to Gail Kingwell of the Alberta Department of Education (personal communication, July 25, 1997), *English as a Second Language* was subsequently produced by a group of educators following a process very similar to that followed by members of TESOL's ESL Standards Project. In order to ensure broad support for the document, a great deal of input was sought and provided by teachers in the field of ESL and bilingual education in Canada.

■ The ESL Standards Project

After repeated efforts to secure funding for the development of additional advocacy tools, including a strong letter-writing effort aimed at state and national legislators by TESOL members at the 28th Annual TESOL Convention, in 1994 the TESOL board approved the restructuring of the task force. A core team was established in an effort to move the project forward, with the primary purpose being to decide if separate ESL standards were warranted and to gauge the interest of the field in their development. Based on conversations with members of the field, the project team agreed to develop a concept paper discussing issues relating to standards-based educational reforms that confronted the ESL field. This core team, consisting of Else Hamayan (chair), Nancy Cloud, Sarah Hudelson, Jean Ramírez, and Deborah Short, began meeting in May 1994 to develop the concept paper. TESOL board members Fred Genesee and Denise Murray also participated in the conceptualization of the standards.

The resulting conceptual framework, later named *Promising Futures* (TESOL, 1996), was a pivotal piece, describing the reasons ESL standards were needed, myths about L2 learning that TESOL wanted to dispel, and general principles of second language acquisition. It also described TESOL's vision of effective education for ESOL students. Writing the conceptual framework required the drafting of three broad goals surrounding the use of the English language.[1] The three goals stress the importance of learning English for the following purposes: (a) to communicate in social settings, (b) to achieve academically in all content areas, and (c) to use English in socially and culturally appropriate ways. The development of the conceptual framework continued throughout the following year, and the framework was presented at the NABE convention in February 1995.

Goal 1 focuses on social and personal uses of English, including interpersonal communication (or what Cummins, 1992, called *basic interpersonal communication skills* [BICS]). Goal 1, Standard 1 deals with students' interactions with other individuals for social purposes, such as talking to a friend about a television show or conducting a sales transaction in a store. Goal 1, Standard 2 refers to a student's use of English for interpersonal reasons, such as reading a book for pleasure, watching and understanding a video, or listening to songs. Goal 1, Standard 3 highlights the importance of students' using learning strategies to extend their ability to communicate in English. Once students are no longer in ESL and bilingual classrooms, they need to rely on these strategies to continue learning English for social communication.

Goal 2, the heart of the standards with respect to educational reform in the United States, focuses on students' ability to use English to achieve academically—in other words, what Cummins (1992) called *cognitive academic language proficiency* (CALP), the English language skills necessary for academic success. These skills are also important for students to learn if they are to meet state content standards. Goal 2, Standard 1 focuses on preparing students to use English for routine classroom interactions—everyday classroom discussions and activities, such as asking a teacher to repeat something, explaining an absence, and negotiating roles when placed in cooperative learning groups. Goal 2, Standard 2 concentrates on the subject matter information in the students' classes. Students need to develop English language skills so they can understand, apply, and demonstrate knowledge of the content being taught. Goal 2, Standard 3 is a critical piece, focusing on the use of effective learning strategies to acquire the language skills and content knowledge necessary for success in school.

Goal 3 shares a conceptual base with the first two goals but was given special treatment to draw attention to the importance of the cultural component in learning language. Speakers use language to communicate humor, irony, and grief, among other concepts; how to express them varies according to culture. Goal 3, Standard 1 explains that language varies and that students must be able to select the appropriate variety, register, and genre according to the context. For example, students need to recognize when to write a friendly letter or a business letter and how to speak to a classmate in the cafeteria versus a potential employer. Goal 3, Standard 2 highlights the fact that nonverbal communication, including tone of voice, voice volume, body language, and gestures, are all important aspects of communication. Goal 3, Standard 3 stresses the importance of students' using learning strategies to develop competence in communicating in socially and culturally appropriate ways.

Another important decision made by the core team was how to define English language proficiency levels. The team realized that districts and states have programs based on differing numbers of English language proficiency levels, usually dependent on the size of the ESOL population within the program. The team based the proficiency-level descriptions on three levels, defined as beginning, intermediate, and advanced, with special attention given to students with limited formal schooling (LFS). The LFS category included students with low or nonexistent literacy skills in their L1, who as a result do not develop English language proficiency as quickly as students who are literate in their L1. The team also decided to include students with physical and learning disabilities in the vignettes.

At the 29th Annual TESOL Convention in Long Beach, California, in March 1995, many events accelerated the further development of the ESL Standards Project. The project members facilitated another meeting of the ESL representatives of SEAs; met with key advisers, most of whom were members of the original task force; and organized a panel of math, science, social studies, and English/language arts representatives to give presentations on their content standards. Most importantly, the ESL Standards Project members presented their draft of *Promising Futures* (TESOL, 1996), the concept paper, to the TESOL membership for review; suggestions for change were welcomed. The TESOL membership was vocally supportive of the effort to produce a concept paper and urged further development of content standards, expressing the benefits such a document would have for the ESL field.

Also at the 1995 convention, the TESOL board realized the need for support and approved a specially funded project managed by Deborah Short with assistance from Emily Gómez at the Center from Applied Linguistics, in Washington, DC, to develop content standards for ESL. The team, using the definition emerging from the larger education field, defined content standards as statements describing what students should know and be able to do. With that, the ESL Standards Project team geared up for the next phase of the project, creating the guidelines for affiliate writing teams and developing a sample standard. It was decided that the sample standard should define the goal and standard and be followed by descriptors, sample progress indicators (SPIs), a vignette, and discussion. (See the box below for definitions of terms used in the standards volume.)

Terms Used in *ESL Standards*

- *goals:* overarching intentions for English language use that are tied to social and academic language and appropriate use

- *standards:* what students should know and be able to do as a result of instruction

- *descriptors:* broad categories of behaviors that students can demonstrate when they meet a standard

- *progress indicators:* assessable, observable activities that students may perform to show progress toward meeting the standard; organized by grade-level cluster

- *vignettes:* brief instructional sequences that show the standards in action

- *discussions:* brief explanations of the teacher's and students' actions in each of the vignettes, linking the vignettes to standards and progress indicators

---

After the ESL standards team drafted the standards statements, some additional decisions about the organization document were made based on issues particular to the ESL profession, including the additional factor of language proficiency. When trying to decide whether the document should be organized by English language proficiency level or by grade-level cluster, as most other content-area standards documents had been, the team realized that the ESL standards document required a three-dimensional organization that was impossible to show on paper. It was clear that, although a 7th-grade math student could be assumed to have a certain level of mathematical knowledge, no assumptions could be made about the English language proficiency level of a 7th-grade ESOL student. Thus, the team had to make decisions regarding how grade levels and proficiency levels would intersect. Grade-level clusters (Pre-K–3, 4–8, and 9–12), similar to those of other content-area standards-writing projects, were defined to broadly represent the organizational structure of K–12 institutions in the United States into elementary, middle, and high schools. The clusters are also related to the testing cycle of national exams, such as the National Assessment of Educational Progress (NAEP), which is given in Grades 4, 8, and 11.

Affiliate and state representatives were then enlisted to form writing teams to develop the descriptors, progress indicators, vignettes, and discussions for the goals and standards. The affiliate and state writing teams were asked to use their own teaching experiences to describe activities that they had undertaken successfully with their students and that addressed the specific goal and standard assigned to them. These writing teams, which were geographically representative of the varying regions of the United States, were asked to describe the school setting (i.e., urban, suburban, or rural location); the teacher's and students' ethnicity and sex; and whether the instruction took place in a self-contained ESL classroom, a content classroom, a sheltered or content-based ESL classroom, or some other type of program.

The ESL standards core team benefited greatly from the experiences of content-area standards-writing teams that were ahead of them in the development process, especially those most closely linked to ESL—the foreign language group and the English language arts group. Drawing on the 1995 draft of the foreign language standards as a model, TESOL's team included the concepts of progress indicators based on proficiency levels and classroom learning scenarios that exemplify the standards in action. The NCTE-IRA English language arts standards (1996) also used classroom vignettes and were the only content-area standards that included ESOL and bilingual students in their vignettes. In addition, the NCTE-IRA standards were important because they emphasized the relationship between L1 acquisition and literacy in the development of English language literacy. The National Council on Social Studies infused multicultural education into its vignettes.

TASK 1

Locate a copy of the NCTE-IRA English language arts standards (see http://www.ncte.org/standards/). How is the relationship between L1 acquisition and literacy depicted? What role do L2 learners play in these standards? How do they compare with *ESL Standards for Pre-K–12 Students*?

TASK 2

Locate a copy of the social studies standards from the National Council for the Social Studies (http://www.ncss.org/standards/too/). How is multicultural education infused into the vignettes? Is the relationship between language and content learning discussed? How might the standards be modified for use with students in sheltered social studies classes?

Throughout the fall of 1995 and into early 1996, the core team revised the writing teams' submissions and created additional vignettes and discussions. By March 1996, a draft of *ESL Standards for Pre-K–12 Students* was ready to be distributed. The team presented the document to the TESOL membership at the 30th Annual TESOL Convention in Chicago. Thirteen hundred copies of the draft document were disseminated, and reviews were requested from many professionals from the wider education community as well as from TESOL members. Based on the reviews received from the TESOL membership and invited reviewers and policy makers, the document was reorganized and additional pieces added over the course of the next year.

The core team grappled with how to show that achievement of the goals and standards would be dependent upon issues relating to both grade levels and proficiency levels. It was difficult to show that the SPIs were both developmental and cumulative in nature. This point was subsequently strengthened by the addition of the SPI charts to the final standards document (TESOL, 1997, pp. 23–25). These charts show how a single SPI, such as "Construct a chart or other graphic showing data," can be used with beginning, intermediate, and advanced students as well as with students with limited formal schooling. It also shows how students would demonstrate proficiency based on developmentally appropriate tasks depending on their grade level. The sample below mirrors a vignette in *ESL Standards*, focusing on a fourth- to fifth-grade classroom scenario in which students read a Native American myth and share myths from their own cultures:

Goal 2, Standard 2: To use English to achieve academically in all content areas: Students will use English to obtain, process, construct, and provide subject matter information in spoken and written form.

SPI: Construct a chart or other graphic showing data.

Beginning	Intermediate	Advanced	Limited formal schooling (LFS)
Draw a sequence chart to illustrate the story line of the myth that was read and describe the chart orally, using words and phrases.	Draw a sequence chart to illustrate the story line of the myth that was read and write simple sentences describing the chart.	Develop a comparison chart to compare two nature myths with regard to characters, setting, and conflict resolution.	Make rebus symbols for key vocabulary and then copy part of the myth using rebus symbols for appropriate words.

The team chose not to develop performance standards, which are statements that describe how well students at certain levels or grades should be able to perform the defined content standards. Two reasons for this decision emerged: (a) the great variety and diversity among programs in which ESOL students learn in the United States and (b) the belief that performance standards should be defined at the local level.

Throughout 1996–1997, copies of *ESL Standards for Pre-K–12 Students* were made available to educators for review, and the document was also posted on the Center for Applied Linguistics' (CAL) World Wide Web site. As the reviews were received, feedback from the field was incorporated before the document was published in June 1997. The team also decided to extend the assessment activities at this point.

■ An Expanded Focus on Assessment

Besides the dissemination of the draft ESL standards, another important event occurred at the 30th Annual TESOL Convention in Chicago: The ESL Standards Project became the ESL Standards and Assessment Project. The assessment team, consisting of Anne Katz (chair), Fred Genesee, Margo Gottlieb, and Meg Malone, had been considering a possible companion document that would focus on assessment. In the year prior to the 1996 convention, the assessment team had developed some guidelines that could serve as a framework for assessing ESOL students' attainment of the ESL standards. Over the course of the next year, the assessment team consulted assessment experts for feedback on the document. After further refining their document, a draft was released in 1997 at the 31st Annual TESOL Convention, and feedback from the TESOL membership was solicited.

After receiving reviews from the TESOL membership, the assessment team made the final changes to *Managing the Assessment Process: A Framework for Measuring Attainment of the ESL Standards* (*MAP*), and it was published by TESOL in 1998. Because *MAP* is essentially a position paper describing what good assessment should look like, the assessment team moved to develop a second assessment document. They asked TESOL members what kind of document would provide additional insight on assessment issues that arise in moving to a standards-based educational system. During the summer and fall of 1998, the assessment team asked teams from across the country to write scenarios around several of the vignettes in *ESL Standards*. These scenarios place the vignette within the assessment cycle that is described in *MAP* and show how assessment needs can be met through a variety of assessment measures. A draft of the second assessment document, *Scenarios for ESL Standards-Based Assessment* (TESOL, in press) was distributed in 1999 at the 33rd Annual TESOL Convention in New York City, and reviews and feedback were invited. (See chapters 5, 6, and 7 for detailed discussions of assessment issues.)

■ Impact of *ESL Standards for Pre-K–12 Students*

The publication of *ESL Standards for Pre-K–12 Students* in June 1997 was a milestone in the history of the ESL profession. This document, published by the international professional organization for teachers of ESL, defined effective education for ESOL students. By reading the vignettes and seeing themselves mirrored in the pages of *ESL Standards*, many teachers confirmed that they were on the right track in the type of education they were providing. Teachers saw that, regardless of the program in which they taught, many of the strategies and techniques they were using to teach ESOL students the skills they needed to achieve in content classes were appropriate.

By using *ESL Standards* and the other standards documents reprinted within it, such as the *Access Brochure* (TESOL, 1993) and *Promising Futures* (TESOL, 1996), as advocacy tools, teachers and administrators could move their school, district, or state in the direction of providing more comprehensive services for ESOL students. Educators saw that much could be done to align their programs to the ESL standards in terms of curriculum and assessment revision and professional development. They realized that the standards document (and its companion documents; see the next section) could provide them with useful additional information in developing their programs. Policy makers and administrators at the district level began to realize that they needed to revise their ESL curricula and assessment systems and align them to the ESL standards.

TESOL has responded by providing many opportunities for educators to learn about *ESL Standards* and the implications of the document. Each year since the release of the draft of the standards document, TESOL has sponsored the following activities:

- TESOL academies (regional 12-hour intensive workshops held at universities during the summer)

- preconference institutes (full-day workshops held before the annual TESOL convention)

- numerous workshops and discussion sessions held during the annual TESOL convention (sponsored by the TESOL Board of Directors and the Elementary Education, Secondary Education, Bilingual Education, and Teacher Education interest sections)

In addition, workshops have been held at regional affiliate conferences and at a number of other national education conferences, including those of NABE, the Association for Supervision and Curriculum Development, and the American Association of Higher Education.

Based on the models of other professional organizations that produced standards, TESOL has recognized the need to monitor the implementation of the ESL standards in states and districts. Members of the project team began to work with selected states and districts to facilitate standards-based reform. Montgomery County, Maryland, agreed to act as an implementation site, and the ESL standards team has monitored the district's process of developing and implementing a standards-based ESL curriculum across the K–12 spectrum.

Many other districts have undertaken curriculum and assessment development projects, including Highline School District (Seattle, Washington), and San Francisco Unified School District (California). Similar projects have been undertaken at the state level in, for example, New Jersey, Tennessee, and North Carolina. (See chapter 4 for a model of curriculum development and an in-depth discussion of several of these projects.)

State and district ESL/bilingual or professional development offices have sponsored workshops for their personnel to aid them in understanding the ESL standards. The members of the ESL Standards and Assessment Project team have been actively involved in providing technical assistance in many of these state and local endeavors. (See TESOL's Web site, http://www.tesol.edu/, and CAL's Web site, http://www.cal.org/, for information on states and districts that have undertaken projects using the ESL standards for curriculum, assessment, and professional development efforts.)

Another concrete measure of the impact of *ESL Standards* presented itself shortly after the release of the draft of the standards in March 1996. For the first time, TESOL was invited from the start, rather than as an afterthought, to participate in an exciting mainstream education project: the development of the National Study of School Evaluation's (NSSE) *Indicators of Schools of Quality, Volume 1: Schoolwide Indicators of Quality* (1997). This venture invited members of content standards–writing teams from almost every discipline to a meeting at which general and discipline-based performance indicators of quality schools would be described. The NSSE, the umbrella organization overseeing the work of six regional accreditation associations, began this project to develop "a research-based self-assessment guide for schools committed to continuous improvement" (NSSE, 1997, cover). As a result of these new indicators, all schools undergoing an accreditation process will have to reflect on the quality of the educational program they provide to ESOL students and improve it as necessary.

■ Additional Companion Documents and Services

Once the standards were published, the TESOL board recognized the need for continued support of the ESL Standards and Assessment Project, based on the experience of other national professional organizations, such as the NCTM and the American Council for the Teaching of Foreign Languages. In addition to *MAP* (TESOL, 1998) and *Scenarios for ESL Standards-Based Assessment* (TESOL, in press), TESOL began to plan for additional publications and support services to ensure that the standards would be implemented in as many districts and states as possible. *Training Others to Use the ESL Standards: A Professional Development Manual* (Short et al., 2000) is intended for teacher trainers throughout the country. It contains black-line masters of overhead transparencies and handouts that the ESL Standards and Assessment Project team has produced and used in training sessions throughout the development and implementation phase of the project. The need for a textbook to be used in teacher education was also recognized. The current volume is the result of that need.

Additional services are also in place. On *ESLSTDS*, the ESL standards implementation discussion list, educators discuss the development and implementation of standards-based curricula that include ESOL students. It is hoped that the dialogue among practitioners will facilitate the implementation of standards-based curriculum and assessments and aid educators in delivering relevant professional development opportunities to educators in districts and states throughout the country.[2]

In addition, the *ESL Standards Implementation Database* (Center for Applied Linguistics, n.d.), available on the World Wide Web, is a searchable compilation of responses from school, district, and state personnel on the status of their standards-based reform efforts. The responses are based on the ESL Standards Implementation Survey (see Appendix B).

TASK 4

Administer the ESL Standards Implementation Survey (Appendix B) to teachers in a local district or in the district in which you currently teach. Analyze the results, and discuss the implications for standards implementation.

The TESOL Publications Committee is overseeing the development of four additional volumes that will provide teachers in four grade spans—Pre-K–2, 3–5, 6–8, and 9–12—with sample units showing how *ESL Standards* can be used in their classrooms.

■ The Future of the ESL Standards and Assessment Project

Because the ESL Standards and Assessment Project has responded to the needs of educators who implement the ESL standards in their schools, districts, and states, the project has continued to evolve. The TESOL board has provided the funding for a large part of the work accomplished thus far and is committed to continuing its efforts. At the same time, the board has made a commitment to other standards projects, such as those for intensive English programs, ESL in adult education, community college ESL, and workplace ESL programs. TESOL hopes to continue to promote the successful implementation of standards-based reforms that benefit ESOL students of all ages well into the future.

■ Conclusion

The original task force established by the TESOL Board of Directors in 1991 found evidence to suggest the need for a separate set of content standards for ESOL students. Task force members felt that ESL standards would provide the ESL profession with a shared vision of what ESOL students should know and be able to do. The fact that schools, districts, and states have so enthusiastically received the standards and have used them as a reference point in evaluating their programs and implementing standards-based reform shows their early impact. Through standards-based revisions to curricula and assessment programs, many teachers and administrators have reflected on the quality of their programs and have been encouraged to participate in professional development.

Although the full impact of the release of *ESL Standards for Pre-K–12 Students* will not be known for some time, the document has clearly led to significant changes in some districts where educators work with ESOL and bilingual students. Other evidence, such as the recognition of ESL in the NSSE's effort, shows that advocacy works. *ESL Standards* has put the educational spotlight on students learning ESL and explains how educators can help these students move from the ESL or bilingual classroom to the mainstream classroom successfully. Once these standards are achieved, ESL students should be ready to meet the other content-area standards, on which they will undoubtedly be assessed at some point in their educational career. As such, the ESL standards can be seen as an on-ramp to success, providing the framework for schools, districts, and states to evaluate their programs and address inadequacies in the education of ESOL students.

■ Notes

[1] There were 10 standards in the first draft of *ESL Standards*, but 2 of the original standards were merged after reviews from the field were received.

[2] To subscribe to *ESLSTDS*, send an e-mail message to request-eslstds@ caltalk.cal.org. In the subject line, type *subscribe*. Leave the rest of the message blank.

■ Appendix A: 1994 National Education Goals

Goal 1   All students will enter school ready to learn.

Goal 2   The high school graduation rate will increase to at least 90%.

Goal 3   All students will leave grades 4, 8, and 12 having demonstrated competency over challenging subject matter including English, mathematics, science, foreign languages, civics and government, economics, arts, history, and geography, and every school in America will ensure that all students learn to use their minds well, so they may be prepared for responsible citizenship, further learning, and productive employment in our Nation's modern economy.

Goal 4   The Nation's teaching force will have access to programs for the continued improvement of their professional skills and the opportunity to acquire the knowledge and skills needed to instruct and prepare all American students for the next century.

Goal 5   United States students will be first in the world in mathematics and science achievement.

Goal 6   Every adult American will be literate and will possess the knowledge and skills necessary to compete in a global economy and exercise the rights and responsibilities of citizenship.

Goal 7   Every school in the United States will be free of drugs, violence, and the unauthorized presence of firearms and alcohol and will offer a disciplined environment conducive to learning.

Goal 8   Every school will promote partnerships that will increase parental involvement and participation in promoting the social, emotional, and academic growth of children.

Source: Goals 2000: Educate America Act (1994, sec. 102).

■ Appendix B: ESL Standards Implementation Survey

Location and Contact Information

Name of program: _____

Name of school district: _____

Address: _____

Contact person:_____Position: _____

Phone number: _____Fax: _____

E-mail: _____ Home page: http://_____

1. Level of implementation (Circle one.):

   State   District   School

   Has your state or district adopted TESOL's *ESL Standards*?

   _____

2. Are you using the ESL standards for: (Check all that apply.)

   _____ Curriculum development or alignment

   _____ Professional development of in-service teachers

   _____ Professional development of preservice teachers

   _____ Assessment revision or design

   _____ As a resource or reference in a state or local standards
   development effort

   Other: (explain) _____

   _____

For Curriculum Development Plans

3. Briefly describe what your state/district is doing to develop/
   modify a curriculum based on *ESL Standards*.

   _____

   _____

   _____

   _____

4. How many people are writing the curriculum?

5. Who is working on the curriculum project?

   _____ ESL or bilingual coordinator

   _____ ESL teachers, bilingual teachers, or both

   _____ Content teachers (Which subjects?)

   _____

   _____

_____ Curriculum specialist
_____ Assessment specialist
_____ Other administrators (Please specify)

_____

6. Please name the person overseeing the project:

_____

7. What content areas are included in the curriculum?

_____

_____

8. For what grade levels are you developing curricula?

_____

9. In what year do you intend to implement the newly revised
curriculum? _____

10. Will the curriculum be expanded? _____
To which grade levels? _____

11. Describe the time line for the process. (When did you start?
What were the significant events during the process?)

_____

_____

_____

_____

12. How is this project being funded (with outside funds, with local
funds for curriculum development)?

_____

13. Is a draft of your curriculum available? (Circle one.)
Yes   No

14. Can people from other districts contact you to get a copy?
Yes   No

15. In what ways might you make the curriculum available to other
districts or states?

_____

_____

_____

_____

For Assessment Development Plans

16. If your district has developed a curriculum based on *ESL Standards*, are you developing assessment aligned to the curriculum? If so, please describe.

_____

_____

17. Are you planning to utilize the guidelines established in *Managing the Assessment Process: A Framework for Measuring Student Attainment of the ESL Standards* for the assessment program? If yes, how?

_____

_____

18. How will you measure student attainment of the ESL standards?

_____

_____

19. For what purposes will you use the student assessment information related to the ESL standards?
    _____ Program placement
    _____ Program exit
    _____ High-stakes decision making (e.g., graduation, grade-level promotion)
    _____ Improve services to ESOL and bilingual students
    _____ Improve instruction
    _____ Monitor student preparation for the mainstream curriculum
    _____ Revise curriculum
    _____ Student/parent feedback
    _____ Other

For Professional Development Plans

20. What training related to standards has been provided to you or other educators participating in the standards-based development efforts in your state or district?

_____

_____

21. How is your state/district using *ESL Standards* for in-service professional development for teachers?

_____

_____

22. What training related to standards has been provided to administrators participating in the standards-based development efforts in your state or district?

_____

_____

23. How is your state using *ESL Standards* in certification (endorsement) plans for preservice teachers?

_____

_____

24. Has your state/district utilized the materials in *Training Others to Use the ESL Standards: A Professional Development Manual*? If so, how?

_____

_____

25. Are there any other educators in your district/state who have actively promoted use of *ESL Standards*? Please provide contact information.

_____

_____

Program and Student Demographics

26. Do you have state-mandated ESL and bilingual program requirements? If so, what are they?

_____

_____

27. How would you describe your state's/district's ESL program? (Check all that apply.)

_____ Part of a bilingual program

_____ Pull-out ESL

_____ Sheltered content

_____ Self-contained ESL

_____ Other (explain)

_____

_____

28. What are the five largest student language groups in your district?

_____

_____

29. What is your total population? (Indicate school or district.)

_____

30. Of the total school/district population, what percentage is limited English proficient?

_____

31. Please share any other pertinent information regarding your local context with us.

_____

_____

_____

_____

_____

_____

_____

_____

_____

Please return to:
Deborah Short or Emily Gómez
Center for Applied Linguistics
4646 40th St. NW
Washington, DC 20016-1859
(202) 362-3740 (fax) or (202) 362-0700
eslstds@cal.org

Developments in Second Language Acquisition Research and Theory: From Structuralism to Social Participation

Bridget Fitzgerald Gersten and Sarah Hudelson

Since 1966, when TESOL became a professional organization, the field's understanding of second language acquisition (SLA) and development has changed radically, particularly with regard to the knowledge base on child and adolescent second language (L2) development outside and inside school settings. This chapter provides a brief historical overview of developments in SLA as a way of contextualizing the publication of *ESL Standards for Pre-K–12 Students* (TESOL, 1997). This overview gives the basis for the field's current conceptualization of language acquisition and use as cognitive, academic, social, and cultural endeavors. As we review beliefs about language learning that have emerged and dominated over time, we identify key points that are relevant to the education of pre-K–12 children in ESL and bilingual settings today.

The presentation of a broad overview of developments in thinking about language is important because teacher education programs often bring together pre- and in-service teachers from varied backgrounds and with varied philosophies of and experience in language education (both first language [L1] and L2). To encourage classroom dialogue and an exchange of ideas in teacher education courses, we emphasize that perspectives on language and learning are multiple and sociohistorically grounded. An examination of theory and research in SLA and bilingualism since the 1960s shows that each approach varies in its treatment of language and learning as cognitive, social, cultural, and academic activity. An understanding of the links between the major trends in the field and pre-K–12 classroom practices can guide teacher education students and practicing teachers in understanding and using the principles and vignettes in *ESL Standards*.

A central aim of this chapter is to highlight how much explanatory power the varied theories and approaches to language and learning have for pre-K–12 instruction. Our own years of experience as bilinguals, teachers, researchers, and teacher educators have influenced our beliefs about the social nature of language and learning; we see a need to underscore the social nature of SLA in teacher education programs. In addition, since the 1960s, the study of children's language acquisition from a social perspective has taken on an interdisciplinary character. Researchers from various fields have begun to ask new questions about the interrelationships of language, literacy, context, and politics. As research has paid more attention to learners' use of language in naturalistic settings, the fact that language use is grounded in sociocultural purposes and social practices of people in interaction has become harder to ignore. This has been true for work in L1 development and in the study of L2 learning, and we examine scholarship in both areas. In our review of the evolution of thinking about children's language acquisition, we draw on findings from disciplines such as anthropology, psychology, linguistics, literacy, gender studies, and critical theory that we believe undergird the principles of language, literacy, and learning in ESL and bilingual settings presented in *ESL Standards*.

■ In the Beginning: Structuralism and Contrastive Analysis

In the United States, early thinking about language acquisition and learning had its roots in the behavioral psychology (Skinner, 1957) and linguistic structuralism of the 1950s and early 1960s. Behavioral psychology viewed language learning as a subbranch of general learning and asserted that the basis of language learning was habit formation and the establishment of stimulus-response patterns. Language learning occurred through drill and repetitive practice, which involved the memorization and error-free production of carefully controlled and sequenced parts of speech. Drill-based pedagogies such as the audiolingual method were used even with young children, and structural notions of language and language learning appeared in treatises on L2 learning (Fries, 1952, 1964; Lado, 1957, 1964) and in textbooks as carefully sequenced learning modules with a primarily grammatical focus. The L1 was viewed as a source of interference in L2 instruction. Because language acquisition was believed to involve the imitation of carefully formed sentence strings, the linguistic study of contrastive analysis aimed to identify and target patterns from the L1 that could help or hinder language acquisition (Corder, 1967; Wardhaugh, 1970).

The behaviorist approach to language learning runs counter to the general principles of language acquisition (see TESOL, 1997, pp. 6–8) in several ways. It acknowledges neither that learners engage in the gradual construction of their L2 by generating, trying out, and refining hypotheses, nor that errors are an inevitable part of this hypothesis generation. It fails to accommodate notions about social, functional, and cultural aspects of language acquisition or account for the role of the L1 and the native culture in the personal and academic well-being of the child. However, despite its decontextualized vision of language, this approach survives in many ESL/EFL classrooms around the world today, especially in traditional settings.

■ Linguistic Viewpoints

In the late 1950s and early 1960s, the publication of Noam Chomsky's *Syntactic Structures* (1957) and *Aspects of the Theory of Syntax* (1965) generated a revolution in thinking about the nature of language and L1 acquisition. Chomsky made a direct attack on the behavioral psychology, operant conditioning perspective on language learning and proposed an alternative: children as constructors of the rules of their language. Chomsky's mentalist or nativist view of language acquisition focused on the universal properties of abstract, formal syntax and the human being's innate capacity for language. His theories were based on what he saw as humans' infinite creative capacity for language. Chomsky proposed that children were equipped from birth with a language-specific language acquisition device (LAD), or *black box*, which wired them biologically for language learning. With this propensity to acquire language in place, a child's task was to use language data from the environment to figure out the rules of any given language. The child as language constructor thus played an active role in the learning process.

Chomsky's theories about the nature of the LAD stimulated further inquiry into the biological nature of language acquisition. Some early, key questions about the role of the brain and maturation in language acquisition included Lenneberg's (1967) hypotheses about a critical period for L1 acquisition, which posited that language acquisition had to occur before puberty. This thinking was related to physiological arguments made by Penfield and Roberts (1959), who concluded that children's brains have a certain plasticity before puberty that makes language learning easy for them. Similarly, researchers of bilingualism began to contemplate the structure of the bilingual brain in cognitive psychological terms (i.e., *perception, memory, learning strategies, storage, retrieval,* and *activation*).

For ESL and bilingual educators, the value of Chomsky's theories lies in their arguments against the tenets of behaviorism and in the proposition that the child is an active, creative hypothesizer of language (not a parrot or a passive automaton). However, Chomsky did not consider the roles of social interaction, culture, or education in language acquisition. He did not theorize about language in terms of its purposes or functions, nor did he consider the ways in which language varies according to context and intention. Credit for language acquisition rested exclusively with the child's brain, that is, with the individual's inner, cognitive processes.

■ Early L1 Acquisition Research

In the 1960s and early 1970s, Chomsky's LAD theory influenced researchers of child language acquisition (who came mostly from the field of linguistics and had a special interest in what they termed *developmental psycholinguistics*), whether or not they were in absolute agreement with his innatist view (see, e.g., McNeill, 1970; Slobin, 1966), to focus on children as active participants in the language acquisition process and as generators and constructors of the rules of their L1. As these researchers began to record and analyze children's spontaneous utterances, it became obvious that young children were not initially using fully formed conventional English utterances, but that ways of speaking were developing and changing in remarkably similar ways across children over time and were becoming ever closer approximations of adult speech (Lindfors, 1987).

One of the most influential early researchers was R. Brown (1973), who, with students and later with colleagues, began to describe a general, predictable sequence of early childhood language development. Brown and others (Bellugi & Brown, 1964; Klima & Bellugi-Klima, 1966) also examined and detailed young English-speaking children's acquisition of such specific aspects of English as negatives and interrogatives. Other researchers (e.g., E. V. Clark, 1973; H. H. Clark, 1970; Clark & Clark, 1977) carried out important work on young children's gradual development of the phonological and semantic systems of English. These researchers and many others demonstrated that children were engaging in the creative construction of their L1 rather than in the simple imitation of those around them. That is, children used available language data from their environments to generate hypotheses about particular aspects of the language, try out these hypotheses, and refine them over time. Thus it became clear that young children's developing language should be seen as rule governed and systematic rather than as "wrong" or "filled with errors."

The developmental psycholinguists were most interested in the work of children in creating their language. However, they readily acknowledged that, to generate their utterances, the children they were studying used linguistic data that came from adult speakers, most often mothers, who were interacting verbally with their children. Studies conducted to determine the special features or qualities of this parent-to-child talk led to generalizations about the linguistic and communicative features of *baby talk,* or *motherese* (Snow & Ferguson, 1977). Researchers discovered that mothers make significant adjustments in their speech to accommodate young children. They use shorter, simpler sentences and enunciate their words carefully. They use repetition, expansion, extension, paraphrase, and questioning to keep conversations going. They interpret the child's behaviors, such as gestures and vocalizations, as meaningful contributions to the conversation. They tend to accept children's contributions as meaningful no matter how unconventional their form. All of these adjustments have been termed a mother-child *jointness,* or partnership, characterized by mother and child working together to understand and to be understood, to use talk as one way of accomplishing and mediating daily activities, and to maintain relationships and communicate with each other (Lindfors, 1987). In an informative collection of papers exploring baby-talk research carried out since 1977, C. Snow (1994) has concluded that a major finding of nearly all of this more recent work is the interactional nature of the talk between adult and child. However, the exact features of the interactions vary across cultures (Ochs, 1988; Ochs & Schieffelin, 1983).

■ Psycholinguistic Research and Models in SLA

By the 1970s, Chomsky's theories about language and the L1 acquisition research that followed had also influenced scholars interested in SLA. Adapting research methods and lines of inquiry from cognitive psychology (and, early on, often conducting research on adult L2 learners and then applying those findings to children and adolescents as well as adults), L2 researchers began to focus on language acquisition from either a developmentalist or an information-processing perspective. The developmentalists adopted an L1-based approach to understanding L2, viewing language acquisition in terms of the sequence and rate of acquisition of certain aspects of language and seeking to explain individual differences in L2 learning in terms of variation in language performance and, in the case of classroom instruction, input.

As with research on L1 acquisition in children, the constructivist views of developmental psychologist Piaget guided the L2 developmentalist view of children as active learners and hypothesizers who act on their environment and gradually construct their knowledge of their L2. In his thorough review of research on SLA in children, McLaughlin (1984) examined the many case studies done of young children acquiring an L2. He noted that most of the earlier researchers (generally pre-1970) provided chronologically based, general descriptions of the linguistic development of children, already fluent users of one language, who were put in situations in which they needed to learn another language. More recent case study research (since the mid-1960s) has tended to examine the acquisition of specific phonological, semantic, or syntactic features of the target language over time. The majority of these studies have found significant similarities between children's acquisition of specific features in an L1 and in an L2, leading many scholars to maintain that L2 development is more like L1 development than different from it in terms of the processes involved and the strategies used. In general, older children tend to acquire an L2 at a faster pace than younger children do because of their advanced cognitive development (McLaughlin, 1984).

Significant individual variation exists, however, in the ways that learners acquire L2 structures, including some reliance on structures from the L1 to predict the L2 (Cancino, Rosansky, & Schumann, 1975; Hakuta, 1975).

Whereas some researchers engaged in case study research, others looked cross-sectionally at larger groups of children, comparing the L2 speech of learners of different ages and levels of language acquisition. For example, researchers such as Dulay and Burt (1973, 1974) examined the acquisition of English language morphemes (e.g., the morphemes for past tense, for the third-person singular of verbs, for plurals) by non-English-speaking children, searching for developmental sequences across children from the same and from differing L1s. Their research, as well as the work of many others, has suggested that child L2 learners, regardless of L1, use similar strategies for L2 (English) acquisition and, again regardless of L1, that there is a high degree of agreement in terms of the order of acquisition of the (English language) morphemes studied. However, the results of some studies have disputed the conclusion that a universal order of acquisition exists, demonstrating that children's L1s influence the ease with which they acquire specific features of English (Hakuta & Cancino, 1977).

At the same time, research on individual differences in language learning came into play as scholars linked sociopsychological factors such as attitude, motivation, aptitude, personality, and social and psychological distance to language learning in naturalistic and classroom settings (Ellis, 1984; Gardner & Lambert, 1972; Giles & Byrne, 1982; Krashen & Terrell, 1983; Lambert & Tucker, 1972; Schumann, 1978; Wong Fillmore, 1976, 1979).

Other researchers tapped into learning theories grounded in the dominant paradigm of cognitive psychology and applied these to language acquisition. These individuals sought to develop accurate information-processing models for language acquisition and learning. When these theory builders talked about language acquisition, they often made analogies between computers and the human mind, using terms such as *input, intake, output,* and *feedback*. Information-processing or input models of SLA emphasized the cognitive functions of the individual, describing L2 learning in terms of perception, memory, and learning and communication strategies (McLaughlin, 1978; McLaughlin, Rossman, & McLeod, 1983).

Krashen's monitor model of SLA (1981, 1982, 1985), an excellent example of the psychological, cognitive view of SLA, has been widely accepted among elementary and secondary school educators. In this model Krashen asserts that children and adults acquire an L2 by receiving extensive amounts of *comprehensible input*, which he defines as input that is a little beyond the learner's ability to produce but that the learner understands. Krashen explains that when comprehensible input gets into the learner's LAD, the learner can generate hypotheses about the L2 and produce language based on these hypotheses, which often results in the production of further input. Although the monitor model may suggest social interaction, Krashen's focus is on the cognitive, inside-the-head work of the individual learner. Krashen's model has been criticized for its claim that acquisition occurs fundamentally because learners receive comprehensible input, as many scholars argue that SLA is accomplished as learners interact with the sources of input (Ellis, 1984, 1997; Hatch, 1978; Wong Fillmore, 1989, 1991) and that consideration must be given to what learners comprehend (Gass, 1988) and to the output learners produce rather than exclusively to comprehensible input (Swain, 1985).

Long's (1981) interaction model also attributes SLA to comprehensible input, but Long emphasizes the importance of what he calls *negotiation of meaning*. When L2 learners demonstrate that they do not understand input addressed to them, linguistic and conversational modifications take place; that is, they are negotiated between the participants in the conversation. These modifications supply the L2 learners with the highest quality comprehensible input, which they then use to acquire the L2. Once again, the efforts of the individual language learner are foregrounded, although Long does seem to recognize that negotiated communication and comprehension, often achieved through the combined efforts of interlocutors, are integral factors in SLA.

Throughout the 1970s and into the 1980s, the dominant paradigm in SLA research continued to be cognitive and psycholinguistic, with its view of language acquisition as a primarily cognitive process, that is, as something that takes place in the heads of individual learners with little regard for sociocultural contexts. Related psychological research during this same period included examinations of the cognitive benefits of additive bilingualism (Cummins, 1976; R. C. Gardner, 1979; Genesee, 1976, 1978; Lambert & Tucker, 1972; Skutnabb-Kangas & Toukomaa, 1976). Other scholars have continued to conduct experiments and develop cognitive theories about SLA and bilingualism (Bialystok, 1987, 1991; Bialystok & Hakuta, 1994; Hakuta, 1986).

Yet even as the cognitive view of language acquisition dominated, some linguists began to envision SLA as a phenomenon that combined cognitive, affective, and social strategies. Wong Fillmore's (1976) study, carried out over the course of a year, detailed the cognitive and the social strategies that first-grade Spanish-speaking children used to acquire English in a bilingual classroom setting. Wong Fillmore's analysis of individual children's language use in their daily social interactions tied together cognitive strategies with communicative competence or social know-how, as she demonstrated that each child's L2 development was influenced by personal style, contacts with other people, and social purposes and needs.

Wong Fillmore's research sent an important message to classroom teachers: that social environment and opportunities for interpersonal interaction play a powerful role in language acquisition. Hatch and her colleagues also combined notions about children's language as involving both social and cognitive functions, as they looked at how discourse with adults and peers influenced young learners' syntactic and semantic development (Hatch, 1978; Hatch, Peck, & Wagner-Gough, 1979; Huang & Hatch, 1978; Peck, 1978; Wagner-Gough & Hatch, 1975). Though taking primarily a psycholinguistic approach to SLA, these researchers and others helped the field to expand its thinking to begin to include connections among social interaction, purpose, language development, and learning.

Psycholinguists have presented substantive data in support of the idea that L2 learning

- is a systematic, rule-governed process of creative construction of the new language

- necessarily involves acting on received language data (comprehensible input) by making hypotheses about, trying out, and making mistakes with the new language

- involves negotiating meaning and interacting with others, thereby using the new language for multiple purposes

- is accomplished by individuals with varied personalities and learning styles who learn their L2 at varied rates

- is a gradual process

These understandings of L2 learning contrast sharply with earlier beliefs about learning as habit formation and the need to control input in carefully sequenced bits.

From these understandings about learners have come implications for bilingual and ESL instruction. For example, classrooms need to be rich environments that provide multiple opportunities for learners to receive and to negotiate comprehensible input. L2 learners need to be encouraged to use their new language in a variety of ways by trying it out in negotiations with peers and adults. Instruction needs to acknowledge individual differences in L2 learners and provide learners with multiple ways of demonstrating their learning. Although psycholinguistics only indirectly pointed at the role of social interaction in SLA and bilingualism, its acknowledgment of the negotiation of meaning paved the way for later discussions of talk, classroom interaction, learning, and language acquisition.

Overall, then, psycholinguistics has contributed some fundamental lessons about the learner's cognitive activity and the importance and inevitability of taking risks and making mistakes in language acquisition. Some of the key notions within the principles of SLA presented in *ESL Standards* have their roots in psycholinguistic research. Although insights from psycholinguistics caused the field to rethink its ideas about learning and language acquisition, it was social approaches to language that filled in important gaps in the knowledge about the relationship among language, culture, and cognition, and underscored social interaction and shared participation in social groups. These approaches are discussed below.

TASK 1

If you have ever lived in a foreign country or studied a foreign language in a classroom setting, discuss how the theories and perspectives presented thus far correspond to your own language learning experiences.

■ Social Interactionist and Sociocultural-Sociolinguistic Approaches to L1 and L2 Acquisition

As we have suggested, in the 1970s and 1980s a more social perspective on language acquisition and learning developed alongside that of psycholinguistics. Vygotsky's (1955/1978) work, first translated into English in the 1960s, began to have more influence. Many language researchers and educators (e.g., Cazden, 1994; Moll, 1995) became interested in his proposition regarding the *zone of proximal development* in learning (the space in which a child learns more in interaction with others who are more skilled or proficient in an activity than the child is). Applied to language learning, the concept of a zone of proximal development would suggest that children would learn more language in social interactions with more proficient adults and children than they would learn on their own.

Bruner (1983) proposed that children's language develops through social engagement with others—that social interaction is fundamental to language acquisition. Berko-Gleason (1989) argued that young children focus on the formal aspects of grammar only after extended social interaction and intellectual development, that language use for social purposes is primary. Their work and that of many others has been termed the *social interaction* view of child language acquisition (Genishi & Dyson, 1984; Lindfors, 1987). This perspective, though recognizing that language resides in the heads of users and that language learners construct their language, maintains that social interaction is central and fundamental to language acquisition. Children acquire language as they see a need to make use of it in their daily lives, that is, as they use language with others to accomplish their purposes.

The study of language acquisition and use also has become more interdisciplinary in nature, as fields such as anthropology, sociology, sociolinguistics, communication, and language education have contributed additional perspectives to the growing knowledge base from linguistics and psychology. Scholars from these disciplines and many others have worked from a socially oriented paradigm that has highlighted the roles of context and community in language acquisition, language use, and bilingualism. They have recognized that abstract, formal models for language acquisition were insufficient to explain the inherently social and interactive nature of language use and communication.

Central to this body of research, in our view, has been the relating of language acquisition to speakers' purposes and functions in using language to communicate with others in socially and culturally appropriate ways. Hymes (1974) introduced the idea that adult users of language, in their daily interactions with others, possess and utilize sociolinguistic or communicative competence. That is, not only do speakers of a language "know" their language phonologically, syntactically, and semantically (linguistic competence), as Chomsky explained, but they also understand and participate in their social worlds through language, and they are able to use their language appropriately in multiple settings (communicative competence). Hymes' notion of communicative competence in adults has led child language acquisition scholars to new discoveries about and understanding of young children's gradual development of communicative competence through membership and participation in speech communities, where they become users of the family and community language as they use the language they are acquiring to serve their social purposes (Lindfors, 1987).

An excellent illustration of children's language development within the context of social interaction in the family is Halliday's (1973, 1977) documentation of his son Nigel's early language development. From very early childhood, Nigel expressed multiple social purposes with the language that he used. For example, Nigel used language to express his individuality, find out about the world, get others to do his bidding, socialize with others, and share information. The specific language forms Nigel used to express his purposes and functions changed over time, but his intentionality—his utilization of language for multiple purposes—remained a constant. Here, Halliday underscored the social functions of language and explained how these language functions were significant factors in the development of language forms.

The earliest work on children's use of language for multiple purposes was carried out with preschool children. However, language educators working in elementary and secondary schools soon became interested in examining the functional nature of students' and teachers' language use in school settings, particularly how students used language as a tool for their learning (Britton, 1973; Cazden, 1972). For what purposes or functions was language used in classrooms? How broad or narrow was the range of language use? Who controlled students' use of language? What kind of classroom organization and activity contributed to children's using language for a variety of purposes to mediate their learning?

Studies of language use in elementary and secondary school classrooms documented that certain kinds of classroom organizations and activities give children and adolescents the opportunities to use language for a variety of purposes that contribute to their learning (Barnes, 1976; Pinnell, 1975; Rosen & Rosen, 1973; Tough, 1977). Not surprisingly, from our current vantage point, these classrooms were organized so that learners had a great many opportunities to talk with peers as well as adults. Additionally, the content studied, which was experientially rather than textbook based, was interesting and challenging to the learners, which meant that they had chosen to engage with others in talking about it. Specifically, talk took the forms of arguing with others about interpretations, making hypotheses and verifying or rejecting them, making predictions and checking them out, defending a position, and using one's imagination (Pinnell, 1975). In contrast, in classes that were almost exclusively textbook based and teacher centered, students had few opportunities to use language for a variety of purposes in their own learning. Instead, the talk they engaged in was limited to answering the teachers' questions (Barnes, Britton, & Torbe, 1969). These findings influenced educational policy documents such as Bullock's Report (1975) in Great Britain, which called for elementary and secondary school classrooms that provided multiple opportunities for learners to engage with others in using oral and written language for a variety of purposes.

Language educators, such as those cited above, first examined talk in classrooms composed of native English speakers, without explicit attention to cultural or linguistic diversity. But concerns were soon raised about culturally diverse and L2 learners (Cazden, 1972; Cazden, John, & Hymes, 1972). Scholars began to document that these learners, too, needed multiple opportunities to use language to learn and that both language learning and content learning were facilitated if teachers structured their classrooms to allow L2 learners both to receive input from and to interact with more proficient adults and L1 and L2 peers around and about meaningful, challenging content (Enright, 1986; Enright & McCloskey, 1988; Tough, 1985; Wong Fillmore, 1982).

Findings from immersion programs with regard to the most effective approach to teaching L2s also became increasingly salient in the move from teaching language in isolation to integrating language and content instruction (Snow, Met, & Genesee, 1989). The immersion studies challenged the field to undertake such integration through systematic planning for language and content learning, explicating how such work could result in classrooms that were more discourse rich and that thus provided greater opportunities for L2 growth (Genesee, 1994a).

Other research has examined the nature of academic language itself, defining it in terms of discrete aspects of language such as vocabulary and syntax, the functions for which language is used in content classrooms (e.g., explaining, persuading), and the particular academic tasks involving language use that students must complete (Solomon & Rhodes, 1995). In addition, scholars examining middle and high school L2 students in content classrooms have found that learners' use of particular learning strategies — that is, particular techniques employed to understand and retain information — has positive effects on the learners' success in academic content classes (Chamot & O'Malley, 1986, 1987; O'Malley & Chamot, 1990). Chamot and O'Malley's findings about learning strategies have influenced many teachers to help students articulate the specific learning techniques they employ and expand their repertoires of strategies. All of this work in integrating language and content learning has become critical in educators' efforts to provide appropriate academic experiences to L2 learners in content classrooms (Short, 1993, 1997b; Snow & Brinton, 1997).

Beyond looking at the content itself, scholars recently have continued to critique traditional textbook- and recitation-based practices in content classes and have proposed that educators need to examine the discipline-based discourses that students in content classes need to learn — for example, the discourse of history, the discourse of mathematics, and the discourse of science (Gee, 1989, 1992; Lemke, 1990; Short, 1997b; Short & Burke, 1996). Learners acquire these discourses not by reading textbooks and memorizing facts or steps but through authentic participation in the discourse community(ies). For example, L2 learners learn the discourse of science as they ask their own questions, figure out ways to investigate these questions, collect and develop their evidence, and construct their own theories. This kind of work is possible for L2 learners within collaborative classroom settings where students work with teachers and peers in a community of practice (Rosebery, Warren, & Conant, 1992).

By considering both home and school settings, educational anthropologists have provided a wider lens through which to view learners' language acquisition and use. They also have been interested in questions of language use in classrooms, particularly in how learners

---

TASK 2

Find vignettes from *ESL Standards for Pre-K-12 Students* that illustrate content-area or sheltered instruction. Make a case for the relationship between SLA and academic achievement.

---

from nonmainstream language and cultural backgrounds have responded to instruction (i.e., ways of "doing school") that has assumed particular ways of interacting in the classroom that might not be similar to those of the learners. Educational anthropologists, for example, have investigated children's development of communicative competence in their home and community settings and then contrasted what were considered appropriate (communicatively competent) ways of interacting within their speech communities to the ways of interacting that were considered appropriate in school settings.

Perhaps the best known example of this work is Heath's (1983) now-classic examination of language socialization and use among children in three communities in the Carolina Piedmont region of the United States: Roadville, Trackton, and Townspeople. Heath's study demonstrated that the ways Roadville and Trackton children were socialized to interact with others in their homes and neighborhoods were significantly different from the interactional expectations of teachers (who were mostly Townspeople) in the schools the children attended. In school, Roadville and Trackton children often interacted (or did not interact) in ways that were considered inappropriate by their teachers, resulting in negative consequences for their learning. For example, children from Trackton did not respond to the known-answer questions (e.g., Who can tell us what day it is?) that Townspeople teachers asked. As a result, the teachers viewed the children as not very attentive or intelligent. Heath's study is one of many that have documented the misunderstandings, communication problems, and negative effects on children's classroom participation and academic learning and achievement that occur when teachers' and students' rules or norms for social interaction (what have been called *participant structures*; Philips, 1983) differ. Au (1980) has documented similar phenomena with Native Hawaiian children in reading groups. Cazden et al. (1972) provide examples of cultural miscommunication and consequent silencing of students in American Indian and African American settings. Michaels (1981) has documented African American first-grade children's interactions in sharing time, which, when deemed inappropriate by their European American teachers, resulted in their being interrupted and cut off as they shared. Philips' (1983) work on the Warm Springs Indian Reservation in Oregon demonstrated that classroom participation structures that were more congruent with Warm Springs community participation structures resulted in more classroom participation by Warm Springs Indian children. More recently, scholars such as Delpit (1995) and Ladson-Billings (1994) have argued for culturally sensitive teaching of minority children.

Bilingual and L2 scholars also have been concerned with how nonnative-English-speaking children negotiate school, not only with regard to the linguistic and academic demands of schooling conducted in and through English but also in terms of the cultural congruence or incongruence (or the cultural match or mismatch) between the family's and school's ways of interacting, values, and expectations. In their examination of an immigrant Spanish-speaking community, for example, Delgado-Gaitán and Trueba (1991) discovered that home and family ways of interacting, accomplishing tasks, and disciplining children contrasted greatly with teachers' expectations of how children would interact with adults, how children would accomplish school tasks, and how children should be disciplined. For instance, Delgado-Gaitán and Trueba detailed the complex and conflicted reality for children whose parents' top concern (value) was that children fulfill their obligations as family members but whose teachers' top concern (value) was that children fulfill their obligations as students. Home-school mismatches and resulting classroom instructional problems for children have been found in other language minority communities and schools as well (Pease-Alvarez & Vásquez, 1994; Trueba, Guthrie, & Au, 1981; Valdés, 1996).

In related research, Cazden (1988) investigated teacher-child interactions in bilingual classrooms in which the teachers shared the students' cultural and language background. She found that these teachers' ways of interacting with children were more socioculturally appropriate than those of teachers from different backgrounds and that the result was fewer teacher-child misunderstandings.

Researchers focusing on child-child interaction at school have confirmed that bilingual children and children put into ESL settings use their language, or languages, for a variety of purposes. Their activity is, above all, social: They learn a new language because it is useful for them; they use two languages and switch from one to the other because their purposes are served (Cazden, 1988; Hudelson, 1983; Wong Fillmore, 1976). A contrasting lesson learned from observing English speakers in bilingual classrooms where a goal was bilingualism for all learners was that they did not acquire much Spanish because Spanish was not necessary (Edelsky & Hudelson, 1980). The idea of authentic purposes is rooted in how individuals and communities value or devalue bilingualism and biculturalism. In bilingual settings, another important lesson is that bilinguals, as individuals and members of dual speech communities and cultures, have unique ways of speaking (Grosjean, 1982). Early research on diglossia, and later research on code switching, helped educators understand that bilinguals make informed decisions on language use based on knowledge about culture, language, context, and purpose (Fishman, 1964, 1972; Jacobson & Faltis, 1990).

Early social approaches to language acquisition and bilingualism looked at how language occurs and serves people's needs in social events across situations and cultures. Scholars examined how language varies in different contexts and speech communities, and described the roles of interactants in the negotiation of meaning. Researchers who focused on the social aspects of language acquisition and development presented findings about how the norms of language use were interrelated and situated in speech communities with sociohistorical roots. One important lesson these scholars presented was that even though language varies, dialects vary, and discourses are multiple, all are rule-bound and serve the needs of their users in multiple contexts (Labov, 1972a, 1972b). Another lesson was that ways of speaking and communicating are an important part of a child's social identity, closely tied to a speech community (Heath, 1983). Also significant is the conclusion that typical, expected ways of interacting in school settings may be strange to learners whose interaction patterns are significantly different from those the schools assume, resulting in cultural mismatches between the culture of home and the culture of school (Au, 1993). These findings have had tremendous significance for the field's understanding of learners' production of language—or lack of it—in particular settings.

A sociocultural perspective on learning also has had some important influences on the creation of the set of principles regarding language learning and use that is found in *ESL Standards*. This perspective is featured in four principles about language acquisition: (a) Language is functional, (b) language varies according to social setting and cultural norms, (c) language learning is culture learning, and (d) bilingualism is an individual and social asset. In our view, this perspective on language acquisition also embraces bilingual learners as individuals whose strengths in their L1 support academic, social, and personal growth in one or more additional languages.

Situate theoretical principles of SLA in pre-K–12 classroom settings by examining vignettes from *ESL Standards.* Using vignettes from each grade cluster, find evidence for SLA as a social, personal, cognitive, and academic endeavor.

■ Literacy Learning in School, Family, and Community Settings

The earliest work on the acquisition and development of ESL in children and adolescents focused on learning and using oral or spoken language. Discussions of literacy were relegated to consideration only after learners were listeners and speakers of English (following the traditional view of a linear sequencing of the language processes: listening, speaking, reading, writing). And, influenced by structural linguistics, suggestions for literacy development emphasized accurate pronunciation, vocabulary exercises, and the utilization of *linguistic readers,* which contained exercises and texts based on spelling-pronunciation patterns of English (Lado, 1964).

This view of literacy was challenged in the mid-1960s by K. S. Goodman's (1967) proposal that reading was a *psycholinguistic guessing game.* Goodman disputed the commonsense notion that reading was a sequential, letter-by-letter process and that the goal of reading was the accurate identification of words on the page. Instead (on the basis of studies carried out with children of various ages who read aloud and retold stories that they had not previously seen), Goodman argued, effective and efficient reading was a language process that involved readers in predicting their way through text by using their prior knowledge and the syntactic, semantic, and graphophonic systems of the language rather than by relying exclusively on the graphophonic system. Goodman discovered that, as readers predicted, what they read was often not exactly what was in the text (Goodman called what the readers produced *miscues*) but that very often these miscues retained the meaning and the grammatical structure of what individuals were reading. In these cases, readers often did not correct their miscues. However, when readers made miscues that disrupted meaning, they were more likely to correct them. This led Goodman to propose that reading was the construction of meaning, not the accurate pronunciation of words. His earliest work was with mainstream native English speakers, but he soon ventured to examine the miscues of children who were speakers of a variety of dialects of English and children who were L2 speakers of English (Goodman & Goodman, 1978; Rigg, 1986).

Goodman's proposals influenced a variety of bilingual and L2 educators to use miscue analysis as a research tool with readers from multiple L1s, resulting in assertions that the reading process is fundamentally the same process of construction of meaning across languages (K. S. Goodman, 1996; Hudelson, 1981). Additionally, miscue analysis research carried out with child and adolescent ESOL learners found that these learners worked to construct meaning as they read texts in their new language. The learners' overall English language proficiency, the structural organization of the texts, and the learners' familiarity with the contents of what they were reading all influenced the meanings that they were able to construct (Rigg, 1986).

Whereas Goodman's research emphasized that reading is a language process and that readers use their language knowledge as they construct meaning, other scholars demonstrated the importance of readers' prior knowledge to their comprehension of text (see Weaver, 1994, for a review of this research). The term *schema*, which comes from cognitive psychology, refers to concepts or constructs in an individual's knowledge base that result from a reader's life experiences. Cognitive psychologists conducting experiments discovered that readers' comprehension of text was affected by their previous knowledge of the contents. Readers remembered more completely and accurately texts that were familiar to them (i.e., for which readers had well-developed schema) than they did texts that were unfamiliar (that is, texts for which the readers had no well-developed schema). Studies conducted with ESOL learners produced the same results: What was most crucial to a reader's comprehension of a text was the reader's prior knowledge base (Carrell, 1981; Carrell & Eisterhold, 1983; Johnson, 1981). As schema theory has been related to the transactional view of reading articulated by Rosenblatt (1938/1983), researchers have advanced views of readers—both native speakers of English and English language learners—as interpreters of text and constructors of meaning (Hudelson, 1994; Samway & Whang, 1995).

Perspectives on the importance of prior knowledge and readers' transactions with texts called into question reliance on readability formulas that proposed using vocabulary and syntactic factors to determine the difficulty of reading material for L2 learners (Rigg, 1986). Instead, L2 educators have been urged to encourage English language learners to read multiple texts around familiar topics or themes (Krashen, 1993). Literature study discussion groups have been examined and proposed as a way in which learners can share their individual transactions with authentic literature and build richer meanings through this social interaction (Ali, 1994; Samway & Whang, 1995). L2 literacy methodology has come to include strategies designed to activate or develop students' prior knowledge in order to facilitate the construction of meaning from texts, especially text materials across academic curricular areas (Schifini, 1994; Short, 1993). Activities that involve learners in developing strategies for constructing meaning and then articulating what these strategies are also have been found to be important for L2 literacy development and for learners' views of their literacy abilities (Janzen, 1996; Jiménez, 1997; Kucer & Silva, 1995).

Another area of literacy research that came to include bilingual and L2 learners is that of children's writing development within school contexts. As English-speaking children moved from home to school settings, researchers began to document the ways that youngsters in process writing classrooms became more proficient writers as they participated in daily writing workshops (Calkins, 1983; Graves, 1983). Scholars demonstrated that children learned to write by engaging in the craft of writing, which included having others—adults and peers— respond to their efforts. Other researchers documented the social nature of children's writing, focusing on the centrality of children's interactions with each other as they wrote and of their social as well as personal purposes for writing (Dyson, 1989, 1993). Understanding how children learn to write by engaging in the craft resulted both in the establishment and development of such groups as the National Writing Project and in the wide-scale implementation and documentation of process writing in classrooms (Calkins, 1992, 1994).

The earliest work on children's in-school writing development involved settings populated by native speakers of English, but researchers in bilingual and L2 instructional settings soon began to ask questions about young children's writing in languages other than English. The researchers discovered that Spanish-speaking children, given opportunities to engage in writing, constructed their understanding of written Spanish much as English speakers did with English (Edelsky, 1982, 1986; Freeman & Freeman, 1998; Hudelson,

1981/1982; Montiel, 1992; Serna & Hudelson, 1993b). They also documented that when learners became comfortable with their writing abilities in their L1, they began to venture with confidence into writing in English (Freeman & Freeman, 1994; Hudelson, 1987, 1989b; Hudelson & Serna, 1994).

Researchers also became interested in how children became writers in their L2, English (Hudelson, 1984, 1989b). Work in a variety of settings soon made it clear that, as with acquisition of the spoken language, there were more similarities than differences between L1 and L2 learning and that L2 learners could begin to express themselves in writing long before they had "mastered" the spoken language (Hudelson, 1984). Over time, examinations of the writing of L2 children and adolescents have made it clear that

- ESOL learners can use writing in their still-developing new language to construct their meanings (Fu & Townsend, 1998; Hudelson, 1989a, 1989b; Peyton, 1990).

- ESOL learners can examine and revise their work based on comments from others (Blake, 1992; Samway, 1987; Urzúa, 1987).

- ESOL learners can often make use of L1 literacy abilities, understandings, and conventions as they write the new language (Edelsky, 1986; Fu & Townsend, 1998; Hudelson, 1987, 1989b; Hudelson & Serna, 1994; Serna & Hudelson, 1993a, 1997).

- ESOL learners benefit from being able to continue to use the L1 and L1 writing while they are developing L2 abilities (Berkman, 1996; Fu & Townsend, 1998; Gee, 1996; Serna & Hudelson, 1993a).

- ESOL learners choose to write in English because the language becomes useful, functional, and enjoyable for them (Fu & Townsend, 1998; Gee, 1996; Hudelson & Serna, 1994; Serna & Hudelson, 1997).

- ESOL learners may need some adjustments in the way process writing is carried out, including a slowing down of the process, lots of opportunities for talk as well as writing, encouragement from teachers, and the opportunity to write from their own experiences (Berkman, 1996; Fu, 1995;

Peyton, Jones, Vincent, & Greenblatt, 1994; Peyton & Staton, 1993).

- ESOL learners develop confidence in L2 writing at different rates (Hudelson, 1989a).

- ESOL learners' reading influences their writing and vice versa, making the processes of writing and reading interdependent (Samway & Taylor, 1993; Taylor, 1990).

As the early childhood language acquisition researchers of the 1960s and 1970s made important discoveries about the social and the cognitive nature of spoken language acquisition in preschool children, their constructivist and transactional perspectives began to influence preschool literacy research (see Weaver, 1994, for a discussion of these connections). As researchers began to view children as acting on their environments to construct knowledge, they discovered that very young children living in environments where print surrounded them and was an integral part of their lives attended to this print, engaged with it, worked to make sense of it, and used it in their daily lives and interactions long before formal schooling (Baghban, 1984; Harste, Woodward, & Burke, 1984). A major finding of the scholars that some have termed *emergent literacy researchers* has been that children come to understand both the functions of reading and writing and written language itself as they see those around them engage in using written language for varied purposes and as they engage in reading and writing themselves, often in the company of others (McGee & Purcell-Gates, 1997; Teale & Sulzby, 1986, 1989).

Young children's early ways of writing and their developing hypotheses about how written language works, including their coming to understand word boundaries and the alphabetic principle, have been documented extensively (e.g., C. Chomsky, 1971; Clay, 1975; Read, 1975; and many others). Young readers' movement from less to more conventional ways of reading texts have also been documented (Doake, 1985; K. S. Goodman, 1996; Weaver, 1994). Once again, the discoveries made with L1 speakers of English led literacy researchers to investigate the writing and reading of preschoolers in languages other than English from a Piagetian constructivist perspective (Ferreiro, Pontecorvo, Moreira, & Hidalgo, 1996; Ferreiro & Teberosky, 1982; Y. M. Goodman, 1991) and also to consider young learners of ESL and their construction of reading and writing through engagement in the processes (Carger, 1993; Fassler, 1998; Seawell, 1985).

Whereas some scholars have focused their investigations of young children's literacy construction on the children's efforts, others have paid particular attention to language and literacy environments, or practices and functions in family settings—what has been termed *family literacy* (Taylor, 1983). These researchers have concluded that, in family settings, regardless of cultural background, socioeconomic status, or L1, family members engage in reading and writing for multiple purposes in their daily lives and that families do have intellectual resources (Taylor, 1997). However, both the variety of functions and the quantity and quality of occurrences vary.

Heath's (1983) previously discussed work in Roadville and Trackton included an examination of written language use in these communities, which she contrasted with written language use by the Townspeople. Taylor and Dorsey-Gaines (1988) later used Heath's categories of written language use in their examination of literacy practices in the lives of urban African American families; they discovered that the families they studied used written language for an even greater variety of purposes than the families studied by Heath. However, practices valued and even assumed by schools, such as reading storybooks to young children and reading novels for leisure, occurred less frequently than in middle-class settings. Additionally, adult-child interaction around storybooks differed significantly from the kinds of interactions schools valued and expected (Au, 1993; Heath, 1983; Michaels, 1981).

Evidence also has been accumulating that families of non-English-speaking recent immigrant families in the United States engage in a variety of literacy practices at home. Given economic circumstances, limited time, and limited L1 resources, these practices have tended to be focused on daily life, survival, and communication with distant relatives. This means that practices such as storybook reading, which are highly valued by schools, tend to occur less frequently, although storytelling and the utilization of forms from the oral tradition are present. The question, according to many scholars, is whether schools recognize some of these practices as legitimate literacy practices (Allexsaht-Snider, 1991; Delgado-Gaitán & Trueba, 1991; Schieffelin & Cochran-Smith, 1984; Valdés, 1996; Vásquez, 1991; Vásquez, Pease-Alvarez, & Shannon, 1994).

An especially intriguing approach toward researching, respecting, and utilizing family literacy practices has been that taken by Moll and his colleagues (González, 1995; González et al., 1993; Moll, 1995), who, with teachers, have examined what they term *funds of knowledge*, meaning those historically developed strategies or bodies of knowledge developed in families and communities that are essential to a family's functioning and well-being. As teachers have spent time in their students' homes and learned about the intellectual and social skills present in families, their understanding of children and their classroom curricula have changed to incorporate what families know and do.

TASK 4

Analyze the role of the native language and native language literacy in selected vignettes from *ESL Standards*.

No one would deny the importance of ESOL learners' developing literacy abilities in school, family, and community settings. But some scholars have gone beyond questions of how literacy develops and how it may be nourished most effectively to challenge teachers to think about why students need to develop literacy. Freire (1970) proposed that these two aspects of literacy are inextricably linked — that the purposes to which people put literacy must be tied directly to literacy development itself. Freire maintained that it was not sufficient to learn how to read the word. Rather, learners needed to use their developing literacy to read the world, that is, to examine their own lives; understand their own situations, realities, and problems; and use reading and writing to act on or resolve their problems. Reading the world means critiquing the world as it is and using literacy to better it. The term *critical literacy* (Freire & Macedo, 1987) has been used to refer to this view of reading and writing. From the perspective of critical literacy, Edelsky (1994, 1996) has written eloquently about using literacy to work for social justice, and she has collected examples from elementary and secondary teachers who have made working for social justice part of their classroom agendas (Edelsky, in press). Bilingual and L2 educators also have shared ways that they have helped their students read the world and then act on it (Peterson, 1991; Walsh, 1996; Wolfe, 1996).

The knowledge base with regard to L1 and L2 literacy learning has expanded tremendously in the past 30 years. It has now become clear that children are active constructors of their own literacy and that they use their language and experiential resources to construct meanings from and with written language. It also has become clear that literacy develops through engagement and that engagement is tied to authentic purposes or functions for literacy within the social worlds (i.e., family, community, school) of learners. Social interaction is central to literacy learning; literacy grows in and through use with others. Talk is essential to literacy. Literacy is social and cultural practice, and the practice varies among social and cultural groups. How we as educators have been socialized to view and use literacy may affect our views of the legitimacy of literacy practices different from our own. In working with L2 learners, teachers must learn about, value, and utilize literacy practices that represent the multiple cultures of students while holding high expectations for students' learning of school literacy.

The knowledge base on literacy that has developed has had an impact on the principles of language acquisition articulated in *ESL Standards* (TESOL, 1997). In addition to the principles that language is functional and that it is learned through meaningful use and interaction, we point specifically to the proposition that language processes develop interdependently. The research on literacy development has made it clear that the profession must discard traditional ideas about a clean separation or sequence of listening, speaking, reading, and writing (Faltis & Hudelson, 1998; Hudelson, 1989b). Spoken and written language cannot be separated. Both are language. The language processes are interdependent, each one facilitating growth in the others. Both spoken and written language are necessarily involved in SLA, and both spoken and written language need to be accounted for in L2 classrooms, which must allow multiple opportunities for learners to use both as they engage with significant content.

We also point to the principle that L1 proficiency contributes to SLA. Early research made it clear that overall L1 proficiency contributes to L2 proficiency (Cummins, 1976). In a related vein, the research on bilingual learners' literacy development has demonstrated repeatedly that L1 literacy learning facilitates L2 literacy development (Edelsky, 1982, 1986; Freeman & Freeman, 1994; Hudelson, 1989b). This finding means that provisions need to be made for learners to develop and maintain proficiency in their L1 even as they are learning a new language.

TASK 5

Examine a series of vignettes from *ESL Standards* for connections between written and oral language and between language and literacy in SLA. Find examples of multiple purposes for reading and writing. How does literacy learning vary according to grade-level cluster? Compare and contrast the vignettes as theories-in-action for the principles of SLA discussed in this chapter.

TASK 6

Analyze the various theories and perspectives on SLA described in this chapter (i.e., psycholinguistic; sociocultural-sociolinguistic; literacy learning in school, family, and community settings), and then examine how principles from each approach appear in "General Principles of Language Acquisition" in *ESL Standards* (pp. 6–8).

■ New Directions for the New Millennium: Rethinking the Social in Language and Classroom Learning

As the field continues to learn more about the nature of language acquisition, learning, and the education of language minority children in Grades pre-K–12, the need to expand the theoretical framework for language and learning in ESL and bilingual settings becomes evident. It is easy to see how the principles of language acquisition in *ESL Standards for Pre-K–12 Students* have their roots in the psycholinguistic and social perspectives of language. As we have shown, the knowledge base on L1 and L2 oral and written language learning makes the following points clear:

- Humans learn language by using it, because it is functional for them; spoken and written language use begins for people in families and communities.

- Language practices vary greatly across families, communities, and cultural groups.

- Learning new "ways with words," both verbal and written, takes time and effort and needs to be supported in classrooms and communities.

- Becoming an effective user of an L2 or additional language is easier with a strong base in the L1.

- Bilingualism serves learners themselves and the society at large.

Given this knowledge base, we challenge ourselves and other teacher educators to use what we know to create conditions that promote the enactment of TESOL's vision of effective education for all students in classrooms across the United States (TESOL, 1997, pp. 3–6). Teacher educators must recognize that the traditional frameworks of educational and cognitive psychology and linguistics that have guided teacher education programs, especially those focused on educating teachers to work with bilingual and L2 learners, do not prepare teachers sufficiently to provide effective educational programs. We need to examine our own programs and, if necessary, restructure them from a sociocultural perspective on learning and language acquisition that takes into account the social, political, and contextual nature of schooling.

In addition, we challenge prospective and current teachers to accept the following tasks:

1. Develop a knowledge base on language acquisition and then consider how these fundamental principles of language acquisition apply to curriculum, instruction, and assessment. Theoretical principles and research take on new life when teachers see evidence for them in the daily lives of children at school (and as represented by the vignettes in *ESL Standards*).

2. Be aware of past and current trends in language acquisition research, giving particular attention to the strong and continuing impact of more traditional psychological, "inside-the-head" views of learning and their prevailing influences in classrooms and schools. Current views of learning show that this research tradition omits the social, contextual, and political nature of learning and language acquisition. Based on that knowledge, teachers need to critique existing views of school learning and advocate for new theoretical frameworks.

3. Advocate for the English language learners in their communities—not only in the classroom but in the public arena as

well. In the face of teacher and teacher education bashing, anti–bilingual education initiatives, anti–progressive education rhetoric, back-to-the-basics advocacy, and high-stakes testing movements, teachers need to speak up about what they know to be effective educational environments for their students. The research base supports well-designed and well-implemented bilingual programs. We know that meaning-based, transactional, culturally sensitive pedagogies provide the kinds of learning opportunities students need if they are to achieve their academic and linguistic potential. When this knowledge is ignored, teachers need to articulate their positions to policy makers and the media. Education is political, and the education of nonnative English speakers is especially so. As uncomfortable as it may be to do so, we need to speak what we know. This volume should help us do that.

TASK   7

Think about some of the key concepts presented in this chapter (e.g., comprehensible input, comprehensible output, negotiation of meaning, motherese, funds of knowledge, communicative competence, attitude and motivation, individual differences, zone of proximal development, schema, participant structures, home/school connection, critical literacy). Review the definitions of these terms. How can these concepts be reflected in your own teaching practices?

Chapter 4

Using the ESL Standards for Curriculum Development

Deborah J. Short

Curriculum development for many ESL programs has been a dynamic process since the 1950s, and for the most part, curriculum changes have been driven by methodological choices and research findings made from within the ESL profession. Teachers have realized over time that students need new instructional approaches in terms of both pedagogical practice and the content of the curriculum. The impetus for some of the changes has been the enrollment in schools of students with varying backgrounds and language learning experiences. What works for students with strong educational backgrounds in their first language (L1) is often different from what works for students who have had limited formal schooling and who lack literacy skills in any language. Other changes have occurred as the result of new expectations that school systems hold for students who exit ESL programs, demanding, for example, that students have both academic language proficiency and basic social and survival skills. Still other changes have been driven by educational researchers and theorists who have examined authentic classrooms and experimental settings with English language learners and made recommendations for new or modified instructional approaches based on their findings.

In the first half of the 20th century, most language curricula relied on the direct method of instruction or a grammar-translation approach. Yet by the 1950s, direct method and grammar-translation languished, and audiolingual methods surfaced. In the 1970s and after, the audiolingual method was displaced by communicative methods for ESL teaching, supporting students to use functional language in meaningful, relevant ways. As districts implemented communicative curricula, students were given opportunities to discuss material of high interest and topicality, which in turn motivated them to learn and participate in class. Students were encouraged to experiment with language and assume greater responsibility for their learning.

The communicative curriculum gave rise to two other types of curricula. Some ESL programs sought to align the ESL curriculum with the district English language arts curricula and developed literature-based language courses. This type of instruction has been supported by commercial publishers through literature-based reading series. Other programs developed content-based ESL curricula to help prepare students better for their transition to mainstream classes. The content-based language approach transformed an ESL class into a forum for subject-area knowledge generation, application, and reinforcement by addressing key topics found in grade-level curricula. The sophistication of the material presented necessarily varied according to the language proficiency of the students in class, but nonetheless they considered this material relevant and meaningful.

Since the late 1980s, an increasing number of programs have begun to develop curricula for sheltered content courses. In these courses, English language learners enroll in a content course with grade-level objectives delivered through modified instruction that makes the information comprehensible to the students. Depending on a school system's regulations, a sheltered mathematics course, for example, might be delivered by an ESL teacher or a mathematics teacher who, preferably, has been trained in such areas as second language acquisition (SLA) and ESL methodology. At the high school level, sheltered content courses are more often delivered by content teachers so that students may receive core, not elective, credit for graduation. The goal of these courses has been primarily to teach content but through a developmental language approach.

As noted above, most of these changes have been internally driven by educators in the field of ESL. Many changes have been welcomed by ESL teachers and by others who recognize the benefits to English language learners. Teachers in mainstream classes who receive students from the ESL programs, for example, are pleased to have students with stronger backgrounds in the content areas. Some changes, however, have been accepted with reluctance. It is difficult, for example, to give up a favored unit in a former curriculum or to learn to teach in a new way. Nonetheless, change has occurred over time and has been widely implemented.

Now, however, a new wind is blowing, and the ESL field is caught up in the same storm of educational reform that mainstream education is experiencing in the United States. As discussed in chapter 2, this is one reason that TESOL undertook the development of the ESL standards. The pressure to change is external; second language (L2) learners are increasingly being held to the same standards, and subsequently must undergo the same assessments of learning, as native English speakers. This is not a negative proposition, but it does require that the profession advocate for ESOL students and inform other educators that although English language learners should be held to the same high standards, they should have the opportunity to follow different pathways to accomplish them. The overall result, though, is another change in curricula and practice for ESL programs.

To meet the new requirements that states and districts are setting forth for all their students, ESL programs are beginning to develop standards-based curricula, using national and state standards as their organizing structures. Some states, such as Tennessee and New Jersey,[1] have adopted *ESL Standards for Pre-K–12 Students* (TESOL, 1997) at the state level and have asked ESL programs to develop curricula based on them. Other states, such as California and Florida, have drawn from *ESL Standards* as they have created their own state English language development standards. Florida, for example, cross-references TESOL's ESL goals and standards within its document and utilizes TESOL's definitions of the English language proficiency levels (Florida Department of Education, 1999). Some states have used *ESL Standards* as the basis for newly revised, state curriculum frameworks and guidelines. As a result of the reform activities at the state level, some district programs have aligned their ESL curricula with the ESL standards (Gómez, Montiel, & Rosenberg, 1998; Leone, 1997; Short, 1997a). Other programs have infused the ESL standards into curricula for such content areas as English language arts, social studies, and mathematics. The section in this chapter called Curriculum Development in Action contains brief descriptions of representative alignment and infusion practices at local district and state levels.

■ A Curriculum Development Process

As part of the implementation work that TESOL has sponsored to help districts and states utilize *ESL Standards for Pre-K–12 Students*, the project team developed a model, known as *ASCRIBER*, for curriculum development. ASCRIBER pulls together the general parameters for any curriculum development project and specifically demonstrates ways to incorporate the ESL standards into any district or state language or content curriculum.

The ASCRIBER model has eight stages: *a*lignment, *s*tandards setting, *c*urriculum development, *r*etooling, *i*mplementation, *b*enchmarking, *e*valuation, and *r*evision. These stages are described briefly below in an example that uses the model to align the ESL and English language arts standards. The model may be enacted after a curriculum development team has been identified for a district or state. If the curriculum will incorporate standards or objectives from any content area besides ESL, representatives from the subject area(s) should serve on the team along with ESL and, if applicable, bilingual educators.

*A*lignment: Align current or adopted standards, curriculum objectives, proficiencies or competencies, and assessments with the ESL standards

Curriculum developers can begin the process by aligning their current or adopted standards, curriculum objectives, proficiencies, or competencies[2] for the course under development with the ESL standards and descriptors. In practice, using the descriptors of the ESL standards has been effective, as these are akin to curriculum objectives. Figure 4-1 illustrates a format whereby the standards, objectives, or descriptors from the district curriculum and the ESL standards are laid side-by-side in two columns and the similarities and differences are identified. First, each similarity is examined individually and a determination is made as to whether it is important and valid for the student population being served. If so, the standard, objective, or descriptor representing the similarity is written down in the composite column. The team may select the wording used in either of the first two columns or rephrase it, as preferred. Second, each difference is examined independently, and those that are also important and valid for the students are noted in the composite column as well. Third, the team reviews the composite column to determine if any standards or objectives are missing.

FIGURE 4-1

WORKSHEET FOR ALIGNING STANDARDS, CURRICULUM OBJECTIVES, PROFICIENCIES, COMPETENCIES, AND ASSESSMENTS

1. Choose the subject areas to align.
2. Compare the standards, objectives, and so forth.
3. Select ones that are similar. Decide which are important, and list them in the composite column.
4. Look at the remaining ones. Decide which are important. Add them to the list.
5. Check for gaps and missed areas of emphasis. Add them to the list.
6. Check the list with others. Revise as needed.

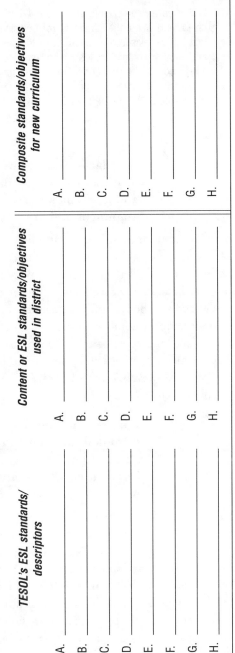

TESOL's ESL standards/descriptors	Content or ESL standards/objectives used in district	Composite standards/objectives for new curriculum
A.	A.	A.
B.	B.	B.
C.	C.	C.
D.	D.	D.
E.	E.	E.
F.	F.	F.
G.	G.	G.
H.	H.	H.

With a partner or a team, use Figure 4-1 to identify composite standards (or objectives). Write the standards (or objectives) either for an ESL curriculum that will be revised or created or for the purpose of infusing ESL standards into another content area, such as language arts. For practice, identify only 10–15 composite standards. Use ESL descriptors from some of the ESL standards. As suggested on the worksheet, when you are finished, share the composite list with others for feedback.

Standards Setting: Establish the state- or district-level standards, objectives, and assessments based on the alignment activity

The curriculum developers establish and approve the standards (or objectives) for the new or revised curriculum based on the alignment activity described above. The composite list is examined for completeness, redundancy, and so forth. Other curriculum specialists and experienced teachers should be asked to review the list at this point. If, upon reflection, some standards or objectives are missing, they should be added. The composite list becomes the standards (or objectives) upon which the new curriculum is built. The list may be categorized as a way to organize the objectives for instructional and assessment purposes.

Curriculum Development Matrix: Complete the matrix to establish agreed-upon courses, years, and program levels in which the individual standards or objectives will be addressed

The next step is to create a curriculum development matrix to select the courses, grades, and program levels in which the objectives will be addressed. Figure 4-2 illustrates a generic matrix that may be modified for any situation. The approved, composite standards or objectives should be listed in the left column, and the ESL proficiency levels or classes offered in the program (e.g., ESL 1, ESL 2, ESL 3), across the top. If this curriculum will address or be used in other content areas, space should be left after the columns headed by the ESL levels, and then the other courses or grades should be listed in

FIGURE 4-2

ESL CURRICULUM DECISION-MAKING MATRIX

Levels and/or grades

ESL composite
standards/
objectives

successive columns. Figures 4-3 and 4-4 below show how this matrix might be applied in an elementary program and in a secondary one.

After the matrix has been designed, stakeholder teachers and district specialists should work collaboratively to identify the courses, grades, and program levels in which the individual standards and objectives will be addressed. It is important for regular elementary classroom teachers and secondary content teachers to participate if they will be asked to address some of the standards. This joint decision-making process is also an important way to generate accountability among educators for teaching English language learners, reflecting TESOL's vision that all school personnel assume responsibility for the education of these students.

In the sample elementary-level matrix (Figure 4-3), the district has identified seven standards, A–G, that the ESL and regular classroom teachers will address in their courses. The district offers three levels of ESL instruction for its students. The ESL teachers have placed the seven standards across their three levels, as appropriate to the developing language proficiencies of the students. It is critical that all the standards be covered in the ESL program. Some standards (e.g., C, E, F, G) will be introduced in one level and reinforced or extended in another level. Other standards (e.g., A, B, D) will be taught in one level with the expectation that students will master it there.

Once the standards have been organized for ESL levels, ESL and classroom teachers examine the grade-level curricula, K–5, to determine appropriate areas where the district ESL standards can be infused. Standard A, which will be taught in ESL Level 1, for example, is most suitable for the kindergarten curriculum. Standard B, taught in ESL Level 2, fits in with curriculum objectives for both Grade 1 and Grade 3. The process continues in this manner, with all the teachers making decisions about appropriate grade-level placements for the standards. When the process has concluded, all seven standards should be addressed across the K–5 spectrum, but each standard is not necessarily addressed in each grade.

The sample secondary-level matrix in Figure 4-4 shows a similar process. In this case, the ESL and social studies departments have decided to work together. Five ESL objectives, V–Z, have been identified as having application to the middle school social studies curriculum. As was done for the elementary matrix, the middle school ESL teachers first place the five objectives in their proficiency-level courses. Then they work with the social studies teachers and examine the

FIGURE 4-3

DECISION-MAKING MATRIX FOR ELEMENTARY-LEVEL CURRICULUM DEVELOPMENT

Composite ESL standards/ descriptors	Level 1	Level 2	Level 3			Elementary					
						K	Grade 1	Grade 2	Grade 3	Grade 4	Grade 5
A	✓					✓					
B		✓					✓		✓		
C	✓	✓					✓		✓		
D			✓								✓
E		✓	✓					✓			✓
F	✓		✓			✓					✓
G	✓	✓	✓			✓		✓		✓	

Using the ESL Standards for Curriculum Development ■ 111

FIGURE 4-4

DECISION-MAKING MATRIX FOR SECONDARY-LEVEL CURRICULUM DEVELOPMENT

Composite ESL standards/ descriptors	ESL			Middle school Social studies		
	Level 1	Level 2	Level 3	Grade 6	Grade 7	Grade 8
V	✓	✓		✓		✓
W	✓				✓	
X		✓	✓	✓	✓	✓
Y	✓		✓		✓	
Z			✓			✓

sixth-, seventh-, and eighth-grade curricula. The five objectives are slotted in appropriately, and the social studies department agrees to address them.

When the curriculum matrix is completed, ESL and regular classroom or content teachers have a clear illustration of their responsibilities regarding particular standards or objectives. At a glance, a curriculum developer or program coordinator can make sure that the language and content knowledge are being presented in a developmentally sound and articulated way. Moreover, the psychological effects are valuable. First, the resulting matrix is a testimony to the agreement of all stakeholder teachers that they are responsible for the education of English language learners. Second, the task of standards-based instruction does not appear daunting. No one teacher is responsible for the entire range of standards and objectives. The process provides a means of determining reasonable responsibilities, recognizing where reinforcement might take place, and avoiding overload at one grade or level. All the standards or objectives will be addressed across the ESL program levels and will be reinforced in the regular, content curricula. Third, teachers often realize that attention to these standards or objectives will be beneficial to all students, both native and nonnative English speakers.

Once the matrix has been completed, the individual sections of the curriculum (or curricula, if an ESL curriculum and a content one are desired) can be written. The process and product may vary from district to district. Some districts may include a philosophical statement about teaching and learning, drawing from the conceptual framework in the introduction to *ESL Standards*. Some districts might organize the standards and objectives thematically and develop a unit-based curriculum. If the curriculum will be used by regular classroom and content teachers, writers should prepare sections in the document on effective methods for content-based or sheltered instruction and provide guidelines for assessing the content knowledge of students who are still learning English. *Managing the Assessment Process: A Framework for Measuring Student Attainment of the ESL Standards* (TESOL, 1998) is a good resource for curriculum developers.

Retooling: Develop an ongoing professional development plan for all teachers

Before the new curriculum is implemented, a professional development plan for all teachers should be in place. The professional development should not consist of an isolated workshop but should be a series of linked sessions that occur over time. Although early sessions might focus on understanding the standards and curriculum, later ones should provide the participants with opportunities to discuss the curriculum in action.

A useful first session would provide all teachers with an overview of the conceptual framework for the ESL standards to give them a basic understanding of effective education for English language learners and the principles of SLA. "Promising Futures" (the introduction to *ESL Standards*; TESOL, 1997, pp. 1–10) is an excellent resource for this type of session. In later sessions, language and content teachers should participate in joint activities that allow them to become familiar with the standards, objectives, new curriculum, and planned assessments. They should share strategies and techniques for the delivery of instruction. Some sessions may be held by subject area or grade level to explore more fully the context within which language learning can take place in a content class.

All teachers might benefit from a reflection and discussion session on the topic, "What would Standard X look like in my classroom?" Often, applying a standards-based lens to one's lesson delivery does not result in radical change. Rather, teachers realize they can maintain much of the instruction they currently offer to students but modify it slightly to focus attention on the standards and objectives of the new curriculum. This type of session can be reassuring to teachers concerned that a standards-based curriculum will require radical shifts in their teaching styles. Teachers might also welcome discussions on other professional development topics, such as how to locate and include appropriate supplemental resources in their lessons, how to teach students learning strategies, and how to scaffold instruction for students in content classes.

Another critical professional development topic is assessment. As teachers implement the new curriculum, they need to consider student learning outcomes, both as a check on their instructional strategies (Am I making the material clear to my students?) and on the students' language growth and progress toward meeting standards. In some districts around the country, small groups of teachers bring samples of students' work (e.g., essays, reports, videotapes of oral presentations) to monthly meetings with colleagues. Together they examine the student-produced items from a standards-based perspective, trying to determine if the student has demonstrated the ability to meet one or more standards. (See the Prologue and chapter 8 for more information on professional development activities.)

*I*mplementation: Plan to implement the curriculum and assessments and identify resources necessary to do so

After districts have written a curriculum based on standards, they need to develop a plan for implementation that takes into account both teacher preparation and the necessary material resources. Teachers should not be asked to implement the curriculum without some professional development and appropriate materials. Administrators and parents should be informed about the new curriculum in advance. The implementation plan might ideally involve field-testing the curriculum in some classrooms at the outset, with central office staff providing support, and observing classes. Teachers who start implementing the aligned curriculum should then share their experiences with the others in their school or district, and that information should be used during the evaluation and revision processes.

*B*enchmarking: Set benchmark levels of progress and achievement toward meeting the standards

Setting benchmark levels of student progress and achievement toward meeting the standards or objectives is a challenging task. Experience from work in other content areas shows that practicing teachers must be part of this process. They can work toward consensus on what is "good enough" when students demonstrate what they know and can do. Some districts might approach this benchmarking process as they would design a holistic scoring rubric (a measurement scale with descriptive criteria for each score point or level that is used to assess student performance, as on a writing or speaking test). The rubric might describe, for example, different levels of progress, from *no evidence of knowledge*, to *evidence of basic knowledge*, to *mastery*.

TESOL believes that setting such benchmarks is a local decision, not a national one. As teachers identify levels of progress and achievement, they should do so with their own students in mind. Expectations for what students can accomplish in a specific period of time may vary across districts. One district, for example, may serve a large number of students with limited formal schooling and no L1 or English literacy skills. Another district might serve students with above-grade-level knowledge in the content areas and some study of EFL in school in their native countries. Both groups of students should meet the ESL standards, but they may travel different pathways and require different amounts of time to do so.

Evaluation: Plan and conduct a formative evaluation of the curriculum implementation

All districts should plan and conduct a formative evaluation of the implementation of the curriculum. This evaluation should be conceptualized at the start of the development process so that data can be collected from the early days of implementation. Such data might include, for example, student work samples; teachers' lesson plans and anecdotal records about the delivery of the lessons; adjustments teachers made to planned activities; students' scores on tests and other achievement data; and interviews with teachers, students, and parents. Through the evaluative process, the district can make decisions about the standards, professional development activities, implementation activities, and benchmarks.

If the curriculum is field-tested, as described in the section on Montgomery County, Maryland, later in this chapter, the participating teachers can be a valuable source of input for the formative evaluation. Their experiences, comments, and suggestions can be used to revise the curriculum effectively.

Revision: Revise the standards or objectives, curriculum, and assessments according to the evaluation

Districts should be prepared to revise the standards, objectives, matrix, curriculum, professional development plan, and benchmarks according to the findings of the formative evaluation. If students are not performing well at the end of 1 year's implementation, each stage above should be examined independently and modified as needed. For example, teachers may find that they are addressing some of the objectives at inappropriate levels of English proficiency. In other words, an objective such as "Students will be able to use persuasive speech effectively in an oral presentation" may have been assigned to the advanced beginning level when it is more suitable for intermediate-level students. If some objectives are misassigned, the decision matrix should be reorganized. As another example, content and regular classroom teachers might find they need more information about SLA theory, so a district might design a new professional development plan, or adjust the time spent on SLA topics and change the activities. Once those modifications have been instituted, however, the curriculum should be reevaluated at regular intervals.

Although the ASCRIBER process appears linear in print, it is cyclical. Feedback and findings from the evaluation and revision stages may loop back to any of the earlier stages for adjustment.

■ Curriculum Infusion

Apart from developing new curricula at the state or district level, the ESL standards can be infused into existing curricula. One approach is to infuse language development awareness and strategies into established curricula for one or more content areas. Another approach is to infuse the ESL standards into established curriculum units.

Some states and districts that seek to infuse the ESL standards into content-area curricula, in addition to or in lieu of developing a standards-based ESL curriculum, may utilize a language implications chart. In this two-column chart, the district or state content-area standards (or objectives or benchmarks) are listed in the left-hand column. Each standard is then considered independently to identify the language implications—that is, what English language learners can demonstrate to attain that standard. These implications are then listed in the right-hand column. The example in Figure 4-5 shows some of the benchmarks for mathematics from the Philadelphia (Pennsylvania) academic content standards (School District of Philadelphia, 1997) with their associated language implications.

TASK   2

Create a template for a language implications chart like the one in Figure 4-5. Choose a content area that you are familiar with, and list the standards or curriculum objectives for that subject in the left-hand column. Now consider the language implications of each standard or objective. Think about key vocabulary, language functions, usage, and so forth. Write these language implications in the right-hand column. If possible, discuss your chart with a teacher of the subject you selected.

FIGURE 4-5

BENCHMARKS FOR MATHEMATICS WITH LANGUAGE IMPLICATIONS

Benchmarks for Philadelphia Mathematics Content Standard 1	Language implications
1. Add, subtract, multiply, and divide whole numbers, and investigate inverse relationships with and without calculators.	1. Students need to listen, read, and write about technical arithmetic vocabulary, such as numbers, symbols, operations and their synonyms.
2. Use numbers and number relationships in problem-solving situations that reflect the experiences of a diversity of groups and contemporary issues. Communicate the reasoning used in these problems.	2. Students need communication skills—they must gather and explain information and justify their process to solve a problem.
3. Estimate, approximate, round off, or use exact numbers, as appropriate, in calculations.	3. Students need to use learning strategies of estimating, predicting, and so on. They need to learn appropriate vocabulary and ways that predictions and estimates are articulated.
4. Use mental computation.	4. Students need to use learning strategies.
5. Use mathematical language to describe problems.	5. Students need to learn math vocabulary including numbers, symbols, operations, expressions like *is larger than, is equal to,* and *let* x *equal . . .* in oral and written form.
6. Relate counting, grouping, and place value concepts to a base 10 number system.	6. Students need to discuss numbers, place value, and movement of numbers from one column to another when regrouping occurs.

Continued on next page

FIGURE 4-5 continued

BENCHMARKS FOR MATHEMATICS WITH LANGUAGE IMPLICATIONS

Benchmarks for Philadelphia Mathematics Content Standard 1	Language implications
7. Describe and compare quantities by using whole numbers, decimals, and fractions.	7. Students need to learn comparative and contrastive language, such as *is larger than* and *is smaller than*; terminology associated with fractions, decimals, percentages; and so on. Students may need to represent comparisons visually and be able to use descriptive language.
8. Describe the need for numbers beyond whole numbers, use adding and subtracting with decimals and fractions.	8. Students need to learn language associated with the addition and subtraction of decimals and fractions, such as *one over three, one-third*, and *twenty-two thirty-seconds*.

Source: Short et al. (2000).

The next step may vary across sites. Some districts or states may choose to add an appendix to an established content curriculum to delineate the language implications and provide suggestions for instructional practice so that teachers help develop the appropriate academic language skills of English language learners in their classes. Other sites might add sidebars or additional pages in the main text of the curriculum or scope and sequence to point out specific instances in the delivery of the curriculum where a "teachable language moment" might take place and how teachers might take advantage of those opportunities successfully. For example, in the section on teaching addition in first grade, advice to the math teacher might read, "Use only one expression to refer to addition, such as *add*, until the students have understood the mathematical concept. Then slowly introduce synonymous words such as *7 plus 8, 7 increased by 8, 7 and 8*, and *8 more than 7*." Some districts might plan professional development for content teachers around the list of language implications. Such training could familiarize the teachers with the language aspects of their curricula and provide an occasion to observe and practice instructional techniques for language development. In addition, this process of identifying the language implications could also be used to help identify the grades and content courses on the curriculum decision-making chart (Step C in ASCRIBER) in which certain composite objectives will be addressed.

The ESL standards might also be infused directly into established curriculum units. This approach to standards-based instruction grows from established practice and thus may be more reassuring to some teachers. Figure 4-6 shows a model of a curriculum unit planner that incorporates the ESL standards.

After identifying the unit topic/theme and ESL proficiency and grade levels for the class, the teacher focuses on the ESL standard or standards that will be addressed. In the example in Figure 4-6, the teacher has selected a standard and appropriate descriptors from *ESL Standards* (i.e., Goal, 2, Standard 2, p. 87). Next, the teacher lists the concepts and skills for the language and content learning that will be taught in this unit. These may be drawn from the existing unit, the sample progress indicators in *ESL Standards*, and the composite objectives list, if the district has created one and the teacher has access to it (see, e.g., Figure 4-1). The teacher then identifies specific instructional activities, both those in the existing unit and others drawn from the progress indicators and vignettes in *ESL Standards* that apply to the standards and descriptors. The teacher continues by listing necessary materials and resources to accomplish the unit and by planning for appropriate assessments of students' learning throughout the unit.

■ Curriculum Development in Action

As mentioned above, there are many ways to incorporate the ESL standards into the curriculum. The type of curriculum development activities that will take place is often decided at the local district level. In some instances, though, state departments of education may participate, offering or issuing curriculum frameworks or guidelines that promote the implementation of the ESL standards.

This section of the chapter explores representative curriculum development processes at the local and state levels. Although the examples in no way capture the rich variety of curriculum development activities occurring across the United States, they demonstrate

FIGURE 4-6

CURRICULUM PLANNER

Theme or unit topic: Heroes
ESL level: Intermediate, middle school
ESL standard(s)/descriptors (Goal 2, Standard 2): Students will • formulate and ask questions • gather information in writing • select, connect, and explain information
Content and language concepts and skills to be learned: Write research questions Locate reference material Read for specific detail Conduct library research Take notes to record information about research topic Use writing process for biographies
Activities: Students will • brainstorm research questions in small groups, then get whole-class feedback • tour the library with media specialist • scan research materials • use tree diagram to record information while reading • draft mini-biographies of their chosen hero • attend writing conference with the teacher for editorial feedback • write final version of mini-biography
Materials/resources: Encyclopedias, biographies, legends, Internet Computer access Tree diagram—graphic organizer Editing guidelines for students
Assessment: Student-developed checklist for process District-developed rubric for assessing student writing
Source: Adapted from Center for Resource Management (1997).

several approaches for creating standards-based curricula. The examples reflect urban and suburban districts with large numbers of students in ESL and bilingual programs, small districts with few learners, and a state with a wide range of L2 populations across its cities, towns, and rural areas. Some of the examples describe the creation of a new ESL curriculum whereas others show how a current curriculum was revised and organized around standards. Two of the sites focused on content-based language learning; one specifically designed a curriculum guide to help content teachers accommodate the needs of English language learners in content classes. One site focused initially on one school and English proficiency level (middle school, intermediate) before moving on to other grades and proficiency levels. The other three sites wrote curricula for all proficiency levels. Two addressed Grades K–12; one, Grades K–8.

The first example explores how a Maryland district aligned its middle school ESL curriculum to the local English language arts curriculum (which in turn had been aligned to the state English language arts standards) and to the ESL standards (cf. Gómez et al., 1998). The second example describes the revision of an ESL curriculum for a New Jersey K–8 bilingual/ESL program that used the ESL standards and descriptors to build a scope and sequence for English language instruction and modeled local vignettes on those in *ESL Standards*, integrating some content objectives from the state standards (cf. Leone, 1997). The third case explains how a local district in Ohio developed a content-based curriculum aligned to state standards and local content-area objectives for mathematics, science, and social studies and to the ESL standards. The fourth example discusses a state-level process that used the ESL standards to develop curriculum guidelines for content teachers who teach English language learners. In the latter two cases, the curriculum developers relied heavily on the ESL standards, descriptors, and progress indicators associated with Goal 2 ("Students will use English to achieve academically").

Montgomery County
Public Schools, Maryland

Montgomery County, Maryland, is a large, suburban district near Washington, DC, with a large ESOL population and a mature ESL program. Maryland had been promoting statewide school reform based on state standards for different content areas, and the Montgomery County Public Schools (MCPS) ESL staff decided to revise the K–12

ESL curriculum to reflect changes in the state and district. During the 1996–1997 school year, staff began the process by revising the middle school ESL curriculum. Middle school was chosen as the starting point because it is a time of transition for many ESOL students in the county and because commercial materials were scarcer. Two goals of the curriculum were "to prepare students for full participation in locally and state mandated assessment programs [and] to facilitate the transition of ESOL students into the general program" (MCPS, 1999, p. 3).

Given district and state requirements for all students, the ESL director and instructional specialists decided the best approach would be to align the intermediate-level ESL curriculum to the eighth-grade English language arts curriculum offered in the county. They felt it was important to incorporate TESOL's ESL standards into the new curriculum as well. Other resources utilized included the instructional guide for the English 8 course; the ESL program's scope and sequence; *Maryland High School Core Learning Goals Skills for Success* (Maryland State Department of Education, 1996), the foreign language program of studies for Levels 1–3; the curriculum framework for elementary science education; and the elementary ESL outcomes, benchmarks, and indicators. A curriculum-writing team was formed, composed of the ESL instructional specialists from the central office and practicing middle and high school teachers, including one who worked in a special district program for low-literacy ESOL students and another with experience teaching ESL content classes. The selected team members represented a variety of schools with differing student demographics.

The team's first activity was to develop pre-K–12 outcomes, benchmarks, and indicators for the ESL program that were aligned with those of the district English language arts program and that incorporated TESOL's *ESL Standards*. The team articulated the curriculum philosophy, drawing from the conceptual framework in "Promising Futures" (TESOL, 1997, pp. 1–2). Second, the ESL curriculum development team prepared an instructional guide for the middle school intermediate ESL curriculum, which was organized around four themes similar to those in the eighth-grade English language arts curriculum: "Hopes and Dreams," "Community," "Discoveries," and "Changes and Challenges." For each thematic unit, teachers are expected to develop lessons around essential questions, common tasks, and language focus points (often language mechanics and grammar).

The curriculum encourages teachers to develop language awareness and critical literacy in the students while teaching and reinforcing the four language skills (listening, speaking, reading, and writing). In addition, the team wrote sample activities and assessments to illustrate the instructional goals for each theme. The activities ranged from reading and writing tasks, to vocabulary development exercises, to discussion topics. Support for assessment included rubrics for student self-assessment, writing prompts and accompanying rubrics for teachers to use in analyzing students' work, and portfolio reflection worksheets. The team also chose the series All Star English, published by Addison Wesley Longman, as an anchor ESL series and supplemented the curriculum with literature from the English 8 course. Figure 4-7 shows a page from the curriculum guide.

The next activity involved the professional development of a small number of teachers who would field-test the new curriculum. Five middle school ESL teachers representing different site locations, school sizes, and years of teaching experience were identified and trained. Only one of these teachers had been on the writing team. The goals of the training were to help the teachers understand the philosophy of standards-based instruction and assessment and to familiarize them with the new curriculum. In the 1997–1998 school year, these teachers field-tested the material and communicated regularly with the district ESL staff and one another via e-mail about their challenges and successes. They kept notes about the classroom implementation, including detailed lesson plans and samples of students' work. ESL instructional specialists observed the field-testers' classes and provided support as needed. The teachers and central ESL staff also held several meetings during the year to discuss the implementation and plan revisions.

The subsequent phase of the process involved districtwide pilot testing. After the Montgomery County Board of Education's Council on Instruction approved the expansion of the program in winter 1998, the ESL central office staff began supporting professional development for all the district's middle school ESL teachers who served intermediate-level students. The office also revised the curriculum based on field-test results. In the 1998–1999 school year, all middle schools in the district implemented the pilot process. Final revisions to the curriculum were made in the summer of 1999 and approved by the board of education.

While the middle school field-testing was taking place in 1997–1998, a similar process began for the elementary school ESL (all

FIGURE 4-7

SAMPLE OUTCOME WITH BENCHMARKS AND INDICATORS FROM MONTGOMERY COUNTY PUBLIC SCHOOLS CURRICULUM GUIDE

OUTCOME V: Demonstrate global understanding, interpretation, and critical analysis in English.

BENCHMARKS	*INDICATORS*
Students will:	Students will:
1. develop global understanding and communicate it in English.	1. identify pattern.
	tell theme, gist, main idea, overview, pattern, author's intent with a rationale for the thought.
2. develop interpretation and communicate it in English.	2. use graphic aids to support interpretation.
locate supporting evidence in information sources.	develop and use own graphic representations to support meaning.
	revise interpretation when necessary.
	use information from a variety of sources.
3. respond critically in English to information.	3. determine author's purpose.
	identify author's and character's point of view.
	evaluate information according to reader's purpose.
	compare and contrast books on the same topic.
	evaluate information.

Source: Montgomery County Public Schools (1999, p. 6). Used with permission.

proficiency levels), the middle school advanced-level ESL, and the high school Level 3 ESL curricula. The outcomes, benchmarks, and indicators were identified, and the curriculum guides were drafted. These curricula were revised for piloting throughout the district during the 1999–2000 school year.

Paterson Public Schools, New Jersey

Paterson, New Jersey, is an urban community located not far from New York City with a large immigrant population and students from diverse cultural and linguistic backgrounds. It has an established bilingual program for students from Spanish, Arabic, Bengali, and Turkish backgrounds, who receive ESL instruction as part of their daily schedule. Students from other language backgrounds participate in the ESL program. Most of Paterson's English language learners receive some type of L1 support during the school day.

Given New Jersey's emphasis on school reform, the development of state content standards, and the need to revamp the bilingual/ESL program, the bilingual director for the district decided to revise the K–8 bilingual/ESL curriculum in 1996 to incorporate the ESL standards, which had been issued in draft form at that time. A team of bilingual and ESL K–8 teachers and consultants was formed to work collaboratively on a new ESL curriculum that would be designed for use by bilingual/ESL teachers and content teachers. The goal was to write a curriculum that would help students learn content while they were acquiring English over the years that they might remain in the program.

The team began with *ESL Standards for Pre-K–12 Students*, planning to build upon the goals, standards, descriptors, and progress indicators. These were modified as needed to generate the scope and sequence of the new Paterson curriculum and to show the connection to the district's K–8 language arts curriculum. Appreciating the inclusion of vignettes in *ESL Standards*, the team decided to include vignettes in the Paterson curriculum. To contextualize the curriculum to the local setting, however, the team members wrote their own vignettes to provide strong, detailed examples of good instruction in Paterson's various ESL and bilingual K–8 classrooms. Language and content objectives (for mathematics, science, or social studies) were written for each vignette and linked to Paterson's K–8 content curricula, which are based on New Jersey state standards. The curriculum developers also drew from the standards and descriptors in *ESL Standards* and identified learning strategies for each vignette.

In addition to the vignettes and curriculum objectives, Paterson's document, *The ESL Pre- K–8 Language and Content Curriculum* (Paterson Public Schools, 1997), included general information, such as the district and program philosophies for teaching and learning; information about the bilingual and ESL instructional models; and principles for sheltered instruction. Other sections provided descriptions of effective teaching strategies for ESL, bilingual, and content teachers; information on learning strategies for English language learners; and examples of lessons that integrate language with science, mathematics, and social studies. One section focused on the evaluation and assessment of students' language and content learning. The document concluded with recommendations for staff development and for curriculum implementation. In autumn 1999, the curriculum was reviewed and piloted by teachers across the district. Board approval was expected in the 1999–2000 school year.

South Euclid–Lyndhurst
City Schools, Ohio

The South Euclid–Lyndhurst City School District, located in a suburban area of Cleveland, Ohio, operates a small ESL program for its language minority students at selected sites. Out of a districtwide student population of 4,500, 35 students are in the ESL program. Most of the students are from the former Soviet Union (Ukraine, Uzbekistan, and Russia), with a few families from other countries, such as the Philippines, Hong Kong, and Liberia. One site serves primary Grades K–4; another, upper elementary Grades 5–6. Both of these sites offer pullout ESL instruction with some inclusion in regular classrooms (with curricular modifications). A third site serves Grades 7–8, and the fourth, Grades 9–12. Secondary-level students may receive ESL instruction in self-contained ESL classrooms in addition to academic content support in ESL resource classrooms for one or two periods per day.

In 1997, the South Euclid–Lyndhurst City School District decided to develop a curriculum for the ESL program that was based on *ESL Standards for Pre-K–12 Students*, as suggested by staff from the Lau Center of the Ohio Department of Education.[3] This was the first ESL curriculum developed for the district. As a first step, the district adopted the three goals and nine standards from *ESL Standards* and added an additional goal, "to communicate effectively with parents." In developing ESL standards for the district, the curriculum team also decided to connect Goal 2, Standard 2 ("To use English to achieve academically in all content areas: Students will use English to obtain, process, construct, and provide subject matter information in spoken and written form"; p. 24) to state standards and local objectives for mathematics and social studies. The district used the State of Ohio Model Curriculum as one of its resources. The resulting document, *Course of Study: English as a Second Language Handbook and Guidelines* (Hartmann, Watson, & Brickman, 1997), is an integrated, content-based curriculum for the K–12 ESL program.

In writing the course of study, the curriculum team organized the district standards first by goal and standard, then by grade-level cluster for each standard. To make the document useful for the local situation, the team reorganized the grade-level clusters as found in *ESL Standards* to the following: K–3, 4–6, and 7–12. The individual pages for each standard provide the following information:

- the goal and standard

- a list of key descriptors drawn from *ESL Standards*

- progress indicators organized by proficiency level (beginning, intermediate, and advanced) in a table, drawing from *ESL Standards* and adding additional indicators as desired

The section of the South Euclid–Lyndhurst document covering Goal 2, Standard 2 is organized slightly differently. After the goal and standard, the section states the local mathematics objective, such as "Strand #1 — Patterns, Relations, and Functions. Goal: Develop an understanding and appreciation of patterns in mathematics and the environment" (p. 14), followed by the key descriptors from *ESL Standards*. The progress indicators, listed next, were written to be more closely aligned to the content objective. For example, under the math objective listed above, one intermediate-level progress indicator is "explore and describe in simple words, patterns in the real world" (p. 14). Finally, a list of key technical vocabulary (e.g., *add, subtract, less,* and *more*) is provided for this combined ESL and math objective. An example from social studies, Grades 7–12, is presented in Figure 4-8.

This handbook also addresses the assessment of the district's ESOL students and explains the ESL program's design and philosophy. Additional information about identification, placement, and grading of students is included. The roles of staff and parents are explained, and suggested instructional strategies and techniques are described. Before the curriculum was finalized, teachers, administrators, and board of education members reviewed it.

FIGURE 4-8

SAMPLE STANDARD FROM SOUTH EUCLID–LYNDHURST CITY CURRICULUM HANDBOOK

ESL Standards

Goal 2: To use English to achieve academically in all content areas

Standard 2: Students will use English to obtain, process, construct, and provide subject matter information in spoken and written form.

SOCIAL STUDIES
Strand #3 World Interactions

GOAL: Locate, represent and describe locations on maps relative to other places. Identify and locate landforms, bodies of water, features of physical environment and reasons for human movement. Cite examples of social, economic, and political interdependence on history.

Descriptors:

- Compare and contrast information
- Respond to the work of peers
- Understand and produce technical vocabulary and test features according to content area
- Represent information visually and interpret information visually
- Listen to, speak, read, and write about subject matter information
- Persuade, argue, negotiate, evaluate, and justify

Continued on next page

North Carolina Department of Public Instruction

In North Carolina, the number of identified limited English proficient (LEP) students grew from 3,000 in 1988–1989 to 25,000 in 1996–1997, an increase of more than 700%. Although the overall numbers of LEP students in North Carolina have not approached those in New York, California, and Florida, the rapid, exponential growth over those 9 years portends the fact that many more L2 students will enter schools in the state over the next decade. In a few of the larger cities, the districts offer full-day ESL programs, but for the most part, English language learners are located in low-incidence districts and receive a

FIGURE **4-8 continued**

SAMPLE STANDARD FROM SOUTH EUCLID–LYNDHURST CITY CURRICULUM HANDBOOK

Grade Level: 7–12

Beginning Level	*Intermediate Level*	*Advanced Level*
• read political and physical maps, identify countries, bodies of water, topographical features	• discuss natural processes and how they affect human activities (i.e., floods, pollution)	• analyze the impact of technology on communication and transportation
• compare climate patterns using graphs or pictures	• examine transportation and communication systems and their impact on people and historical events	• examine reasons why people have gone to war against each other
• view and listen to works of literature and the arts that describe particular places	• search for ways in which people borrow and loan cultural characteristics and present an oral presentation in class	• justify proposed solutions to international problems
Vocabulary: drought flood pollution	transportation politics economics technology	interdependence war solution

Source: Hartmann, Watson, and Brickman (1997, p. 46). Used with permission.

limited amount of ESL services during the school day. At the elementary level, they are often in regular classrooms with some pullout ESL support. At the secondary level, students may have a period of self-contained ESL but spend most of their day in mainstream content courses. In some rural areas of the state, ESL teachers are responsible for providing instruction in more than one school.

Because the language minority population has traditionally been a small percentage of North Carolina's students, the state's Department of Public Instruction does not have mandated ESL curriculum guidelines for districts to follow as they plan an ESL program or deliver instruction. ESL certification has been an add-on credential for practicing ESL teachers; moreover, most content teachers have had little or no training in meeting the needs of English language learners. Yet North Carolina, like many other U.S. states, has been undertaking school reform as part of the Goals 2000 process. The state has developed standards in all subject areas. Required state assessments exist in reading, writing, and mathematics for Grades K–8. Voluntary assessments are available in science and social studies. In high school, end-of-course tests exist for many required courses.

Interested in helping English language learners succeed in state-mandated courses and on state tests, the state Department of Public Instruction developed one approach through which mainstream teachers of English language learners in the content areas could improve their instruction. With the sponsorship of the Department of Public Instruction, ESL coordinators and exemplary ESL teachers from around the state formed a curriculum coordination team. This team decided to create a curriculum guide for classroom and content teachers that would demonstrate ways to accommodate English language learners in content-area courses and meet their language development needs. The source materials for this process were the state standards documents for mathematics, science, social studies, and English language arts; *ESL Standards for Pre-K–12 Students*; some local ESL curricula; and course textbooks. Content teachers acted as informants and reviewers throughout the development.

The curriculum coordination team came together several times over 2 years to develop the structure and generate the curriculum guidelines for English language learners in the content areas. To make the document most useful for the content teachers, the team infused the ESL standards and ESL strategies into the content-area objectives and tasks. Given limited time and resources, the team could not address all of the state standards for each of the content areas. Instead, they created a representative sample. Figure 4-9 depicts the framework they developed.

The team members divided into grade-level clusters, each cluster working on a document for elementary, middle, or high school teachers, and established the following procedure:

FIGURE 4-9

FRAMEWORK DEVELOPED FOR NORTH CAROLINA'S *GUIDE TO THE STANDARD COURSE OF STUDY FOR LEP STUDENTS*

Subject: _____

Content objectives	Content tasks	Language considerations	Language strategies	Progress indicators
[Selection from North Carolina state content-area standards]	[Sample real classroom tasks]	[Implications regarding the language needed to do the tasks; organized by technical vocabulary, usage, functions, and thinking skills]	[Strategies teachers can use to help students; organized for novice, intermediate, and advanced proficiency levels]	[Ways teachers can determine student progress; organized for novice, intermediate, and advanced proficiency levels]
Source: state standards documents	Source: textbooks, content teachers, experience	Source: *ESL Standards for Pre-K–12 Students*, textbooks	Source: ESL teachers, *ESL Standards for Pre-K–12 Students*	Source: ESL teachers, *ESL Standards for Pre-K–12 Students*

Source: North Carolina Department of Public Instruction (1999, n.p.). Used with permission.

1. *Select a sample of objectives from the content-area standards.* At least two objectives from each content area would be chosen for each grade level (K–8) or each high school course, and they needed to cover different topical areas.

2. *Identify an associated, real classroom task.* The tasks would be drawn from course textbooks, content teacher informants, and the ESL teachers' knowledge about activities their students are asked to accomplish in content classes. As they considered potential tasks, the team members needed to make sure the overall complement of tasks would reflect different levels of cognitive challenge. For example, not all tasks selected for U.S. history should require independent research and writing.

3. *Consider the language implications of the task.* The team would determine what aspects of language the students would need in order to accomplish the task. These considerations were then to be categorized to help content teachers understand the multiple language development needs of LEP students: *technical vocabulary* that pertains to the subject; *usage* like past tense and question formations; and *language functions* like requesting, recording, and comparing. A fourth category, *higher order thinking skills*, was also selected to highlight the language implications of articulating these skills. To generate these language considerations, teachers would rely on textbooks, their experience, and *ESL Standards for Pre-K–12 Students*, with particular attention to the descriptors found in the three standards for Goal 2.

4. *Identify instructional strategies that teachers might incorporate in their lessons to help English language learners understand the task and objective, and correlate these strategies to appropriate proficiency levels of the students (novice, intermediate, and advanced).* This part of the framework would demonstrate how teachers could infuse ESL methods into their lessons in order to make the content more comprehensible. The curriculum team members would use their knowledge of ESL strategies and techniques as well as information found in the vignettes in *ESL Standards* to identify the strategies. The vignettes under Goal 2 proved to be useful resources because they were designed to address different content topics, grades,

and student proficiency levels. The range of sample strategies listed included writing directions on the board in addition to giving them orally, preteaching vocabulary, pairing ESOL students with native-English-speaking students, and using graphic organizers like semantic maps before beginning a new topic and Venn diagrams when comparing similar things.

5. *Recommend sample activities for teachers to use in class to determine students' progress, and organize them by student proficiency level.* This column in the framework would help content teachers understand what might be reasonable for students to accomplish at different levels of proficiency. For example, if the task required students to write a time line of events leading to the American Revolution and explain the causes and effects of these events, a novice ESOL student might list events without written explanation. However, advanced students might be able to complete the task in much the same way as native English speakers, although these students might exhibit some grammatical inaccuracies in the written explanation. To develop these activities, the curriculum team would draw from its own experience, textbooks, and the sample progress indicators and vignettes under Goal 2 in *ESL Standards for Pre-K–12 Students*.

6. *Solicit feedback on the framework and representative samples from practicing teachers in the different content areas.* The curriculum coordination team met only a few times each year. After each meeting, the staff would prepare a revised draft along with a feedback form, and the teachers and ESL coordinators would share the draft with content teachers and coordinators in their districts. In addition, content specialists at the Department of Public Instruction examined the guide as it was being developed. All of these content experts would review the material, fill in gaps, and make suggestions for improvement. After the team was satisfied that the framework was viable and a number of standards had been worked through the full process, local teams that included content teachers were established at several district sites in order to develop the curriculum guide more fully.

When the curriculum guide (North Carolina Department of Public Instruction, 1999) was finished in the 1998–1999 school year, the North Carolina Department of Public Instruction began to conduct regional professional development activities to familiarize the content teachers and their ESL counterparts with the new guidelines. Other support would be provided as needed. The state also embarked on a complementary project to train teacher education faculty so that preservice teachers in North Carolina would learn how to infuse the ESL standards and ESL strategies in their instruction before they began working in schools.

TASK 3

Once a curriculum has been developed, retooling and formative evaluation are necessary. For the teachers in your school or in one you are familiar with, draft a general retooling plan for ongoing professional development on the new curriculum before and during implementation. Similarly, outline a formative evaluation plan for monitoring the implementation process. Be sure to identify the stakeholders for the evaluation and address their concerns in the plan.

■ Conclusion

The school reform movement in the United States has created an exciting opportunity for ESL professionals to revitalize their curricula and programs for English language learners and provide professional development to various educators who work with these students. *ESL Standards for Pre-K–12 Students* provides a common framework for communication among educators to generate attention to the needs of ESOL students. The presence of Goal 2, with its focus on academic English, has served as a bridge between language and content educators in many school districts across the country.

Curriculum development using the ESL standards is in its infancy, but as more districts and states undertake the process, we are learning more and more about what works. The examples in this chapter demonstrate some approaches districts and states with different student demographics, program types, resources, and curricular goals have taken to complete the process. At all of the sites, teachers have actively participated on curriculum-writing teams, and a wide range of educators have reviewed drafts of the new standards-based curricula. The goal of all curriculum development is to create an instructional and assessment program that will help English language learners achieve high standards. The ESL standards provide an excellent resource to accomplish this goal.

TASK 4

Compare and contrast the approaches to standards-based curriculum development in the three examples provided. How were they similar? How were they different? Why do you think different approaches were used?

■ Notes

[1] Tennessee adopted the ESL standards in a slightly modified version, organizing the standards around four grade-level clusters instead of the three found in the national document. New Jersey has placed the ESL standards into the bilingual education administrative code, thus requiring that all bilingual and ESL programs in districts across the state align their ESL curricula to TESOL's *ESL Standards*.

[2] Terminology varies widely across districts in the United States. Some sites organize curricula around objectives, others around learning proficiencies, student competencies, or benchmarks. For the purposes of this discussion, *standards* refer to local, state, and national standards; *objectives* refer to instructional goals for students in the curricula; and *descriptors* refer to the behaviors described in the ESL standards.

[3] South Euclid–Lyndhurst City School District also received a small grant from the Ohio Department of Education to write its ESL curriculum.

Chapter 5

Changing Paradigms for Assessment

Anne Katz

Creating ESL standards is merely the first step in rethinking and restructuring the delivery of instruction to ESOL students. Educators interested in charting their students' success in achieving those standards must

- begin to document what students know and can do

- examine the effectiveness of learning environments for students and reflect on how best to adapt those environments to enhance students' learning

- be able to judge how to match students with appropriate levels of instruction and decide when students are ready to move on to other program levels or services

When ESL standards form the core of designing the teaching and learning environment, assessment data can provide the information needed for educators to examine critically how students are progressing in attaining those standards.

To assist teachers in utilizing assessment data in useful ways, this chapter first outlines some of the major changes in assessment theory that undergird current practice and inform the conceptual framework underlying the development of sound assessment practices for ESL programs. It then presents the model at the heart of this framework: a four-step assessment process that can provide teachers with the information they need to make decisions about teaching and learning in the classroom.

To gain a greater understanding of students' learning, teachers can draw on information gathered in two ways: through traditional testing and through classroom assessment. Traditional testing (see chapter 6) includes (a) commercially available language proficiency instruments used to determine students' language levels and (b) large-scale assessments prescribed by state or district mandate as part of an accountability system set up to monitor students' achievement in content areas and the delivery of program services. Complementing traditional testing are classroom assessments (see chapter 7) that are woven into instruction and often designed by classroom teachers. Because both approaches to gathering information about students' achievement are part of the everyday life of most ESL teachers, a clearer understanding of the assessment process will help educators determine how to make use of all information collected.

■ Changing Trends in Assessment

The 1990s witnessed major changes in how educators think about assessment (Herman, Aschbacher, & Winters, 1992; O'Malley & Valdez Pierce, 1996). Many of us associate testing with multiple-choice tests administered to large groups of students periodically during a student's career (Bachman & Palmer, 1996). Although exams much like the ones most teachers remember from their own school experiences continue to provide information needed by students, parents, teachers, and administrators, alternatives to these tests are appearing alongside the fill-in-the-bubble answer sheets. Students are creating portfolios of their work, performing tasks, mounting exhibitions, and developing projects with peers. Instead of relying solely on machine-generated scores to judge these student outputs, educators are enlisting students' peers to provide feedback and designing local rubrics to determine appropriate performance levels.

Not surprisingly, these new assessment practices reflect the larger context of schooling. These expanded ways of thinking about assessment reflect deeper changes in conceptualizing what teaching and learning are all about, especially in classrooms designed to provide rich instruction to diverse learners. In today's classrooms, learning is seen as socially constructed, developmental, and complex; the many languages and cultures embodied in a diverse student population are viewed as resources that can enhance learning (Tharp, 1997). These changes in the way educators think about instruction have implications for assessment design, especially when assessment is regarded as contextualized *within* rather than as separate from the teaching and learning environment. Figure 5-1 illustrates the connection between assessment and instruction and their relationship to the ESL standards, all within the context of teaching and learning.

Based on current thinking about teaching and learning, assessments are interwoven with instruction, reflect the sociocultural context of the student population being assessed, can be ongoing and complex, and involve multiple ways of demonstrating students' competence. This vision of assessment also recognizes the importance of the teacher's role. Within this new model, teachers are active agents in creating, administering, and analyzing results from such assessments.

The History of Testing

Assessment as a procedure for gathering information about somebody or something in order to make a decision or take an action has been around for a long time. Bertrand (1991), for example, illustrates the longevity of testing with an example drawn from the Bible:

> Jephthah (Judg. 12:5) ordered that all those who approached the Jordan fords unable to pronounce the word "shibboleth" should be killed. By doing so, he distinguished between his own men and those of the enemy, who could not say the sound "sh." Thus, those who came with the password pronounced as "sibboleth" failed a very effective, early, criterion-referenced achievement test and received immediate feedback. (p. 18)

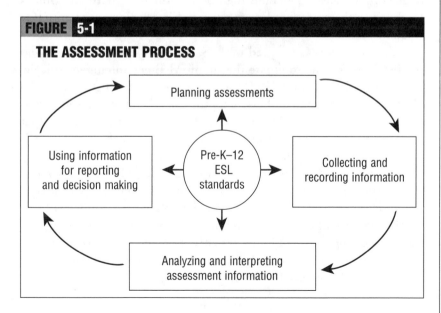

FIGURE 5-1

THE ASSESSMENT PROCESS

Planning assessments

Using information for reporting and decision making

Pre-K–12 ESL standards

Collecting and recording information

Analyzing and interpreting assessment information

This example can be seen as describing a language learning hurdle similar to the ones faced by ESOL students or even as another instance of high-stakes assessment; it also shows that people have been collecting data to make decisions for a long time.

Understanding the context for current trends in assessment, however, requires a look at more recent history. Wolf, Bixby, Glenn, and Gardner (1991) place any understanding of assessment in the context of an understanding of learning and education. From this perspective, assessment is not an isolated part of an educational program but reflects how learning and teaching are conceptualized within the curriculum and through instructional practice. At the beginning of the 20th century, theories of learning were intertwined with work on intelligence testing carried out by Alfred Binet, director of the psychology laboratory at the Sorbonne. Acting at the behest of the minister of public education, Binet was asked to develop a way to identify children who were unsuccessful in everyday classrooms and would benefit from special education. To carry out this assignment to sort children by ability, Binet developed an extensive series of short and varied tasks that were linked conceptually, he theorized, to basic reasoning processes. Trained examiners administered the tasks. Because tasks were arranged on a scale of difficulty and age levels were assigned to each, children's "mental" ages could be determined by the tasks they could complete. Children whose mental age did not match their chronological age could then be identified. Eventually, Binet's work led to the more familiar construct of intelligence quotient (IQ) (Gould, 1981).

Binet's work was adapted by U.S. educator Lewis Terman, who revised Binet's scale to create the Stanford-Binet Intelligence Scale, characterized by Gould (1981) as the standard for IQ tests in the United States. Terman and his generation of educators viewed intelligence as a fixed and unitary entity. It was an innate quality that seemed to vary only by specific social categories such as race, class, and gender. Higher intelligence, then, was associated with being White, of higher rather than lower class, and male. As public schools faced increasing numbers of immigrants from southern and eastern Europe, these ideas about intelligence provided a convenient empirical basis for sorting the children of these immigrants into different programs or tracks receiving different kinds of instruction and educational materials. The sorting and ranking were based on the results of compulsory testing (Farr & Trumbull, 1997).

Although not all standardized tests derive from the Stanford-Binet, H. Gardner (1991) argues that without it and other "widely esteemed" (p. 79) examples of intelligence instruments, the widespread testing culture of today would not have been possible. He points out that the focus in the United States on features of this testing culture, such as quantitative markers and educational efficiency, have driven the market for any and all tests, including tests of language proficiency and achievement and those that measure content knowledge (see also Barnwell, 1996). The numbers of such tests have also mushroomed. Bertrand (1991) notes that by 1928 there were more than 1,300 published tests, and by 1944 more than 60 million standardized tests were administered to more than 20 million people. Today, of course, nearly all schools administer tests to students on a periodic basis to collect evidence of learning, and negative consequences for immigrant children continue to occur as a result of testing.

This testing culture can be described in terms of certain features:

- an emphasis on ranking students against one another rather than according to what they know or can accomplish

- a preference for items that are easily quantifiable rather than ones requiring complex displays of skill or knowledge

- a perspective that values individual performance over collaborative endeavors as indicators of progress

- an image of testing as a scientific means of evaluating educational progress (Wolf et al., 1991)

Many of these features of the testing culture still permeate U.S. educational institutions. Certainly standardized tests with their uniform testing conditions and scoring procedures offer ostensibly more objective ways to assess students' learning, thus reducing teacher bias in evaluating students' work. Yet, as in examining current theories of knowledge and learning, ESL teachers need to question how applicable this older paradigm is to their classrooms today.

The classrooms envisioned in *ESL Standards for Pre-K–12 Students* (TESOL, 1997) are different locales for learning than the ones assumed above. Based on general principles of language acquisition that emphasize equitable access to rich educational opportunities, these classrooms require a range of approaches to assessment.

The Influence of Language Classrooms on Language Testing

Pointing out the close connection between classrooms and assessment, Bachman (1990) notes that "advances in language testing do not take place in a vacuum; they are stimulated by advances in understanding of the processes of language acquisition and language teaching" (p. 3). Since the 1970s, the ESL field has seen some major changes in the conceptualization of how learners acquire language. Describing developments in current thinking about second language acquisition, in chapter 3 Gersten and Hudelson articulate the influence of a sociocultural perspective on learning, noting that this perspective is reflected in TESOL's set of principles regarding language learning and use (TESOL, 1997, pp. 6–8) as well as in the ESL standards themselves. In the language classroom, this sociocultural perspective has been implemented through communicative and learner-centered approaches, with a focus on how learners communicate meaning, how they recognize and respond to social and cultural cues, and how they manage their own learning.

As one might expect, this change in language classrooms has presented a challenge to language testing. In weighing the demands on language testing brought about by broader notions of language, language use, language teaching, and language acquisition, Canale (1984) states,

> Evaluation within a communicative approach must address, for example, new content areas such as sociolinguistic appropriateness rules, new testing formats to permit and encourage creative, open-ended language use, new test administration procedures to emphasize interpersonal interactions in authentic situations, and new scoring procedures of a manual and judgmental nature. (as cited in Bachman, 1990, p. 297)

The focus on communicative approaches has influenced language testing. In the 1960s, in one of the earliest attempts to capture authentic language use through testing, Carroll (cited in Barnwell, 1996) made the distinction between *integrative* and *discrete-point* testing approaches. Discrete-point testing reflected a structuralist, form-centered notion of language that assumed that if learners were linguistically competent, they were then communicatively competent. Such testing required the learner to produce isolated bits of language that could be scored as either right or wrong responses. With such a fixed and compartmentalized view of correct versus incorrect language use, scoring was a highly objective process. Integrative testing, on the other hand, attempted to measure the total communicative effect of an utterance. Cloze tests and dictations are examples of integrative tests. On these tests, learners draw on several language skill areas—for example, reading, syntax, and morphology—as well as the context of the language text used in the testing situation. Scoring of such tests is less straightforward because more than one answer may be acceptable.

The 1970s and 1980s witnessed the increased use of essays, yet another highly integrative language test, for gauging language competence. During this time, for example, the Test of Written English was added to the Test of English as a Foreign Language. Because the scoring of essays is less controlled than that of discrete-point tests, much of the focus in developing these tests was on ensuring a high degree of interrater reliability. Clear scoring criteria were developed that embodied both communicative and linguistic features of language. To make sure these criteria were understood, essay test scorers were trained intensively with sample essays that illustrated the different scoring points on the rating scale.

The 1980s also marked the emergence of the proficiency movement in language testing. Led by the development and publication of the American Council on the Teaching of Foreign Languages guidelines (1996), language testing incorporated the use of oral interviews as a means of assessing language proficiency. Students' oral language in these interviews was scored according to four scales: speaking, listening, reading, and writing. Thus, the language assessed was language in use in a communicative setting. As with the scoring of essays, these samples of oral language were evaluated against criteria embodied in rating scales.

In the 1990s, two new trends in language testing continued the push for greater authenticity and a focus on communicative competence: (a) the use of *performance assessments*, which A. Brown (1995) characterizes as an estimate of language proficiency as demonstrated in a specific context, and (b) an increasing reliance on the learner's self-assessment of language ability to provide information about the development of language proficiency. Innovations in language testing in the 1990s show the influence of the paradigm shift occurring in the larger context of educational assessment, from a psychometric approach focused on traditional standardized testing to alternative assessment methods that are classroom based (Genesee, 1994b).

This brief review of language testing illustrates the close connection between the development of theories of language and language acquisition and the development of theories of language testing. Focusing on communicative competence changed the thinking about what language proficiency entailed and challenged the field to create new teaching methodologies and new testing technologies to measure that competence. Certainly, many of the forms of testing referred to above can be found in today's classrooms, as many teachers use a variety of assessments. Students take vocabulary tests, write essays, perform debates, and provide feedback on their own learning and that of their peers. Brown and Hudson (1998) note that "virtually all of the various test types are useful for some purpose, somewhere, sometime" (p. 657) in today's classrooms. Yet in choosing how to incorporate assessment into language classrooms, teachers need to remember the necessary link between instruction and assessment. The methods teachers use to assess students should be the result of the deliberative process described in the next section. Teachers need to ask themselves if they are testing in a manner that allows them to understand something about their students' learning and not merely because the test is at hand and easy to administer.

Reflecting on the future of language testing, Barnwell (1996) points out that most teachers have little interest in the theoretical debates in professional journals devoted to language testing. Much of the testing that takes place in classrooms often comes with the textbook adopted or from school, program, or departmental sources. To be careful users of any information gathered through classroom tests, however, teachers must acknowledge the degree of congruence between what and how they teach and what and how they test.

Current Educational Assessment Practice

The educational reform movement that has swept in the standards movement has coincided with major changes in assessment theory and practice. Critics of standardized testing have pointed out that results from such testing programs end up disenfranchising large segments of students, primarily students from diverse backgrounds. Though designed to sort children, these tests seem to place disproportionate numbers of immigrant children, poor children, and children of color into lower tracks and special-needs programs and prevent them from participating in gifted and talented programs. To explain this outcome, García and Pearson (1993) identify norming, content, and linguistic and cultural biases as key factors in skewing formal, standardized tests in favor of mainstream students and against children from diverse backgrounds.

TASK   1

Examine a test (e.g., a commercially available, norm-referenced standardized test; a textbook chapter quiz; a departmental exam) used in your local district or school site. How appropriate is it for ESOL students in your area? Consider cultural assumptions embedded within the items. Also consider how well it covers the curriculum taught.

At the same time that testing has come under fire for acting as a gatekeeper that prevents equal access to educational opportunities for immigrant students and students of color, the structure and content of tests have also been examined according to redefined notions of language and learning. Instead of viewing learning as the transmission (and, it is hoped, reception) of information, current thinking posits that students must construct knowledge in active and meaningful ways through transactions with other learners and within rich instructional contexts. A theory of language envisioned as communicative competence requires more complex assessments, ones situated in contexts that are meaningful for learners (Canale & Swain, 1980).

Assessments that purport to measure such learning may take the following forms:

1. *multiple assessments:* New assessment practices assume that teachers will gather information about students' learning from a variety of sources and on several occasions over time, because one score or one performance provides only a partial view of what students know and can do.

2. *authentic assessments:* New assessment practices are relevant and meaningful to students. Problems or tasks are drawn from the instructional context of students' classrooms and may permit more than one correct answer.

3. *dynamic assessments:* New assessment practices focus on the process of learning as well as on products. Assessment tasks may be complex and require multiple steps. Students need to be active participants in constructing meaning as they engage in these tasks.

4. *individual and group assessments:* New assessment practices encompass both individual and group performances to show students' learning.

5. *standards-referenced assessments:* New assessment practices measure achievement not by ranking individual students relative to one another but by charting students' growth against specific instructional targets tied to high standards for all students.

The assessment principles presented in the next section show the influence of these new assessment practices on the conceptual framework for assessment.

■ The Assessment Process

The paradigm shift in assessment, outlined above, has changed the field's understanding of how to uncover what students know and can do and expectations of what teachers must know and be able to do. Within this new paradigm, teachers assume a more active role in designing and implementing assessment plans in their classrooms. To help teachers in this new role, this section describes a four-phase assessment process.

The key premise of the approach to assessment presented here is that assessment data can assist educators in understanding more fully what is going on in classrooms as students and teachers engage in learning and teaching processes. Such information provides a window on how and to what extent the ESL standards are operationalized. More specifically, collecting assessment data can help

- teachers track how well students are learning lessons

- program administrators determine the effectiveness of particular instructional approaches

- district personnel make decisions about how to allocate educational resources

- students reflect on their progress

- parents understand how well their children are doing in school

The heart of this approach is the assessment process. Just as the development of effective instruction involves multiple steps in planning and implementation, gathering useful assessment data involves a multiphased process of (a) planning, (b) collecting and recording, (c) analyzing and interpreting, and (d) using relevant information for reporting and decision making (see Figure 5-2).

Although this model can be used to examine any instructional context, whether for ESOL or for other students, each phase of the process described here is accompanied by a series of principles reflecting the linguistic and cultural complexities involved when assessing ESOL students. These principles help illuminate how attention to linguistic and cultural features should infuse each step of the assessment process to ensure the best possible fit between the assessment and the learners.

Phase 1: Planning Assessments

Although each phase of the assessment process involves many specific activities to implement that phase, the first phase—planning the assessment—is perhaps the most crucial step in the model. Even though at times in schools it seems as if tests just happen, good assessment practice requires thoughtful planning of when and how best to collect information. Without comprehensive planning, it becomes difficult to implement and manage data collection. Because the assessment process is dynamic and cyclical, assessment plans will be reexamined and revised over time. However, even preliminary well-thought-out plans will assist educators in integrating assessment into classrooms with a minimum of disruption. In fact, well-planned assessments should support learning and teaching. The following are some activities associated with the planning phase of the assessment process.

Identifying Stakeholders and Purposes

Assessment planning grows out of identifying the stakeholders and their purposes for collecting assessment information in the first place—or more simply, identifying who wants to know and why. Before much more planning can take place, educators must have clear answers to these questions because those answers will influence the design of the assessment plan. The kind of data that will satisfy students' curiosity about their learning of a specific point in a lesson is different from the information that will satisfy a district's interest in the level of achievement a student attains after a semester or year of

FIGURE 5-2

ACTIVITIES ASSOCIATED WITH EACH PHASE OF THE ASSESSMENT PROCESS

Phase 1: Planning assessments

- Identifying purposes and audiences
- Devising a time line for data collection
- Selecting standards and instructional strategies
- Setting performance levels or benchmarks
- Designing and/or selecting performance/ proficiency/commercially developed, norm-referenced tests and tasks
- Modifying and/or selecting rubrics

Phase 2: Collecting and recording information

- Using journals and feedback forms
- Conferencing with students
- Using performance tasks and assessment documents
- Administering commercially available, nationally norm-referenced tests
- Observing students and maintaining anecdotal records

Phase 3: Analyzing and interpreting assessment information

- Applying standards to information collected
- Interpreting scores for students, classes, programs, districts, and states
- Judging performances using scales, rubrics, or both
- Examining progress across time with multiple assessments
- Using a data management system

Phase 4: Using information for reporting and decision making

- Modifying instructional plan
- Sharing student progress with students and parents
- Creating additional program support for ESOL students

instruction. Table 5-1 shows some of the different stakeholders and their purposes for collecting assessment data.

Collecting Information About Students

As the principles suggest, information about students' home contexts, proficiency in their primary language, learning styles, and schooling history all provide important background information for designing appropriate assessment collection tools and for understanding the information once it is collected. Information-gathering tools, such as a home language survey (see Appendix A), which is filled out by a family member when a student enters a district, can tell much about a student's primary language as well as other languages spoken in the

PRINCIPLES OF ASSESSMENT: PLANNING

1. The students' ages, learning styles, levels of proficiency and academic achievement in their first language (L1) and second language (L2), educational continuity inside and outside the United States, and amount of time receiving ESL or bilingual support provide the background information for assessment.

2. Assessments draw on the social, cultural, and academic experiences of ESOL learners.

3. Assessments are based on current educational research, especially in the areas of L1 and L2 acquisition.

4. Assessments allow ESOL students to demonstrate complex learning in contextualized ways, such as through the use of real objects or graphics (e.g., pictures, charts, tables, diagrams, photographs, and graphic organizers).

5. Classroom assessments mirror the language(s) and content of instruction and instructional practices.

6. Classroom assessments enable students to demonstrate their learning in multiple ways from multiple perspectives, thus serving as learning experiences themselves.

7. Classroom assessments, such as thematic projects, promote student involvement and reflection on learning and require students to use a variety of learning strategies and resources.

8. Assessment documents or rubrics represent the full range of student performance and are designed with a set of clearly defined criteria against which the standards are measured.

TABLE 5-1

STAKEHOLDERS AND PURPOSES FOR COLLECTING ASSESSMENT DATA

Stakeholder	Purpose
Students	Recognize their own strengths and areas for development
Teachers	Assess students' progress in attaining ESL standards
Parents	Understand their child's growth in academic areas
Principals and school administrators	Monitor equitable access to school resources
Program administrators	Determine appropriate placement into program services

home. For administrators, setting up databases that can disaggregate data by, for example, amount of previous schooling will help determine the appropriateness of instruction for different groups of students. Figure 5-3 shows one version of a student information form. Data collected from home language surveys and other student records can be recorded on this sheet.

Creating Time Lines for Data Collection

Time lines for data collection and analysis will help ensure that assessment data are collected when scheduled. This is particularly important when introducing new assessment approaches. Juggling lesson planning and the introduction of a new assessment activity can be difficult. Establishing a time line with suggestions on how to implement the assessment activity takes some of the burden off teachers. Depending on the level of implementation for the assessment plan, a time line can be as simple as the one shown in Figure 5-4. This kind of plan might be appropriate for a program administrator who wants comparable sets of information about students across several classrooms. A more complex time line might be designed to assist classroom teachers in balancing the myriad activities of learning and assessment that take place on a day-to-day basis. In these plans, assessment data may be collected daily and by students and their peers in addition to the teacher. (See chapter 7, Figure 7-1, for a classroom-based example.)

FIGURE 5-3

SAMPLE STUDENT INFORMATION FORM

Student name: _____

             Surname   First given name   Second name

Student identification number: _____

Date of birth: _____ Current grade level: _____

Home language: _____

Current language proficiency classification: _____

Present schooling:

- Type of program of instruction _____

- Medium of instruction (English/native language) _____

Previous schooling:

   In the United States

- Number of years _____

- Type of program of instruction _____

- Medium of instruction (English/native language) _____

   Outside the United States

- Number of years _____

- Type of program of instruction _____

- Medium of instruction (English/native language) _____

FIGURE 5-4

SAMPLE TIME LINE FOR DATA COLLECTION

September	*October*	*November*	*December*	*[etc.]*
• Writing sample	• Group observation	• Oral language proficiency test	• Writing sample	
	• Reading inventory			

Creating Linkages Between Standards and Assessment

For assessment to help educators measure attainment of the ESL standards, those standards and accompanying descriptors need to be clearly articulated and infused into classroom instruction. Assessment activities can then be aligned with instructional activities. Forging explicit linkages across standards, descriptors, and assessment activities allows teachers to feel confident in drawing inferences from the assessment data about how successfully students are progressing in their attainment of the ESL standards. The checklist in Figure 5-5 illustrates the steps in creating this linkage.

Deciding How to Report Data

As illustrated in Figure 5-2, the last phase of the assessment cycle underscores the need to do something with the information collected in classrooms. To serve the specific purposes for which students are assessed, the data need to be reported to the stakeholders interested in them. In addition to teachers, a variety of other stakeholders are interested in students' performances. Ensuring that the information reported back to those stakeholders is understandable and useful requires careful consideration of the reporting method. As shown in

---

FIGURE 5-5

CHECKLIST FOR ALIGNING STANDARDS AND ASSESSMENTS

Steps in alignment	Completed? (yes or no)
1. Determine standards to be assessed	
2. Determine how standards will be reached through specific activities and contexts	
3. Design or select an assessment (or assessments) for each instructional goal	
4. Set outcome levels	
5. Provide adequate professional development to promote reliable assessment	
6. Ensure the assessment tool is measuring the standard it claims to be testing	

chapter 6 with regard to large-scale assessments, the need to plan how to explain assessment data is even greater when communicating the results of assessment.

Report cards are traditionally used to provide information on students' achievement to parents. However, reporting can take place in other formats and at other times during the school term. For example, students' work might be shared with family members during a back-to-school or parents' night when translators are available to ensure clear communication and give parents a channel for voicing their questions or expressing their concerns. Parent conferences provide another venue for sharing information. Exhibitions of students' work, student performances, and individual or group projects offer possibilities for sharing students' achievement not only with parents but also with other students and teachers.

Assessment data can provide necessary information as ESL teachers consult with other school personnel to ensure appropriate planning for curriculum and instruction and equitable access to resources. Other members of the school community, such as school boards, are also interested in student achievement data. Across these stakeholders and their purposes, educators need to consider how best to report results. Figure 5-6 shows a template for this kind of planning.

FIGURE 5-6

PLANNING TEMPLATE FOR REPORTING RESULTS TO STAKEHOLDERS

Stakeholder	Type of assessment	Method of reporting	Language and cultural considerations
Students			
Parents			
Teachers			
Department heads/ program coordinators			
School administrators			
District administrators			
State administrators			

PRINCIPLES OF ASSESSMENT: COLLECTING AND RECORDING INFORMATION

9. Multiple types of assessment, including both criterion-referenced and norm-referenced measures, are used to form a composite picture of ESOL students' performance over time.

10. Information from classroom assessment for the purpose of monitoring student progress is gathered within the instructional cycle (i.e., lesson, theme, project, or unit).

11. Assessments use multiple sources of information, including teachers, parents, and students themselves, to provide a clear picture of students' performance.

12. Assessment data are collected and recorded systematically with a uniform set of procedures and guidelines for administration.

Phase 2: Collecting and Recording Information

The next phase of the assessment process involves conducting assessment. Once assessment plans have been made, they can be implemented in the day-to-day activities of classrooms. Teachers and students may work together to create portfolios; students may complete performance tasks or take tests; students may provide feedback to one another using class-created checklists. Although formal testing procedures mandated by programs, districts, or states will require teachers to schedule specific testing times during the school year, the majority of assessment should be intertwined with learning and take place on an ongoing basis. The following questions can serve as a guide in deciding how to collect and record information useful to teachers and other stakeholders.

What Is Assessed?

Traditional notions of testing tend to focus on traditional academic content areas, such as a student's reading comprehension, ability to solve differential equations, or even ability to spell grade-appropriate vocabulary items. Both *ESL Standards* and current thinking about learning, however, have expanded the "what" of assessment. Teachers using *ESL Standards* are interested in gathering information about how successfully students are acquiring the language skills needed to engage in lessons in science, language arts, or math. Now, in addition to academic content, they want to know how students use learning strategies to grapple with that content. They note how well students utilize cooperative groups to complete individual and group tasks and how students solve their math problems, not just whether they have the right answer. To conduct useful assessments, then, educators need to explicitly identify the instructional objectives they wish to measure, understanding at the same time that any one measurement will provide only a partial snapshot of that achievement.

The sample progress indicators in *ESL Standards* offer an array of observable behaviors that illustrate the kinds of instructional objectives teachers may want to measure. Figure 5-7 shows one of the standards and selected sample progress indicators for students in Grades 9–12.

How Is It Assessed?

Depending on the purpose and stakeholder, as discussed in the section on planning assessments above, the method of collecting information about students' learning will vary. The range of methods is limited

---

FIGURE 5-7

WHAT IS ASSESSED?

Goal 2, Standard 3

To use English to achieve academically in all content areas:

Students will use appropriate learning strategies to construct and apply academic knowledge.

Sample Progress Indicators:

- take notes to summarize the main points provided in source material
- practice an oral report with a peer prior to presenting it in class
- preview assigned textbook chapters and generate questions to explore the topics to be presented
- take risks with language

Source: TESOL (1997, p. 91).

---

only by a teacher's creativity in designing approaches and then deciding how to blend them into ongoing instruction. Within the new assessment paradigm, assessment is no longer relegated to a place at the
end of the unit or chapter; rather, it is seen as way to carry forward the
learning agenda. Figure 5-8 shows some of the ways to collect information about students' learning.

Who Assesses?

Just as variety is an important characteristic of new approaches to
collecting assessment information, who participates is no longer a
given either. Whereas teachers or other educational personnel administer higher stakes tests like departmental exams or state-mandated
achievement tests, classroom assessments can be administered and
even created by students as well as teachers. When students engage in
self-assessment, they assume responsibility for their own learning and
have an opportunity to reflect on it. This technique may also ease the
burden on teachers. For example, for a lesson in which students give
oral presentations on a specified topic, several stakeholders can assess
the performances (see Figure 5-9 for a sample assessment plan). The
teacher uses a rubric designed by the department to assess growth in
oral proficiency. In addition, as each student speaks, the rest of the
students record their assessment of the performance on a checklist
containing certain features of the oral presentation. In this instance,
students have discussed earlier what criteria would be relevant for
measuring the performance and selected key features to incorporate

---

FIGURE 5-8

HOW IS IT ASSESSED?

- Writing samples
- Homework
- Interactive journals
- Literature logs
- Learning logs
- Games
- Debates
- Brainstorming

- Story retelling
- Anecdotal records
- Checklists
- Cloze tests
- Criterion-referenced tests
- Norm-referenced,
  standardized tests

FIGURE 5-9

WHO ASSESSES?

Assessment plan for oral presentation

Who assesses?	What is assessed?	What kind of recording tool?
Peers	Persuasiveness Style Following "rules"	Checklist
Teacher	Language growth	Rubric

into the checklist; thus, the students have a clear sense of how to assess each other's presentations.

How Often Is It Assessed?

With assessment woven into instruction rather than being relegated to an end-of-unit event, teachers can take advantage of multiple opportunities to sample what students know and can do so using multiple methods, as shown above. Some growth may be monitored daily, some weekly, and some monthly; the frequency needs to be determined during the planning process, depending on the purpose of the assessment and other planning factors. Sometimes teachers have little choice in the frequency of assessment, as in, for example, a departmental examination or district testing. Frequency is also affected by such practical matters as whether teachers have appropriate assessment tools readily at hand or have sufficient time not only to collect information but also to analyze and interpret results. Assessment procedures that are reasonable and realistic have a greater chance of being implemented.

How Is Information Recorded?

Teachers can utilize a range of formats to record information about students' performances. Checklists, grade books, anecdotal notes, rating scales, and rubrics are just some of the ways to capture students' progress. For examples of these kinds of tools, teachers can consult an extensive literature dealing with classroom assessment (e.g., Genesee & Upshur, 1996; O'Malley & Valdez Pierce, 1996). Some teachers keep a Polaroid camera available to capture three-dimensional group projects. The form in which information is recorded is less important than the fact that it is recorded consistently and in a timely manner. Figure 5-10 shows an instrument for planning the way information from assessments is recorded.

Phase 3: Analyzing and Interpreting Assessment Information

By this point in the assessment process, a teacher has planned for, collected, and recorded a variety of information about students' progress. The next step is determining what all of the information means. This is a crucial phase of the assessment process. Describing students' work or performances using some of the tools noted in Figure 5-8 above is a necessary but insufficient step in assessment. For the work or performances to have meaning within an educational system, they must be weighed in some way. Teachers and programs — as well as students and parents — need to have clear and explicit criteria for considering students' work. Clear and explicit criteria also ensure that work is consistently assessed across performances and across students.

Looking at Individual Students' Performances

One way to analyze and interpret assessment information is by comparing individual students' performances against (a) a *norm*, or expected outcome based on other students' performances on the same task, or (b) criteria or scoring guides geared to instructional objectives.

As an illustration, consider a student's performance on a required districtwide exam consisting of a multiple-choice test in mathematics

---

FIGURE 5-10

ASSESSMENT ORGANIZING MATRIX

Instruction/ assessment activity	Frequency	Individual, pair, or group	Recording tool/recorder
Students engage in debate	2 times/term	Group	Peer critique checklist/peer developed and used

---

and language arts plus a writing sample. The scores are returned to the school as a set of numbers: 62 on the math test, 77 on the reading test, and 4 on the writing sample. Before these numbers can be meaningful, as noted, they need to be related in some way to a scoring scale or a set of criteria. Large-scale tests provide several different ways of ranking or interpreting scores. For the sample student, the math score of 62 can be translated into a percentile showing how that performance compares with that of other students taking the same exam. The raw score of 62 placed this student in the 75th percentile, meaning that the student scored higher than approximately 75% of the other students but not as high as approximately 25% of them. (All scores contain what test makers call a *margin of error*; that is, any score is an approximation of a student's performance.) The score on the reading test can be interpreted in the same way as the math score because it is also reported as a percentile.

The writing score, however, is based on a different scale. The student's performance of 4 is referenced to a 5-point holistic writing rubric; a score of 5 on this scale is *exemplary*. In addition to an overall performance level, the rubric provides specific characteristics for each level. To be scored 4, or *accomplished*, on this particular rubric, a writing sample must show clear evidence of organization, a variety of vocabulary including figurative language, reasonable development of the topic, and a reasonable degree of fluency. This student's score of 4, then, can be interpreted in terms of how well the criteria in the rubric map onto the curriculum at the student's grade level.

Many newer assessment approaches use rubrics, such as check-lists, holistic and analytical scoring guides, and rating scales, as the criteria for understanding student performance. Navarrete and Gustkee (1996) recommend asking the following questions to evaluate the quality of scoring criteria:

- Are important, teachable outcomes addressed by the criteria (e.g., if writing is to be judged, are all the important competencies, elements, or benchmarks included)?

- Are the criteria clearly written and in a usable form (i.e., are the criteria written in concrete terms that are understandable to students, parents, and teachers)?

- Do the criteria reflect current thinking on excellence in the content areas?

- Have the criteria been examined for developmental, ethnic, gender, and linguistic diversity?

- Are the criteria generalizable to other, similar tasks or performance in other content areas?

- Do the rating strategies applied to the criteria match how the assessments will be used (e.g., holistic scoring for global outcomes or analytic scoring for diagnostic purposes)? (p. 33)

Looking at the Performances of Groups of Students

In addition to interpreting individual students' performances, educators can also compare performance across different groups of students—for example, how one group of students in a school compares with another. This process is particularly important for ensuring that all students are making progress toward achieving the standards set out in the curriculum. Unfortunately, many programs do not break out achievement data. Disaggregated data, however, can provide the basis for arguing that additional services are needed or showing how existing services should be modified.

Student data not only tell something about how students are performing and, it is hoped, achieving, but can also serve as an indication of the effectiveness of instruction. If all the students in a class do poorly on a test or assignment, it may well mean that the teacher needs to consider reteaching the lesson. This accountability function

Gather some test scores for a group of ESOL students. Practice sorting the scores by different student characteristics, for example, gender, first language, English language proficiency. Do you see any patterns emerging? What do you predict will happen after one semester of instruction? After a year of instruction? How could this information help you plan for the next year of instruction?

of assessment data is an important one—it provides a pathway to ensuring that all students, including ESOL students, have access to the best instruction possible.

Phase 4: Using Information for Reporting and Decision Making

The last phase of the assessment cycle is the culmination of the hard work of collecting and analyzing assessment data. Using information—either to report to specific stakeholders for certain purposes or to make decisions about instruction—is ultimately why educators engage in the assessment process in the first place. Figure 5-6 is a starting point for determining how to use assessment data. It illustrates the ways in which assessment data can be used, depending on who wants to know about students' performances and why. Before

PRINCIPLES OF ASSESSMENT: USING INFORMATION FOR REPORTING AND DECISION MAKING

16. Results from assessments are used to enhance instruction, improve student performance, and aid in educational decision making.

17. Results from assessments are understandable and useful to students and the greater educational community. Information is presented clearly and in the appropriate language(s).

18. Results from assessments are reported to stakeholders with reference to ESOL students' performance of designated standards.

19. Results are reported in a timely fashion to stakeholders (i.e., while information is still current and applicable), and all relevant information is compiled and considered before a decision is rendered.

implementing this plan, however, educators need to consider the strengths and limitations of the information they plan to report.

Is the Information Collected Believable?

No matter how carefully planned for, collected, and analyzed, no set of assessment data is flawless. Information collected using one measurement tool may be appropriate for one group of students, for example, but inappropriate for others. It may serve one purpose very well yet be inadequate for other purposes. Teachers need to be able to recognize how closely the information collected fits with students' abilities and the instrument's intended use. Clearly, the limitations of any one measure underscore the need for multiple sources of information about students' developing skills, and each measure used needs to be considered in terms of what it can and cannot reveal about students' performances.

The traditional measurement terms *reliability* and *validity* are relevant here. Consistent with other TESOL publications related to the ESL Standards and Assessment Project, the terms are defined here in this way:

- *reliability:* a technical measure to determine an assessment's ability to produce consistent results

- *validity:* a technical measure of an assessment's match between the information collected by the items and its specified purposes

The assessment literature provides much more detail on what these terms mean and how to determine whether specific assessments meet those conditions (see, e.g., Bachman, 1990, for a discussion of these terms in regard to language testing; Genesee & Upshur, 1996, for classroom-based examples of reliability and validity; Herman et al., 1992, for an explanation of these terms in relation to alternative assessment).

In the classroom, assessments are considered reliable when they can supply similar information again and again. If a teacher determines, for example, through an assessment on Monday that a student can successfully write an essay explaining his or her views, the teacher expects that student to be able to do it again on Wednesday. Assessments are considered valid when they are connected to the purposes for collecting information: Does the assessment measure what it is intended to measure? If the teacher believes that the student's successful essay provides evidence of the intended learning goals, then the assessment is valid.

Reliability and validity become even more important in relation to the consequences resulting from the use of assessment data. Checking off whether students have completed homework assignments as a way to chart students' effort in a class has a different level of consequence than a final exam does. The higher the stakes, the more effort needs to be invested in ensuring the use of a well-designed or appropriately chosen assessment. One way to increase the trustworthiness of an assessment is to collect additional information. Herman et al. (1992) call this *corroborating evidence* and note that it can come from other assessments, other teachers, or even the research literature. Do the patterns of performance match what is expected, given students' performance on other assessments or in classes with other colleagues? Again, an assessment plan that incorporates multiple sources can provide useful corroborating evidence.

Because any assessment, even an assessment shown to be reliable and valid, can provide only a limited picture of a student's performance, teachers should exercise caution in drawing inferences about that performance, noting the assessment's strengths and limitations, especially when used with ESOL students. For example, some assessments may be more or less appropriate for certain groups of ESOL students depending on their background and educational experiences. The following questions provide some direction in identifying an assessment's strengths and limitations:

- Does the content reflect the instructional objectives?

- Will the results be interpreted in terms of clearly defined and agreed-upon educational standards?

- Are the assessments free of biases (i.e., cultural, racial, class, or gender)?

- Are the exercises or tasks involved in the assessment reflective of the kinds of activities students engage in in the classroom?

- Are the procedures for assessment understandable and easy for teachers to use?

- Will it be easy for teachers to score the assessment or summarize the data collected?

- Will the results from the assessment be understandable and easy for teachers and other stakeholders to use in evaluating program effectiveness as well as students' progress?

How Can Information From the Assessment Be Reported?

Because a range of stakeholders may receive information about students' performance, a variety of methods may be used for reporting that information. Often, the reporting method will depend on the purpose for looking at that particular piece of information. Assessment data are often reported as summarized scores or numbers. For example, a school might show how many students have moved from ESL services into mainstream classes. This information could be reported as the number of students in each category from one time period to the next; the numbers could also be presented as percentages of students who have made the transition within each time period. The presentation of the numbers can also vary: They can be presented in graphs, pie charts, or tables and can represent a moment in time, a period of time, or a trend over time.

A few criteria gleaned from the assessment principles can help educators frame the data in ways that will prove most effective for communicating with various stakeholders and for various purposes:

- *clarity:* Results should be presented as clearly as possible. Pie charts with different colors for each section may look good and impress a school board, but if the audience does not understand how to read those charts, they will not be meaningful.

- *appropriate language:* Results are best understood if they are presented in a language understood by the stakeholder. This caveat echoes the need to ensure that all written communications from school, especially assessment data, are in the language of literacy for relevant stakeholders.

- *timeliness:* Results that arrive while they are still current and relevant are more meaningful than ones that are reported long after the fact.

■ Next Steps

Coming to the end of Phase 4 of the assessment process does not signal the end of language educators' responsibility. As Figure 5-2 above illustrates, the process is a cyclical one. After gathering and thinking about the assessment data, educators must take the next step: to start over at the planning phase. This step is part of the ongoing search for ways to improve students' learning, teachers' instruction, and the delivery of services in schools. As professionals focused on improving their craft, teachers can utilize the information provided by the assessment process discussed in this chapter to sharpen their judgment and inform their decisions. The consequences of these decisions are not trivial, for they affect the lives of children and their families. The responsibility of educators, then, is to make sure those decisions are informed by the highest quality information possible.

■ Appendix A

Sample Home Language Survey
English

_____   _____
Date   School

                                _____
                                Teacher

The California Education Code requires schools to determine the language(s) spoken at home by each student. This information is essential in order for schools to provide meaningful instruction for all students.

Your cooperation in helping us meet this important requirement is requested. Please answer the following questions and have your son/daughter return this form to his/her teacher. Thank you for your help.

Name of student: _____
                    Last   First   Middle

Grade _____   Age _____

1. Which language did your son or daughter learn
   when he or she first began to talk?   _____

2. What language does your son or daughter most
   frequently use at home?   _____

3. What language do you use most frequently to
   speak to your son or daughter?   _____

4. Name the language most often spoken by
   the adults at home.   _____

5. Has your child received any formal English
   language instruction (listening, speaking,
   reading, or writing)?   _____

_____

                    Signature of parent or guardian

_____

Source: Adapted from State of California Department of Education (1987).

Chapter 6

Standards-Based, Large-Scale Assessment of ESOL Students

Margo Gottlieb

The success of the standards-based reform move-ment depends on the accurate and equitable measurement of students' achievement, which must be tied to challenging academic content. How states and school districts assess their students, in particular those students for whom English is an additional language, forms the core of educational accountability. Large-scale assessment is the mecha-nism that communicates to stakeholders the extent to which students have attained educational standards.

Large-scale assessment involves standard procedures for data collection, analysis, and interpretation across multiple classrooms. Although it may be implemented at a grade level, large-scale assess-ment generally functions at a program, school, district, or state level. It is summative in nature, is based on accumulated learning, and is administered on a specified schedule (such as annually). Either as-sessment internal to classrooms or assessment imposed from the out-side, such as by a district or state (external assessment), can qualify as large scale. In either instance, the measures that constitute large-scale assessment must have sound psychometric properties (i.e., proven reliability and validity) that yield defensible results. Large-scale as-sessment requires rigorous technical qualities, as it often carries high stakes for students and teachers as well as sanctions for schools and school districts.

Substantive issues surround large-scale, standards-based assess-ment of ESOL students. In this chapter, I explore how the current assessment paradigm can be made more meaningful for linguistically and culturally diverse students. After examining the relationship be-tween language proficiency and academic achievement for ESOL students, I discuss how the standards-based movement currently drives large-scale assessment efforts, argue for the reconceptualization of the most efficacious forms of assessment, and present several frameworks for incorporating ESL standards within a school district's or state's assessment model. I then introduce performance assessment as a viable alternative to standardized achievement testing and analyze the use of *ESL Standards for Pre-K–12 Students* (TESOL, 1997) by states and school districts. In this context, I discuss the sources of documentation and the types of information gleaned from different measures. Last, I highlight portfolio assessment as one approach that holds promise for ESOL students within a standards-based system.

■ Understanding the Relationship Between Language Proficiency and Academic Achievement for ESOL Students

For ESOL students, the distinction between language proficiency and academic achievement is central to assessment decisions. Standards-based, large-scale assessments are measures that reflect a student's conceptual development and the access the student has had to rich academic content in school. The primary purpose of this type of assessment is accountability for learning. Measures of language proficiency tap a student's acquisition of language, typically in the areas of listening, speaking, reading, and writing, inside and outside school. In large part, the purpose of language proficiency assessment is to monitor an ESOL student's progress in English language development.

Educators are well aware of the difficulty of obtaining a true picture of ESOL students' academic achievement, in large part because of its interaction with language proficiency. In other words, ESOL students' academic performance in English may be masked by their English language proficiency. This problem is exacerbated in assessment that is literacy dependent (i.e., in which meaning can be constructed only from the printed word). Incorrect responses marked on a test, for example, may mean that the ESOL students know the concept but lack the English labels for it, do not know the concept, or do not have the test-taking strategies to answer properly.

Educators also realize that assessing students in their first language (L1) or home language may shed little light on ESOL students' academic achievement. First of all, many large-scale measures have suffered in translation from English to another language. Direct translation of any test renders it invalid unless the test is originally conceived within a dual-language framework or blueprint. Otherwise, the linguistic and cultural nuances that are idiosyncratic for one measure cannot be captured by the second, the norming population for one test cannot apply to the second, and the validation studies on one test are inappropriate for the second.

Second, L1 assessment for summative or accountability purposes is only appropriate to the extent to which the students have had opportunities to continue learning in that language. In other words, the language of assessment should mirror the language of instruction. Unless the students are in dual-language, two-way immersion, or maintenance programs, in which their L1 is sustained and enriched, there is generally not sufficient L1 support to justify large-scale assessment in a language other than English.

The most appropriate criterion for determining eligibility for meaningful participation in a large-scale assessment of academic achievement is the students' level of English literacy. A deterrent to the success of ESOL students on this type of assessment is the heavy reliance on decontextualized information available only through print. School districts or states need to formulate policy based on empirically determined thresholds of literacy in English for ESOL students at specified age-grade clusters. In that way, students will be identified as qualified to take large-scale assessment based on data rather than on an arbitrary criterion or surrogate variable, such as years in the United States or years of bilingual or ESL services. Literacy screening in English more accurately identifies ESOL students and ensures that the large-scale assessment is a valid indicator of their academic achievement rather than of their language proficiency.

Until ESOL students have reached a predetermined level of literacy in English, the ESL standards should remain as guideposts for ESOL students and ESL teachers. At that time, data should indicate that ESOL students are approaching attainment of the ESL standards, district or state content standards, and academic parity with their native-English-speaking peers. Participation in large-scale assessment would provide confirmatory evidence that ESOL students are indeed ready to make the transition from ESL services and succeed in mainstream classrooms.

Until ESOL students are performing at a rate commensurate with their native-English-speaking peers, accountability for ESOL students' learning should rest with the measurement of ESL standards. Alternate means, outside of standardized norm-referenced measures, should be used to assess students' attainment of ESL standards that account for their English language proficiency and academic achievement. These assessments, in large part, should be performance-based measures, in which students demonstrate their language acquisition and content knowledge in direct ways through activities and tasks, which, in turn, are interpreted according to specified criteria. The characteristics of performance-based assessment activities and tasks and the role of ESOL students in a standards-based system are outlined below.

In a standards-based system, performance-based activities and tasks

- represent standards, curriculum, and instruction

- integrate language and content

- draw from the students' personal experiences, cultures, and real-life situations

- have multiple avenues to reaching solutions

- raise questions that lead to related topics and issues

In a standards-based system, ESOL students

- are aware of their goals for language and content learning

- have opportunities to engage in higher level thinking

- actively participate, using authentic materials and resources

- are encouraged to explore new ideas

- are challenged, energized, and excited about learning

■ Using Standards in Large-Scale Assessment

By and large, states have developed content and performance standards for their general school populations. As a matter of course, the alignment of curriculum and instruction comes to match that of the mainstream educational program. Consequently, standards-based assessment becomes an expression of the performance of average native-English-speaking students. Assessments that are designed for, piloted, normed on, and benchmarked (translated to assigned performance levels) on standards for the general education population cannot serve ESOL students in the same capacity. These assessments are not fair, valid, or useful for ESOL students until they are approaching the academic performance of their native-English-speaking peers.

Unfortunately, many ESOL students are subjected to local and state assessments under inequitable conditions, and ESL and bilingual educators must conform to assessment policies that run counter to research and best practices. Still worse, when the stakes for an assessment are high, ESOL students may pay dire consequences for results that do not truly reflect their content knowledge. There are several explanations for ESOL students' struggle with large-scale assessment. First, ESOL students' scores may be depressed as a result of their low levels of English language proficiency. Second, ESOL students may not have full access to the general educational curriculum with which the assessment is aligned. Third, in opposition to principles of sound educational assessment, important decisions about ESOL (and other) students are often based on a single test administration. Last but not least, ESOL students most probably are not test-wise, nor are they thoroughly familiar with the testing culture of the United States.

The advocacy role ESL educators assume for ESOL students and parents must be extended to the assessment arena. ESL professionals need to clarify to the public that although requiring all students to attain standards is an admirable goal, by definition ESOL students are at the beginning rungs of the developmental ladder and require time and support to climb to the top. In addition, ESL educators have to explain assessment data within the context of demographic and program characteristics. Various stakeholders (e.g., students, parents, teachers, administrators, boards of education, and the media) have to understand assessment results and their implications for the education of ESOL students. Ultimately, ESL, bilingual, and classroom teachers must be able to translate information from large-scale assessment (whether it entails student, classroom, district, or state data) into improved instructional practices.

Find out the policy of your local school district or state in regard to the large-scale assessment of ESOL students. Do you consider this policy fair or equitable for ESOL students? Why or why not?

Shifting the Conceptual Focus

Since the mid-1990s, the treatment of ESOL and ESOL special education students in statewide assessment has received much attention (Butler & Stevens, 1997; Olson & Goldstein, 1997). This interest has been prompted by federal legislation, the most prominent being the Goals 2000: Educate America Act (1994), Titles I and VII under the Improving America's Schools Act (1994), and the Individuals With Disabilities Education Act (1997). This series of federal mandates has placed tremendous pressure on states and school districts to substantially increase the participation rate of special student populations in their assessment programs.

If this dilemma is to be resolved and if, in fact, standards are indeed intended for all students, then the performance criteria associated with content standards have to be broadened to capture the entire student spectrum. The ESL standards were developed specifically to provide direction in bridging the gap between what ESOL students can do and what the general student population can do.

For ESOL students, reaching a state's content standards is desirable and to be expected within an expanded time frame. However, some older students with limited formal schooling or with severe cognitive disabilities may never fully attain challenging content standards. To maximize the inclusion of ESOL students, assessments would ideally be revamped to more accurately reflect the extensive range of ESOL student performance.

The ideal is not reality. Diverse policies and practices from state to state have resulted in varying participation rates for ESOL students in assessment programs. Currently, states and districts follow several courses of action:

1. exclusion based on English language proficiency, time in an ESL and bilingual education program, or time in the United States

2. partial inclusion according to subject area as stipulated by time in the program

3. full inclusion without accommodations

4. inclusion with accommodations

5. exemption with use of alternate assessment

The advantages and disadvantages of each of the five options for ESOL student participation in state or district assessments are outlined in Table 6-1.

For the most part, the first four options perpetuate the historically marginalized status of ESOL students. The reason is simple: States have continued to create conceptual frameworks for assessment without regard to the unique characteristics of this student population. Measures have been constructed or selected without consideration of ESOL students' language and academic proficiencies, their multicultural backgrounds, and their educational experiences.

Exclusion from large-scale assessment (Option 1), although appropriate in a technical sense, eliminates ESOL students from the accountability equation altogether and perpetuates their isolation from the mainstream. With or without testing accommodations (Options 2–4), ESOL students, by virtue of their linguistic, cultural, and academic profiles, are unable to demonstrate the attainment of standards in English with the same facility as their native-English-speaking peers. An inclusion requirement makes ESOL students assume membership in the larger group and provides baseline data on ESOL students. However, more likely than not, the ESOL group will remain stigmatized as low achievers and bear the brunt of attention for lowering a school or district's average.

Managing the Assessment Process: A Framework for Measuring Student Attainment of the ESL Standards (TESOL, 1998) gives educators who work with ESOL students a model for analyzing their current assessment practices. In it, assessment is defined as a multiphased, iterative process that entails planning, collecting and recording information, analyzing and interpreting information, and using information for reporting and decision making. A set of principles for ensuring fair and equitable assessment of ESOL students accompanies each phase. This document may be useful to states and school districts that are currently employing one of the first four options in Table 6-1 and are contemplating how to assess ESOL students more appropriately. (See also chapter 5.)

In contrast, Option 5 recognizes the value of ESOL students in an accountability system that has indeed been crafted for all students.

TABLE	6-1

OPTIONS FOR ESOL STUDENT PARTICIPATION IN LARGE-SCALE ASSESSMENT

Option	Advantages	Disadvantages
1. Exclusion	• Students are not subjected to invalid assessments • Students who would be frustrated with assessment are not included	• Students are not part of the accountability system • ESL teachers are not validated as professionals • ESL's programmatic worth is not recognized
2. Partial inclusion	• Students get experience with high-stakes assessment • Baseline data are collected on ESOL students	• Students' proficiency is not necessarily sufficient to succeed on achievement tests • All ESOL students are assumed to progress according to the same timetable • Students often face consequences for poor performance
3. Full inclusion without accommodations	• Students are a part of school, district, and state accountability • All stakeholders assume responsibility for student learning	• Students are subjected to inappropriate and invalid assessments • Students' language and cultural backgrounds are not considered
4. Inclusion with accommodations	• Assessments are modified to meet needs of ESOL students • Students can use a variety of strategies to enhance comprehension	• Accommodations may invalidate the assessment • Students may be just as frustrated with accommodations as without them
5. Exemption with use of alternate assessment	• Students are assessed with reliable and valid tools • ESL teachers and administrators contribute to assessment development	• Alternate assessment is not valued as highly as other state assessment • Alternate assessment is not necessarily statistically equated with other state assessment

Alternate assessment complements nonalternate or traditional assessment, and together they constitute a state or district's assessment system. These alternate assessment measures address the variability of ESOL student performance. If properly designed, alternate assessment simultaneously captures the performance of ESOL students at the lowest and highest ends of a scale. Thus, the alternate assessment for ESOL students must be aligned with and must dovetail with large-scale assessments of native-English-speaking students in order to create a seamless series of educational services and achievement measures.

The difficulty of selecting a reasonable large-scale assessment option for ESOL students is exacerbated in states with a high-stakes graduation test (Rivera & Vincent, 1998). Although exclusions, accommodations, translations of the test, or alternate assessments are permitted in some states, these practices represent other instances of states' reacting to assessments that are already in place. The consequences are often great for ESOL students who, by all other counts, have earned a high school diploma. With a growing number of states moving in this direction, the potential influence of *ESL Standards* on assessment practices warrants examination. ESL and bilingual teachers need to be cognizant of program, district, and state policies in order to prepare their students well for large-scale, high-stakes assessment.

TASK 2

Find a review of a commercially available, norm-referenced test. Read the review, and determine the tests' usability with ESOL students. What recommendations would you make about the use of this test to classroom teachers? To parents? To school board members?

Selecting a Framework for Implementing ESL Standards

Standards, in particular ESL standards, help shape the curriculum, instruction, and assessment of ESOL students. For districts and states to comprehend the potential impact of these standards, an ESL curricular framework that defines the role of ESL standards in relation to state or district content standards has to be formulated. States and school districts with large numbers of ESOL students generally utilize *ESL Standards* within one of four contexts or frameworks (see

Table 6-2). Teachers should be aware of the impact of a district's philosophical orientation toward ESL and bilingual education, exemplified in the treatment of *ESL Standards*, on classroom practices.

In the first framework, states or school districts may directly adopt the three goals and nine standards in *ESL Standards*. This frame-

TABLE 6-2		
FRAMEWORKS FOR USING THE ESL STANDARDS FOR INSTRUCTION AND ASSESSMENT		
Curricular framework for ESL standards	*Philosophical assumptions*	*Implications for instruction and assessment*
1. Adoption as stated	• ESL is a recognized content area, and ESOL students are unique • ESL standards match school, district, or state needs	• Applicable to a variety of models and methods • Easy to align classroom assessment with district and state assessment
2. Amplification, reordering, or restatement	• ESL curriculum may be isolated from other content areas • ESL standards are foundation for state or local ESL standards development	• Often perceived as independent of the general education program • Molded to match specific needs of a district or state
3. Adaptation and alignment with English language arts	• ESL standards serve as a precursor to English language arts standards • ESL standards bridge with English language arts standards	• Emphasize collaboration between ESL and language arts teachers • Often focus on students' acquisition of and measurement of language proficiency
4. Application or integration with content areas	• ESL curriculum is woven into all content areas • ESL standards are linked with other content standards	• Encourage coordination of effort among ESL and classroom teachers • Integrate language and content with dual goals of language proficiency and academic achievement

work views national ESL standards as the backbone for the development, implementation, and evaluation of local ESL and bilingual curriculum, instruction, and assessment. The second framework involves the choice to amplify, reorder, or restate the national ESL standards. The Chicago Public Schools, for example, have added a standard, "Students will acquire English across the curriculum through the use of technology," as part of Goal 1, "to use English to achieve in all academic areas and settings," in their field-test version of ESL goals and standards (Office of Language and Cultural Education, 1998). Assessment within these two frameworks generally serves a purpose directed specifically at the provision of ESL and bilingual education services, such as monitoring student progress, and is not necessarily connected with other large-scale assessment efforts.

A third curricular framework envisions the integration of ESL and language arts standards to create composite ones, or the formation of a parallel set of ESL standards to augment existing language arts standards. In this vein, the state of Illinois, for instance, has created a standardized language proficiency test in the areas of reading and writing for ESOL students as a precursor to its state achievement testing. To document ESOL students' literacy development for up to 3 consecutive years, students in state-approved ESL and bilingual education programs in Grades 3–11 take this standardized measure, which is anchored in the state's language arts reading and writing standards.

The fourth option uses ESL standards as an umbrella for content standards in the major learning areas. An example of this type of framework is the work undertaken by the state of Wisconsin. As part of an extensive professional development effort, teams of bilingual/ESL, special education, and content-area specialists have devised alternate performance indicators for language arts, mathematics, social studies, and science content and performance standards. ESOL and special education students who are not eligible for the state assessment will take alternate performance assessments developed from these indicators and suggested alternate performance activities and tasks.

Aligning the Elements Within the Assessment Process

Once states and school districts have a general framework for ESL standards, the next step is matching the purposes for assessment with the types of appropriate instrumentation. As stated earlier, aligning assessment measures with specified standards during the planning phase helps ensure that the measure collects valid information and inspires confidence in the results. Stakeholders at the classroom, program, school, district, and state levels rely on different kinds of data for educational decision making. Table 6-3 outlines a sampling of the purposes of assessment, the types of measures, and sources of documentation at each level of implementation. It is assumed that assessment is operating within a standards-referenced system and that some purposes, although not repeated, apply to multiple levels.

In large-scale assessment at the state, school, district, and program levels, summary information on ESOL students is aggregated from a standard set of criteria delineated in a rubric (a scoring guide) or from a standardized administration of a test that yields standard or scale scores. Uniformity in the methods of data collection, analysis, and interpretation yields results that are generalizable to the ESOL student population as a whole. According to the principles of assessment (see chapter 5), teachers and administrators have the obligation to disseminate information on ESOL student performance in meaningful ways.

The higher the level of implementation (from the classroom to the state), the stricter the enforcement of standard procedures to ensure high reliability of measurement. ESL and bilingual teachers must comply with the administration requirements stipulated for all teachers, or any information gleaned from the assessment will be rendered meaningless. Professional development affords teachers and administrators the opportunity to work with other teachers in developing a sound standards-based assessment system for their district and implementing uniform assessment policies.

■ Considering Alternate Forms of Assessment

Because standard conditions for data collection are required in order to produce reliable results in an efficient and timely manner, states and school districts rely heavily on nationally norm-referenced tests. The information obtained from these standardized measures is consistent or reliable, but it often is not valid for ESOL students. Therefore, ESL and bilingual services should rely on quantitative and qualitative data, linked to the ESL standards, for their ESOL students. In this way, teachers can gain insight into where their students lie on the ESL standards' continua as well as be informed of the effectiveness of their

TABLE 6-3

ELEMENTS WITHIN THE ASSESSMENT PROCESS, BY LEVEL OF IMPLEMENTATION

Level of implementation	Purpose of assessment	Types of measures	Sources of documentation
Classroom	• Self-reflect on learning • Monitor student progress • Inform instruction	• Student work • Performance tasks in L1 and L2 • Observation	• Narratives, checklists, journals • Task-specific and general rubrics • Teacher-made or unit tests • Anecdotal records
Program	• Screen, place, and transition students • Ascertain extent of academic achievement • Determine growth in language proficiency	• Home language survey • Achievement tests in English (and L1) • Language proficiency tests in L1 and L2 • Performance measures in L1 and L2	• Survey information • Standard scores • Percentiles, language levels • Rating scales, general rubrics
School or district	• Document student learning • Determine effectiveness of services	• District standardized tests • District performance assessments	• Normal curve equivalents, stanines, percentiles • General rubrics
State	• Be accountable for student learning • Develop policies based on trend data	• State assessments • Alternate state assessments	• Standard scores • General rubrics

instructional program. In addition, the information from multiple data sources may be used to make educational decisions for individual students.

The ESL standards are global in nature so that multiple avenues of instruction and assessment may be pursued. Assessments related to Goal 1 ("To use English to communicate in social settings") and Goal 3 ("To use English in socially and culturally appropriate ways") may rely on teachers' observation of classroom routines or student-centered tasks. ESOL students may interact in pairs or small groups to demonstrate social and cultural aspects of language proficiency. Self-assessment through oral or written journals may offer additional insights and perspectives into how ESOL students are acclimating and acculturating to a new educational system.

Attainment of Goal 2 ("To use English to achieve academically in all content areas") should also initially rely on alternate assessment. The support materials and resources utilized by bilingual/ESL teachers for instruction, such as pictures, charts, diagrams, maps, and graphic organizers, should be incorporated into performance tasks and projects as a means of assessing students' mastery of concepts within the content areas. ESOL students should have opportunities to relate their conceptual understanding through exhibits, models, demonstrations, displays, and experiments.

In classrooms where assessment of ESOL students is interwoven with performance-based instruction as well as aligned to standards and the curriculum, alternate assessment may yield results that are valid but not necessarily reliable. Variation from teacher to teacher and from task to task makes it difficult to reach agreement regarding the scoring of students' work. Therefore, ESOL students and ESL and bilingual educators should rely on a variety of measures, representing standardized and standard administration, at the classroom, program, and district levels.

A key that may unlock some of these inequities for ESOL students is the use of *rubrics* (scales or scoring guides with descriptive criteria at each score point or level by which the student's performance is interpreted; see Gottlieb, 1999) in performance-based tasks and projects in which students construct a response, create a product, or demonstrate their knowledge in other direct ways. Together, the performance and the rubric constitute the assessment.

A rubric's criteria serve as documentation of student performance and a barometer for standards attainment. There are two broad classifications for rubrics: (a) general or developmental, with criteria applicable across numerous tasks or projects, and (b) task-specific, with defined descriptors for one particular task or project. For summative, large-scale assessment, general rubrics are preferred, whereas task-specific rubrics are more often utilized for formative or classroom assessment. The different types of rubrics (e.g., focused-analytic scales, holistic scales, rating scales, checklists) may qualify as either general or specific.

General or developmental rubrics are global in nature and provide an overall indication of students' performance. Those designed for ESOL students may assume a subset of descriptors or sample performance indicators as their criteria, thereby directly connecting to the ESL content standard(s) and goals. Being developmental in nature, general rubrics are broad based and offer summary information on areas of student learning. Teachers commonly use developmental rubrics for summative assessment—at the end of a marking period or semester, for example—to detect trends over the span of ESL and bilingual services.

Task-specific rubrics are geared to a predetermined instructional sequence or curricular segment, such as a theme or project. The criteria in these rubrics are discrete, applying performance indicators in designated ESL standards to a particular unit of study. For ESOL students, the criteria in this type of rubric are bound to the language elements and academic concepts currently being taught. Teachers may use task-specific rubrics as an organizational guide for students during instruction and, subsequently, as a diagnostic tool for ongoing, formative assessment.

To maximize the reliability of assessment results, teachers who work with ESOL students in a standards-based setting should reach consensus regarding

1. the type of rubric most appropriate for the task

2. the match between students' work and the rubric's criteria

3. the benchmark or score point that designates attainment of the standard(s)

4. the number of pieces or work necessary to constitute meeting the standard(s)

Professional development should afford all teachers ample opportunities to collaborate within a standards-based system. Much time should be devoted to alignment that firmly anchors the major components of the system; standards and curriculum, curriculum and instruction, and instruction and assessment must be securely aligned.

Using Portfolios for Standards-Based Assessment

Once aware of the added responsibility of performance-based assessment, teachers and administrators may consider the benefits of an assessment management tool: the portfolio. A historical precedent was set when Vermont and Kentucky launched their statewide portfolio initiatives in the early 1990s as part of their educational reform packages. In Kentucky, legislation stipulated the development of a statewide performance assessment system with portfolio tasks incorporated into the accountability strand for each school (Guskey, 1994). Previously, portfolios had been utilized for classrooms, programs, schools, and even districts, but never before had they been applied at the state level for assessment purposes.

An assessment portfolio

1. is a systematic collection of the processes and products of original student work with their associated documentation (usually in the form of rubrics)

2. has an accompanying set of defined targets (or content standards) with clear-cut criteria (performance standards or indicators) that forms the basis for referencing the assessments

3. contains accumulated, direct evidence that is representative of student performance, growth, or achievement at a specified level of implementation (Gottlieb, 1997)

As the use of assessment portfolios grew, it became obvious that the definition of *portfolio* needed to be broadened to accommodate the enlarged circle of its use. School reform, state and school accountability, and the educational standards movement all led to this change in perspective. Portfolios were no longer merely collections and reflections of student work but began to assume characteristics in line with large-scale assessment.

An expanded definition of portfolios encompasses several features. A large-scale assessment portfolio whose primary purpose is accountability must have proven reliability and validity. If educational decisions are based on its contents and scores, then the assessment portfolio must be technically sound and legally defensible. In a standards-based, large-scale assessment portfolio, the content or entries are organized and referenced to specified content and performance standards. Some of the features, suggested content, and uses of this type of assessment portfolio for ESOL students are presented in Table 6-4.

The value of portfolio assessment for ESOL students is well documented (Genesee & Upshur, 1996; Gottlieb, 1995; O'Malley & Valdez Pierce, 1996; Valdez Pierce & O'Malley, 1992). Navarrete (1990) envisions portfolios as repositories for both informal and formal assessments; she suggests combining information from large-scale and classroom measures to create a composite picture of an ESOL student. Farr and Trumbull (1997), on the other hand, see portfolio assessment as a potentially powerful tool in promoting equity for ESOL students. Overall, portfolio assessment, whether at the classroom or the district level, should reflect instructional practices deemed effective and worthwhile for ESOL students.

Large-scale assessment portfolios designed for ESOL students serve several distinctive purposes. The ESOL student portfolio for Fairfax County, Virginia, for instance, is intended to aid in the placement, reclassification, and transition of students from its ESL program (T. Predaris, personal communication, 1998). The entries in a two-way developmental portfolio, created by a consortium of unified school districts in southern California in the early 1990s (*Two-Way Immersion Portfolio Assessment*, n.d.), support and document a student's dual language development. Each language area is represented by a developmental rubric that traces the growth in a student's proficiency in two languages over the course of a school year.

A large-scale assessment portfolio for ESOL students might feature a cassette with oral language samples accompanied by a focused-analytic developmental rubric to interpret different components of listening and speaking. Perhaps this student cassette contains samples of oral reading that are interpreted with a holistic reading rubric chronicling a student's relative reading proficiency in the L1 and the second language (L2). Other entries may include samples of the student's journal writing that are matched with a developmental checklist for journal writing; this form of documentation traces a student's

TABLE 6-4

STANDARDS-BASED, LARGE-SCALE ASSESSMENT PORTFOLIOS

Features	*Contents*	*Uses for ESOL Students*
• Defined purpose and stated level of implementation	• Original student work, dated and arranged in chronological order and accompanied by a developmental rubric, that is matched to standards	• Management tool for student- and teacher-selected pieces
• Content and performance standards aligned with entries and rubrics		• Documentation of student performance over time based on identical criteria (or indicators) used on multiple occasions
• Referencing system that defines the relationship among the standards, student work, and documentation of student performance	• Direct evidence of student performance, such as audiotapes (for oral language and reading), videotapes, photographs of projects and exhibits, and computer disks	• Alternate form of assessment for students who do not participate in large-scale district or state assessment
• Substantiated validity	• Self-assessment and reflection attached to work samples	• Expression of what students can accomplish while approaching ESL standards, such as academic projects and community service
• Proven reliability among the tasks selected to be represented	• Summary sheet informing stakeholders of assessment results in relation to standards attainment	
• Proven interrater agreement on scores assigned to students' work		• Appropriate and equitable
• Standard procedures and guidelines for collection, analysis, and interpretation of data		
• Opportunities for professional development in which teachers discuss, refine, and modify contents		
• Collaboration and articulation among participating teachers and administrators		

writing development in the L1 and the L2 on a systematic basis throughout the year.

Older students may digitize their assessment portfolio by maintaining writing and oral samples on a computer disk. Results from projects may be recorded on a holistic scale accompanied by a photo of an exhibit, a student self-reflection, or both. Ultimately, school districts should craft assessment portfolios that represent the standards being addressed. A student portfolio summary sheet serves to capture the information within the portfolio and facilitates the aggregation of data across students.

As a response to the shifting assessment paradigm, portfolios come to reflect more authentic performance assessments that require students to demonstrate what they know and are able to do rather than to show their knowledge and skills indirectly through traditional, multiple-choice tests. As an alternate assessment, portfolio data derived from actual student work serve to complement standardized test data. In a standards-based system, each assessment is criterion referenced to specified standards, and results are reported in that context. Without content standards, a norm-referenced tool serves only as a means of ranking students and comparing the performance of one student against that of the norming group. In contrast, when assessment is standards based and all the elements of the system are aligned, validity is maximized for all students.

TASK 3

Arrange to visit a school that has implemented portfolio assessment. Talk to teachers about their reactions to this form of assessment. What are the benefits? Challenges?

■ Conclusion

Teachers have the difficult task of balancing the demands of accountability that accompany large-scale assessment with the monitoring of individual students' progress within a classroom. All stakeholders, especially teachers, need to understand why assessment is necessary (its purpose), what is to be assessed (the measures), and how the information is to be interpreted (the sources of documentation) and used (the decisions). ESL standards help define and shape the assessment process, the success of ESOL students in pre-K–12 educational programs, and the future of ESL and bilingual education. A standards-based, large-scale assessment system that is inclusive of ESOL students is rigorous, useful, and meaningful for all who strive for education reform.

Chapter 7

Using Standards for Classroom-Based Assessment

Margaret E. Malone

Different approaches to assessment provide different kinds of information. Chapter 5 presents an approach to assessing ESOL students, and chapter 6 addresses the dilemmas inherent in including ESOL students in—and excluding them from—large-scale assessments. Large-scale assessment, while offering a broad perspective on students' performance, particularly in academic areas such as math and language arts, by its very nature cannot provide a diagnostic picture of students' progress within a classroom setting. Classroom assessment is thus very important in providing this information. For ESOL students, the issue is far more complex: How can teachers know that students are ready to take a large-scale assessment without forcing them to take a high-stakes test for which they are not prepared? Moreover, if students are not participating in a large-scale test, how can teachers ensure that the students continue to make progress on the ESL standards or on content-area standards?

In *Managing the Assessment Process: A Framework for Measuring Student Attainment of the ESL Standards* (TESOL, 1998), principles of and priorities for equitable assessment of ESOL students are presented. This chapter explores and exemplifies the assessment approaches taken by teachers working at a variety of educational levels and serving diverse types of students as they strive to meet the ESL standards.

The chapter focuses on the implications of *ESL Standards for Pre-K–12 Students* (TESOL, 1997) for assessments in classrooms serving the ESOL student. First, I outline relevant features of the assessment cycle. I then discuss different approaches to and purposes for classroom assessment and its implications for stakeholders at all levels. Finally, I present a sample scenario based on real-life examples to illustrate the implications for standards-based assessment in the class-room and the issues raised throughout the process, including context, background, and the placement of assessment within the assessment cycle.

■ The Assessment Process

The approach to assessment presented here emphasizes an assessment cycle consisting of four stages: (a) planning assessment, (b) collecting and recording information, (c) analyzing and interpreting assessment information, and (d) using information for reporting and decision making (see chapter 5). All assessment occurs within the wide context of teaching and learning and measures the attainment of standards by individual students or groups of students. The four phases of the assessment cycle provide ample opportunity for teachers, students, parents, school personnel, and other stakeholders to participate in student assessment in appropriate ways.

■ Approaches to Classroom Assessment

Classroom-based assessments include a variety of measures, from teacher- or district-made written tests, to student journals, to peer assessments. In approaching classroom assessment, teachers should consider the following issues:

1. *What is the purpose for assessment?* Though the general purpose may be to assess students' progress toward attaining the ESL standards, the more specific purpose may be to determine to what extent students have understood a portion of a lesson. Because students in the same class may have different levels of English proficiency and content-area achievement, assessments should accommodate students at all levels. In addition, teachers of math or language arts, for example, may have the same purposes for assessment as ESL specialists do or may have different ones.

2. *Who should be involved in the assessment?* Traditionally, class-room assessment involves the student and the teacher. However, the standards movement emphasizes the involvement of more stakeholders in assessment. Other stake-

holders—guidance counselors, mainstream teachers, principals, district personnel, and program directors, in addition to ESOL students and ESL specialists—should be apprised of ESOL students' progress to ensure that informed decisions are made later about those students' involvement in large-scale assessments.

3. *What should be assessed?* In large-scale assessments, the content of the assessment is clear. In classroom assessments, various students may be assessed differently depending on their background and language proficiency. The teacher may use a paper-and-pencil test, a classroom observation, a portfolio, or a student self-assessment, for instance, to obtain different information about students' progress.

4. *How should assessment take place?* Teachers may assess students formally or informally, and students may assess themselves or each other. Assessments may be developed by a group of teachers according to a district plan, by an individual teacher, or by a group of students.

5. *When should assessment occur?* As mentioned earlier, assessment should be ongoing. The timing of different types of assessment is important. A student self-assessment or teacher observation should precede a district paper-and-pencil test. Timing is also important in communicating with school and district personnel about ESOL students' progress toward attaining the ESL standards.

Types of Measures

The key to success in classroom-based assessment is to rely on a variety of approaches so that teachers, students, and other stakeholders gain valuable information on students' progress toward attaining standards. Just as a large-scale assessment provides a particular kind of information about students' progress, each classroom assessment provides a different piece of information on students' progress.

Teachers can use many different kinds of classroom assessments to assess students' progress. Though some assessments are formal and shared with multiple stakeholders—such as students, ESL specialists, content-area teachers, program administrators, parents, and principals—still others provide simple, ongoing, diagnostic information to students and teachers. Below are some types of assessments, the purposes for which they may be used, and relevant stakeholders:

- *district paper-and-pencil tests:* These tests are developed district- or programwide, usually by a team of teachers and program specialists, to determine students' progress toward meeting district or state standards. Such tests are administered to large groups of students at similar times during the school year. The results of these tests are shared with district personnel as well as with students, teachers, and parents.

- *teacher-made tests:* Teacher-made, pencil-and-paper tests may be developed by one teacher or by a team of teachers to determine progress in a specific instructional area. The main stakeholders for such a test are teachers and students, though other personnel may be advised of the results.

- *performance tasks:* Performance tasks allow students to demonstrate how they do in specific learning situations, including on language and other content-area tasks. Students' progress is often rated according to a specific rubric (a scale with descriptive criteria at each score point or level) used to document students' performance. Rubrics may be language or subject-area oriented and may be used at different points within a student's school career, the school year, or the semester to show progress. Progress may also be determined according to checklists developed for specific instructional purposes (Genesee & Upshur, 1996).

- *student observations:* Informal or formal observations allow teachers to note students' progress as shown in their classroom behavior. Teachers may record their reactions to observations in anecdotal notes or by using a checklist or rubric as a point of reference. To ensure that such observations are systemic and manageable, teachers must develop a strategy for classroom observation. For example, a teacher may select a day of the week on which to observe specific students and take notes on their performance (Genesee & Upshur, 1996).

- *portfolios:* A portfolio is a systematic collection of the processes and products of a student's original work along with associated documentation. The contents are determined in part by students themselves based on a set of defined targets with clear-cut criteria and a specified purpose (Valencia, 1991). A portfolio allows students and teachers to work together in showing a student's work over time. For the approach to work, students must be involved (O'Malley & Valdez Pierce, 1996).

- *self-assessments:* Classroom-based assessments include not only teachers' reflections on students' work but also students' reflections on and analysis of their own work. Students may reflect on, for example, the processes and strategies used in creating the final product, either focusing on one point in time or comparing work over time (Paris & Ayers, 1994).

- *peer assessments:* Classroom-based assessment may allow students to work together to assess each other's work. Clear parameters must be established for such assessments, and the processes through which such assessments occur must be explained to all participants (Genesee & Upshur, 1996).

- *journals:* Students and teachers may keep journals to communicate with each other or for their own reflection on the learning process. Journals may be written, visual, or even oral (O'Malley & Valdez Pierce, 1996).

■ Sample Scenario of Classroom-Based Assessment

The sample assessment scenario below (adapted from *ESL Standards for Pre-K–12 Students*, TESOL, 1997, pp. 128–130), which describes an 11th-grade civics class, provides an overview of one teacher's approach to assessment. The sample progress indicators show the kind of tasks students are expected to perform during this instructional period. The parts of the scenarios are in boxes, each followed by discussion. Following the scenario is an illustration of how this real-life classroom setting incorporates the four phases of the assessment cycle.

Goal 2, Standard 2, 9–12th Grade

Assessment Scenario

The scenario first defines the goal (Goal 2: To use English to achieve academically in all content areas) and standard (Standard 2: Students will use English to obtain, process, construct, and provide subject matter information in spoken and written form) in *ESL Standards* (p. 127). This information is important in helping identify the purpose or purposes of assessment. Indicating the grade level targets the approximate age group of the students in the scenario.

Sample Progress Indicators

a. locate information appropriate to an assignment in text or reference materials

b. research information on academic topics from multiple sources

c. take a position and support it orally or in writing

d. prepare for and participate in a debate

The indicators above specify how students will show to what extent they have attained the goal and standard. For any lesson, teachers can identify multiple indicators of students' progress. This scenario identifies four: (a) one performance indicator, the ability to locate information; (b) a research indicator, which allows students to demonstrate how well they can find information in a library or via the Internet; (c) an oral or written indicator for arguing a point; and (d) a classroom participation indicator, that of preparing for and taking part in a debate. Each of these indicators is measured in different ways during the scenario.

Context Information

Grade level:	11th grade in a mainstream civics class
English language proficiency level:	Advanced
Language of instruction:	English
Focus of instruction:	Civics

The context information allows the teacher to tailor assessments to the specific grade level (11th) and class (mainstream civics). This information tells who the teacher is (a mainstream civics teacher); it also reveals that not all the students in the class are ESOL students. Knowing the English proficiency level is important for ensuring that assessments are targeted to students at that level. In addition, the context information gives the language of instruction, which is usually (but not always) the language of assessment, and the instructional focus.

Background

The scenario takes place in an 11th-grade, one-semester civics course. Most of the 24 students in the class are of Hispanic background. Most ESOL students speak Spanish; other language groups include Haitian Creole and Chinese. Mr. Philippe, the teacher, is certified in civics and ESL. He is proficient in Haitian Creole and English and has a working knowledge of Spanish. Most of the students in this class are true advanced-level students, although some are at the intermediate level. The students' ages range from 16 to 19. It is near the end of the school year.

The background information takes the context one step further by providing specific information to consider in planning the assessment process. Knowing that the course lasts only one semester allows the teacher to establish a time line for planning assessments across a

4-month period. Like many ESL classes, this classroom includes students from at least three language groups. Though the broad context claims to include only students with advanced levels of language proficiency, the additional information about the students' actual language level shows that the teacher has to address a fairly broad range of proficiency levels within the assessment context. Also, the students range in age from 16 to 19, which means that the class includes adolescents from a fairly broad age span. Such age spans are not unusual in ESL classes.

Additional important information is provided on the teacher's background. When planning assessments, many teachers are generous in considering students' needs but sometimes less so in considering their own. The teacher, Mr. Philippe, has a good background in the content area and ESL as well as holding teaching certificates in both subjects. It is hoped that he will bring a deep understanding of both content and language to his assessment-planning process. Mr. Philippe's extensive background does not mean that he should not consult with other content-area and language teachers; it may suggest instead that he has colleagues in both departments with whom he can collaborate.

A final piece of information is the time of the school year: the end of the semester. If the unit covered by the scenario falls at the end of a semester, Mr. Philippe may wish to integrate skills or knowledge attained throughout the semester into the assessment plan for the unit. This information may also indicate that Mr. Philippe needs to follow up on earlier assessment activities and emphasizes the need for a long-term assessment plan. Furthermore, a department-level or even statewide assessment may be scheduled soon, and Mr. Philippe needs to consider such assessments in planning for the assessment of portions of the unit.

Allocation of Time

This unit is approximately 3 weeks in duration. The first week is devoted to researching the topic and organizing the information. Week 2 centers on preparation and delivery of the debate. The last week includes essay writing and reflection along with practicing for the departmental exam.

This section provides a still richer picture of the classroom context. Three weeks is ample time for Mr. Philippe to integrate multiple forms of assessment into his unit. The fact that the last week includes practicing for the departmental exam suggests that it carries slightly higher stakes than most teacher-made tests do. This unit allows the students to progress gradually toward the departmental test: 1 week of research, 1 week for the debate, and 1 week for essay writing in addition to exam preparation.

The 3 weeks of instruction can now be matched to the sample progress indicators. Table 7-1 shows the timing of assessment in this unit.

Instructional and Assessment Cycle

Planning

Mr. Philippe plans a sequence of instructional activities leading to the culmination of this unit on civic responsibility. He decides that students will

1. collect articles from different sources on the topic

2. talk about different ideas in six groups of four students

3. record ideas on newsprint and share them with the class

4. develop a graphic organizer for ideas

TABLE 7-1	
SAMPLE PROGRESS INDICATORS AND TIME FRAME FOR ASSESSMENT	
Sample progress indicator	*Time frame for assessment*
a. Locate information appropriate to an assignment in text or reference materials	Week 1
b. Research information on academic topics from multiple sources	Week 1
c. Take a position and support it orally or in writing	Week 2 (orally) Week 3 (in writing)
d. Prepare for and participate in a debate	Week 2

5. answer his questions as a group

6. engage in a class discussion

7. practice debating

8. debate (some students debate, others prepare questions, others critique)

9. critique the debate

10. write two essays: one discussing the debate, one focusing on a specific issue

11. compile a list of references

After reviewing his instructional goals and activities, Mr. Philippe reflects on how he can monitor students' progress in this unit as well as in the civics class. Because sample progress indicators are generic ones designed to be used across content areas, Mr. Philippe must develop specific assessment activities that reflect the content of his class. Table 7-2 shows his outline for integrating assessment into his instructional plan.

Next, he selects collection and recording tools that correspond to the instructional activities and decides on ways to analyze the information collected. He also sketches how the results will be shared with students and other stakeholders. Finally, he consults with his social studies and ESL colleagues to select a department-developed writing rubric with which to grade the students' essays. He also realizes that he has to allot time during the unit to work with students on developing a peer-critique form for them to use during the debates.

Mr. Philippe has used the planning phase of assessment carefully. Although planning for multiple measures means that he can use more than one form of assessment, Mr. Philippe is judicious in selecting forms of assessment that fit this context and his students. He has developed a thorough assessment plan that may help prevent unnecessary surprises at the end of the unit. He will begin by assessing students informally to note their progress on the first sample progress indicator, collecting research information. After noting students' progress in this area, Mr. Philippe will note their group interaction and their abilities to communicate with each other on academic topics. At this point, the students' differences and similarities may come into play, particularly with regard to language proficiency. Mr. Philippe

TABLE 7-2

STAKEHOLDERS AND RELEVANT AREAS TO ASSESS

Stakeholder	Areas to assess

Student	• Progress toward achieving sample progress indicators
	  a. Monitor students' progress in finding sources for debate
	  b. Assess students' class discussion
	  c. Evaluate students' performance on debate
	  d. Assess students' ability to support a position in writing
	• Ability to follow directions
	• Ability to work collaboratively in small groups
	• Achievement of content material for state graduation requirement

Teacher	• Effectiveness and comprehensibility of instructional sequence • Appropriateness of different activities for different learning styles
Department	• Accountability for graduation requirements

may note that students with lower levels of language proficiency, regardless of their level of preparedness, are more reluctant to join group discussions. Conversely, he may notice that quieter students feel less inhibited about speaking about civics in small groups rather than with the whole class.

Mr. Philippe has also developed a group check-in system for students to use as they plan newsprint presentations to the whole class. This checking-in will allow him to chart groups' progress and provide assistance before the debate. Students will also have ample opportunity to seek help before the debate. Finally, Mr. Philippe will be able to see students' progress at the end of the unit by evaluating their essays.

In addition to providing feedback to individual students and the debate groups, Mr. Philippe has allowed for opportunities to evaluate different approaches to assessment. Because it is the end of the semester, he has probably already observed students engaged in different assessment activities, such as observations, group work, and peer assessment. This unit will allow Mr. Philippe to reflect on the more effective forms of assessment he has used with this group. He may find that the students needed time to become accustomed to some approaches but that, over time, these approaches worked well.

Finally, this unit will provide feedback to the social studies department on the class's progress in meeting departmental standards. The end-of-unit test, standard across departments, will also provide feedback to Mr. Philippe and his students on their progress relative to other 11th-grade civics students.

TASK 1

Think about a lesson and its instructional goals. Using some ideas from the scenario in this chapter, outline three different approaches to assessment you can use to determine students' progress in attaining these goals.

Collecting and Recording Information

Because Mr. Philippe wants the instructional activities to progress naturally, he has tried to insert the assessments into the flow of each day's instructional events. He collects and records assessment information as the students participate in the planned instructional activities:

- Using the observation sheet he selected when planning the instruction and assessment sequence, he takes notes on how students interact in their groups. He also notes each group's ability to stay on task.

- He reviews students' journals to chart their progress in collecting sufficient information for the debate.

- He has students critique each other's performance in the debate using the class-generated scoring checklist.

- He assigns two essays to the class. In the first, students are to evaluate their performances in the debate; in the second, they are to take a position on a proposal for a toxic waste dump.

- At the end of the semester, students take a departmental exam linked to state standards for the history graduation requirement. The exam consists of half multiple-choice items and half open-ended short-answer and essay questions, with the two sections weighted equally.

TABLE 7-3

PURPOSES AND TOOLS FOR COLLECTING AND RECORDING INFORMATION

Purpose	Collection tools	Recording tools
Assess students' class discussion	Observation sheet	Grade book
Monitor student progress in finding sources for debate	Students' journals; list of references	Grade book; comments in journals
Evaluate student performance on debate	Peer critique checklist Teacher checklist	Exchange of checklists among students
Assess students' ability to support a position in writing	Student essays scored by departmental rubric	Portfolio; grade book; student conferences
Chart progress toward graduation requirements	Departmental exam: multiple-choice and open-ended questions	Sharing of scores with students; disaggregation of ESOL student data

In this phase of the assessment process, Mr. Philippe selects specific tools for collecting and recording information (see Table 7-3).

1. *observation sheet:* The Student Oral Language Observation Matrix (SOLOM; U.S. Department of Education, 1978) shows five increasing levels of oral proficiency, from 1 (least proficient) to 5 (approximately that of a native speaker) (see Figure 7-1). The matrix also assesses students' comprehension and four domains of production (fluency, vocabulary, pronunciation, and grammar). Mr. Philippe will reflect all criteria in rating his students' proficiency. He will collect this information as students meet in groups. He may walk from group to group to listen to their interactions and may also watch how the groups interact to determine if levels of involvement change when he is not with the group. If he does not have time to record all the observations during the class period, he will need to take some time at the end of the

FIGURE 7-1

STUDENT ORAL LANGUAGE OBSERVATION MATRIX

☐ Social domain
☐ Academic domain

Student's name _____ Grade _____ Signature _____

Language observed _____ Date _____

	1	2	3	4	5
A. Comprehension	Cannot understand even simple conversation.	Has great difficulty following what is said. Can comprehend only "social conversation" spoken slowly and with frequent repetition.	Understands most of what is said at slower-than-normal speed with repetition.	Understands nearly everything at normal speed, although occasional repetition may be necessary.	Understands everyday conversation and normal classroom discussions without difficulty.
B. Fluency	Speech is so halting and fragmentary as to make conversation virtually impossible.	Usually hesitant; often forced into silence by language limitations.	Speech in everyday conversation and classroom discussions frequently disrupted by the student's search for the correct manner of expression.	Speech in everyday conversation and classroom discussions generally fluent, with occasional lapses while the student searches for the correct manner of expression.	Speech in everyday conversation and classroom discussions fluent and effortless, approximating that of a native speaker.
C. Vocabulary	Vocabulary limitations so extreme as to make conversation virtually impossible.	Misuse of words and very limited vocabulary; comprehension quite difficult.	Student frequently uses the wrong words; conversation somewhat limited because of inadequate vocabulary.	Student occasionally uses inappropriate terms and/or must rephrase ideas because of lexical inadequacies.	Use of vocabulary and idioms approximates that of a native speaker.

D. Pronunciation	Pronunciation problems so severe as to make speech virtually unintelligible.	Very hard to understand because of pronunciation problems. Must frequently repeat in order to make himself or herself understood.	Pronunciation problems necessitate concentration on the part of the listener and occasionally lead to misunderstanding.	Always intelligible, though one is conscious of a definite accent and occasional inappropriate intonation patterns.	Pronunciation and intonation approximate that of a native speaker.
E. Grammar	Errors in grammar and word order so severe as to make speech virtually unintelligible.	Grammar and word-order errors make comprehension difficult. Must often rephrase and/or restrict himself or herself to basic patterns.	Makes frequent errors of grammar and word order that occasionally obscure meaning.	Occasionally makes grammatical and/or word-order errors that do not obscure meaning.	Grammatical usage and word order approximate that of a native speaker.

Based on observation, for each of the five components at the left, mark an "X" or write the date across the box which typically describes the student's performance.

day to record his observations and transfer notes into his grade book.

2. *peer critique checklist:* Developing this checklist (see Figure 7-2 for a sample) may take a good portion of a class period. The checklist allows students to critique each other on their performance. The students have input into both developing the checklist and evaluating each other's performances. Mr. Philippe should first ensure that students have a firm understanding of what a debate is. Then he can take suggestions for different categories on which students will be assessed. Students should see a final version of the checklist before the debate. During the debate, students who are not actively debating can use the checklist to take notes on different students' performances.

3. *writing rubric:* The Composition Profile for Writing Samples (adapted from Wormuth & Hughey, 1988; see Figure 7-3)

FIGURE 7-2

STUDENT PEER CRITIQUE CHECKLIST

Debater _____

Comments _____

_____

Student name: _____

	Assessment factor	Yes/no (Circle one.)
	Has clear facts	Y N
	Speaks clearly	Y N
	Does not interrupt other speakers	Y N
	Keeps to time limit	Y N
	Uses relevant facts	Y N
	Has a clear rebuttal	Y N
	Does not get angry	Y N
	Does not read from notes	Y N
	Consults team for support	Y N
	Makes eye contact	Y N

is an analytical scale requiring the rater to assign points in five categories: content, organization, vocabulary, language use, and mechanics. The writing rubric, which should have been used at other times during the semester, can show students' writing attainment for this portion of the unit. This type of assessment tool gives students feedback on specific areas in which they need to improve their writing. Mr. Philippe will collect the essays on the appointed day, match the criteria with the writing sample, and compare individual students' papers with the criteria, which categorize students from the least proficient level (challenger) to the most proficient level (champion).

4. *student journals:* Mr. Philippe will assign topics for journal entries and collect them on the assigned day. He may write comments on journal entries.

5. *departmental exam:* Mr. Philippe will administer and collect the departmental exam.

Analyzing and Interpreting Information

As he collects information about students' performance on each of the activities in this unit, Mr. Philippe analyzes the information so that he can adjust his instruction and provide feedback to students.

- To check on students' participation in class discussions, Mr. Philippe reviews the observation sheets. When he records this information in his grade book, he compares each student's participation in two ways: against other students' level of participation in the activity and within the individual student's participation history. He may use this analysis later in the semester, for example, in a student and parent conference.

- He returns completed peer checklists to debaters for their review.

- He reviews student journals, writing his own comments and adding comments from the group interaction observation sheet. He also records in his grade book whether or not students have completed journal assignments on time.

- To determine the effectiveness of instruction, he examines student journals for comments on comprehensibility of

FIGURE 7-3

COMPOSITION PROFILE FOR WRITING SAMPLES

Name: _____ Language: _____ Date: _____ Assessment task: _____

Language component	Champion	Contender	Competitor	Challenger
Content	30–27 ☐ Suits audience/purpose, one idea expressed, specific development, relevant to topic, creative	26–22 ☐ One idea loosely expressed, some specific development, mostly relevant to topic	21–17 ☐ Nonspecific statement, incomplete development, little relevance	16–13 ☐ Not related, no clear development
Organization	20–18 ☐ Effective lead/topic sentence, logical order (time-space-importance), effective connecting/transitional words, conclusion	17–14 ☐ Adequate lead/topic sentence, logical but incomplete order, some connecting/transitional words, sketchy conclusion	13–10 ☐ Weak or no lead/topic sentence, illogical order, no connecting/transitional words, weak or no conclusion	9–7 ☐ No main idea, no organization
Vocabulary	20–18 ☐ Correct word forms, meaning clear, effective word choice/description/figurative language	17–14 ☐ Mostly correct word forms, meaning understandable, adequate word choice, some description, figurative language	13–10 ☐ Many incorrect word forms, meaning obscure, some variety in word choice, little description/figurative language	9–7 ☐ Limited word choice, little or no meaning

	25–22	21–18	17–11	10–5
Language use	Sentence variety, complete sentence, correct verb tenses, word order, agreement ☐	Simple sentences, mostly complete sentences, several errors in verb tense, word order, agreement, article, negatives, run-ons ☐	Few complete sentences, inconsistent verb tense, word order, agreement, articles, negatives, run-ons ☐	Largely phrases, random verb tense, word order, agreement, articles, negatives ☐
Mechanics	5	4	3	2
	Mastery of spelling, capitalization, and punctuation ☐	Occasional errors in spelling, capitalization, and use of commas, periods, and apostrophes ☐	Frequent errors in spelling, capitalization, and use of commas, periods, and apostrophes ☐	Dominated by errors in spelling, capitalization, and punctuation ☐

Total: ☐

Genre:
Descriptive _____
Expository _____
Narrative _____
Persuasive _____
Poetry/rap _____

Source: Adapted from Wormuth and Hughey (1988).

instruction, listens to comments students make while working in groups, sees how well they follow instructions, and uses the results of the departmental exam to compare his class's performance with that of other classes.

- He assesses students' essays using a writing rubric shared with students and enters the scores in his grade book.

- He and other civics teachers grade the departmental exams of all students, using a scoring key for the multiple-choice questions and a department-developed scoring guide for short-answer and essay questions.

Mr. Philippe uses the following tools in his analysis:

1. *observation sheet:* Mr. Philippe knows that most of his students (based on their proficiency level) probably cluster around similar levels on this classroom-based rubric. However, he checks the information he gains on their progress against earlier assessments of their language proficiency; he may find that some students have progressed across all levels (holistically) and in different subcomponents of language. Such information can be shared with students either in their journals or in conferences. Students should be familiar with the rubric and should be aware that they have progressed over the course of the semester. The rubric that accompanies the observation can also provide feedback to Mr. Philippe on new approaches he can take with this class and with future classes. Because the rubric has been used in the past, it can provide important feedback to Mr. Philippe on how ESL Goal 2, Standard 2, is being met.

2. *peer critique checklist:* The checklist has allowed students to give feedback to each other on their performance in the debate. Mr. Philippe may allow the feedback sheets to go directly to individuals, or he can write notes on them and return them with the journals. Depending on the level of trust among members of the class, students may also provide feedback directly to each other.

3. *writing rubric:* By using the same writing rubric throughout the course, Mr. Philippe can provide consistent feedback to

his students on their progress in writing. In addition, he can use information on students' progress as feedback on areas on which he should focus his instruction.

4. *student journals:* The journals are an effective diagnostic tool. Mr. Philippe's journal assignment for Week 1 of the unit might be for students to list in their journals at least five sources of different types (e.g., journal articles, newspapers, books) and their bibliographic information. Looking at the journals is a fairly quick way for Mr. Philippe to determine which students need additional encouragement to visit the library or need clarification on different kinds of publications. In addition, he can provide a sample bibliographic format for the students. The journal may also be an opportunity for Mr. Philippe to talk informally with students about their group work. He might comment to one usually quiet student, "It's nice to see you participating in your group! Maybe you can try to speak up more in class."

5. *departmental exam:* Mr. Philippe can compare his class's outcomes on the departmental exams with those of other students. He can also look for trends among items students got wrong and note whether some items could have been worded more sensitively for nonnative speakers of English.

All the information in these tools can provide an excellent picture of the individual student and the class as a group. Mr. Philippe can look back to earlier observations conducted with the same rubrics for oral and written proficiency to see students' progress on meeting the standards over time. This information will allow him to formulate reasonable expectations for this group of students for his own planning and communicate them to the department, school, and district.

Reporting and Decision Making
Mr. Philippe uses the information he has collected in several ways:

- He enters the scores from the essays in his grade book. He then returns the essays and scoring rubric to the students and meets with a few who are concerned about the results.

- He has the students choose one of the essays to include in their civics portfolio, which will count for 50% of their grade.

- He uses the portfolio when he talks with students, parents, and counselors in conferences.

- Because the students' essays are very short and tend to treat the topics somewhat superficially, he decides that the next time he teaches this unit he will ask students to write one longer essay defending their position rather than assign the two shorter essays. In addition, during a class discussion he will also review and critique students' performances in the debate.

- He receives the results of the departmental exam and shares them with the students. ESOL students' scores are separated for comparison with those of other students.

- The department head reviews the exam results, including those of ESOL students separated from those of mainstream students. These data are also reviewed by the ESL specialist in the school.

Reporting the results of assessments, a necessary part of the assessment process, often receives the least attention. It is not enough to report results to stakeholders; to be helpful, results must be reported in meaningful and appropriate ways. In the last phase of the assessment process, Mr. Philippe, his students, and his colleagues review the results of the assessments conducted. Mr. Philippe gives feedback to students in different ways: through journals, conferences, and a writing rubric. In addition, he shares information with parents by showing them the portfolios during conferences. He may also wish to explain the results of the departmental exam. Because he speaks Spanish and Creole, he can communicate directly with some parents who do not understand English. He may find a translator for parents of other language backgrounds, if necessary.

The assessments have provided important information not only to the students about their progress in the class but also to Mr. Philippe and the school. Mr. Philippe has discovered that assigning two essays in a 1-week period does not result in the quality of work he had expected. He now knows he must modify his expectations. In addition, the department is focusing on ESOL students' performance on the civics test, which may help the department develop a better test in the future.

Come up with a plan for collecting, analyzing, and reporting the information resulting from the assessment plan you prepared in Task 1. Be sure to include a range of stakeholders in your plan.

■ Conclusion

This scenario illustrates how assessment activities can be interwoven within an instructional sequence. It shows how Mr. Philippe

- attends to a variety of assessment purposes, both those related to monitoring students' attainment of ESL standards and those related to other desired educational outcomes;

- utilizes a variety of assessment approaches

- includes students in both instructional and assessable activities

- links one task within a unit with longer term instructional objectives, such as the end-of-semester departmental exam and the graduation requirements

Ongoing assessment is part of the fabric of the classroom. Information gained from students' everyday interaction, such as participation in class discussion, is internal to the functioning of that classroom. The students and teacher receive feedback that reinforces students' behaviors and informs instruction.

Assessment that occurs at intervals, such as at the end of a unit, is more directly tied to specific instructional goals and district standards. Information gained from students' process writing, for example, assists teachers in determining the extent to which the students have demonstrated the knowledge and concepts associated with specific performance indicators. Mr. Philippe has used the assessment process to (a) plan, (b) collect data, (c) analyze information, and (d) report key findings to stakeholders, selecting appropriate kinds of assessment for each situation.

The scenario above shows how one teacher uses the ESL standards in one unit for assessment purposes. Because the teacher assesses different aspects of the unit through different approaches, all stakeholders—students, teachers, parents, and program administrators—receive varied information on students' progress toward attaining Goal 2, Standard 2. This information may allow teachers to modify instruction; make decisions about including students in large-scale, standards-based assessments; and make other decisions based on a wealth of information rather than on only one test.

Chapter 8

Disseminating the
ESL Standards

Else V. Hamayan

In this chapter, I examine the purposes of disseminating the ESL standards and describe strategies of dissemination as they apply to five possible audiences: (a) teacher educators in university settings, (b) colleagues beyond the local university setting, (c) local school personnel, (d) educators beyond the local school, and (e) parents and community members.

■ Purposes of Dissemination

The purposes of disseminating standards for ESOL students range from raising awareness and increasing knowledge to effecting change in the educational environment created for ESOL students and advocating for the improvement of the education they receive. At a preliminary level, by disseminating the standards, teachers and others involved in the education of ESOL students can be informed of what can be expected from these students. At another level, the dissemination of the ESL standards can serve an important advocacy function: to ensure a quality education for a group of students who are often ignored in the larger school community or to ensure high-quality working conditions for their teachers. The educational and advocacy functions of dissemination are obviously closely related, in that advocacy cannot happen without education. A better informed teaching staff can advocate for students and for themselves more effectively. Parents who are better informed about their children's language development can demand better educational programs for them. Both roles for dissemination are necessary.

Education

Because the ESL standards were developed by a grassroots movement, without the support of the federal government, they have not received the exposure that standards in other content areas have received. Mainstream educators, that is, administrators and teachers who do not see themselves primarily as ESL educators, are likely not to have seen or heard of the ESL standards. However, mainstream classroom teachers, principals, and superintendents must become familiar with the standards because they must form the context for learning not just ESL but for all parts of the curriculum. Furthermore, because the ESL standards were developed on a limited budget and through mostly volunteer efforts, even the primary audience for *ESL Standards for Pre-K–12 Students* (TESOL, 1997) — ESL educators — may not be familiar with the document or even know that the standards exist. Encouraging colleagues to join state TESOL associations and international TESOL is one way to improve access to information on the standards. The reason this group needs to know about the ESL standards is obvious: The standards need to inform and guide the development of English language skills that these teachers are primarily responsible for.

Advocacy

Disseminating the standards plays an extremely important advocacy role because of the status of the student population to which the standards refer. Typically, ESOL students have a minority status in their school, and their parents hold a minority status in the larger community. They typically do not play a significant role in the decision-making process in the school or community. ESOL students are often overlooked in decisions regarding assessment, academic subject-area standards, and graduation requirements. Mainstream educators often do not see themselves as being primarily responsible for these students and perceive them as falling within the domain of the ESL or bilingual program. Mainstream educators often do not know enough about the services offered to ESOL students. In fact, the special program offered to ESOL students is sometimes seen as a separate entity within the school.

Members of the larger community, affected by the general malaise regarding immigrants, not only may see themselves as separate from the minority population but may have negative attitudes toward it. Thus, the larger community may need to change its views regarding

ESOL students. The Unz initiative, a ballot initiative passed in California in June 1998, is a good example of the public's misconceptions regarding second language (L2) development and intolerance of the support that ESOL students need. The fact that California voters expected students to become proficient enough in English to survive in a mainstream classroom after only 1 year of ESL instruction shows extremely distorted expectations of L2 learners. For all of the above reasons, it is important to advocate on behalf of ESOL students.

The low status of ESOL students is also reflected in the status conferred on their teachers. ESL and bilingual teachers often do not enjoy the best working conditions within the school community. Many ESL teachers do not have classrooms that are on a par with other teachers', and sometimes ESL teachers are expected to work miracles with the students' L2 development in a very short period of time. Dissemination for the purpose of advocacy should incorporate the improvement of working conditions for teachers of ESOL students.

■ A Framework for Dissemination

A framework that incorporates the educational and advocacy purposes discussed above serves as a useful guide to dissemination. In describing their framework for advocating for enriched language and culture education for all children, Cloud, Genesee, and Hamayan (in press) suggest that advocates need five crucial components to demonstrate successfully to others that the changes they propose are desirable:

1. knowledge of the content of what is disseminated

2. an understanding the application of the content to the specific educational context under discussion

3. knowledge of how the audience would be affected by the content of what is being disseminated

4. knowledge of the attitudes of the audience toward the content

5. familiarity with supporting evidence

Dissemination for the purpose of mere education requires at least the first three components of this framework; dissemination for advocacy also includes the last two conditions, which involve attitudes and persuasion. Table 8-1 describes the five components as they apply to dissemination for educational purposes and for advocacy.

Disseminating the Standards to Teacher Educators in University Settings

Audience

Within the university setting, the ESL standards could be disseminated to several groups of educators, some more closely tied to the ESL field than others. The primary audience within this setting consists of ESL and bilingual teachers. These teachers need to have an in-depth understanding of the content of the standards as well as of the principles of language learning and the vision of effective education. They will use this knowledge not only to establish an effective learning environment for their students, as demonstrated in the other chapters of this book, but also to advocate on behalf of their students with teachers who are not as positively inclined toward linguistically and culturally diverse students.

Another group to whom the standards must be disseminated is the faculty of the department of education. As the number of language minority students increases in schools all over the United States, all educators need to learn about L2 learners. Immigration and secondary migration patterns have changed since the late 1980s: ESOL students now enroll in schools located in socioeconomically well-off suburban and rural areas at a much higher rate than in the past, when they were concentrated mostly in urban and poorer suburban schools (Crawford, 1997). Thus, it is not only teachers who are planning to work in poorer urban schools who need to know about the ESL standards and the theoretical foundation on which they are based. Most teachers will, at some point in their career, encounter students who are learning ESL.

Part of the knowledge that mainstream classroom teachers, principals, and superintendents need relates to their expectations of ESOL students. The implication of mainstream classroom teachers' becoming familiar with the standards and using them is that these teachers will change the way they teach to incorporate sheltered instruction strategies. Administrators might make the district- or schoolwide assessment more flexible to accommodate the special linguistic or cultural needs of ESOL students. (See chapter 6 for detailed suggestions.)

This group of non-ESL specialists is very important in the context of advocacy. Their support for ESOL students is crucial, as is their

TABLE 8-1

COMPONENTS OF DISSEMINATION

Component	To educate others about the standards,	To advocate on behalf of students and teachers,
Knowledge of the content	Become familiar with the content of the standards, and understand how they will be used in the existing educational system	Become familiar with the changes that would result by using the standards, and understand the implications of the changes for people in the existing educational system
Understanding of the application of the content	Understand the classroom, school, district, regional, or statewide context in which the standards are to be applied	Understand the general social, political, economic, and cultural climate in which the changes resulting from the use of standards would occur
Knowledge of how the audience would be affected by the content	Know what changes would be necessitated by standards-based instruction and assessment	Know the stakeholders who will be affected by the changes resulting from the use of standards
Knowledge of the attitudes of the audience	Know the people—teachers and administrators—who will use the standards	Know the stakeholders' attitudes, feelings, or predisposition with respect to the changes resulting from the use of standards
Familiarity with supporting evidence	Keep up to date on current research and practice on the effective instruction and assessment of language minority students	Identify evidence that will counteract opposition, and reassure reluctant and resistant stakeholders that the changes are desirable

feeling of responsibility toward those students. Schools where the non-ESL specialists know about the program set up for the ESOL students and take responsibility for teaching them are more effective than schools where the achievement of ESOL students is seen as primarily the responsibility of the ESL specialists (Ramírez, 1992). However, to advocate effectively on behalf of language minority students, teachers need to be cognizant of the social and political thinking that exists within the culture of mainstream education. Many among the mainstream teaching force do not see the education of language minority students as a top priority for themselves; hence, ESL teachers need to present ideas so that these teachers perceive them as pertinent to their work.

Faculty outside of departments and schools of education can also benefit from learning about the standards and the principles on which they are based. Several fields related to the education of language minority students, for example, child psychology, public health, and communication disorders, need to be included in the dissemination plan. Each of these fields deals with language minority children from a different perspective. If advocacy is the goal of dissemination, it may well be worth the time to develop materials that specifically relate to the particular field. For example, if the audience consists of child psychologists, teachers might focus on the cultural aspects of language use or the possible misinterpretations of behavior that result from lack of proficiency in the language.

How to Disseminate the Standards

Within a university setting, the standards can be disseminated through courses and course addenda. As described in the prologue to this book, courses based on *ESL Standards* can be established for teachers who are specializing in the education of language minority students. Aspects of *ESL Standards* can also be added to existing courses that all teachers take. The issues surrounding the education of language minority students must become part of the regular course work in any teacher education program, and the standards can serve as a vehicle for developing units on the topic. In addition, institutes, seminars, and special lecture series can be organized throughout the year.

Faculty meetings are another venue for possible dissemination of the standards; fact sheets that summarize parts of the standards document can be passed out to faculty. As well, short articles written for newsletters can help inform the whole faculty of the latest developments in ESL education.

Disseminating the Standards to Colleagues Beyond the University Setting

Audience

The ESL standards can be disseminated to educators in related professional fields across the country, such as members of the International Reading Association, the National Science Teachers Association, or the American Association of School Librarians. These groups include faculty from other universities and colleges and members of professional organizations that are related to the field of ESL. Some professional organizations are a primary audience in that their field is directly related to the teaching of language or the instruction of language minority students. These organizations not only constitute an audience for the standards but may themselves have material that can help in the dissemination of the ESL standards to secondary audiences.

Secondary audiences that can benefit from learning about the ESL standards fall into the following categories (see Appendix A for lists of these types of organizations):

- professional organizations of teachers of the various academic subject areas

- general educational organizations

- professional organizations representing different types of educators

- national centers of research in education (These centers can in turn provide newsletters, fact sheets, and research summaries to use as supportive evidence in the final component of advocacy.)

How to Disseminate the Standards

The standards can be disseminated to colleagues beyond the university setting through two main venues: conferences and publications. Publications include newsletters, journals, magazines, and special reports. Both venues can be explored at the local or the national level, as most professional organizations have state or regional chapters that may have their own publications and conferences.

Disseminating the Standards to School Personnel

Audience

Student teachers or teachers who attend graduate school and work in a school setting should attempt to disseminate the ESL standards to their colleagues in school, including other ESL specialists, mainstream classroom teachers, and administrators at either the school or the district level. When disseminating the standards to other ESL specialists, teachers should focus on the development of the three aspects of language: (a) everyday language for interaction, (b) the language needed for academic content-area learning, and (c) the cultural aspects of language use. When disseminating the standards to mainstream classroom teachers, teachers may want to focus more specifically on the development of academic language and the cultural misunderstandings that may occur as a result of ESOL students' lack of proficiency in English.

Administrators, on the other hand, may be interested in more general issues of how to support cultural diversity across the whole school setting and, more specifically, how to change assessment procedures to take into account the expectations of ESOL students, as they appear in the standards. They may want to consider possible changes to regular testing procedures and in the interpretation of test results that make more sense for students who have not attained a certain level of proficiency in English.

How to Disseminate the Standards

Within a school setting, teachers can raise the awareness of colleagues through in-service professional development sessions. These can be full-fledged sessions that focus solely on the issue of L2 development or add-ons to other sessions in which adaptations for ESOL students are considered. For example, in a workshop on the use of graphic organizers, teachers may want to discuss how some organizers are conducive to the development of certain language skills. Teachers may also want to establish partnerships in classrooms where an ESL specialist works closely with the mainstream classroom teachers or a content-area teacher to adapt material and teaching activities to the needs of ESOL students. The standards could serve as the context for these activities. Action research based on the standards is also an excellent way of getting ESL and mainstream classroom teachers to become aware of the special language needs and expectations of ESOL students as outlined by the standards.

Dissemination of the ESL standards to school personnel primarily serves the function of raising awareness, especially among staff who do not have extensive training in L2 development. However, it should also serve an advocacy purpose by ultimately changing the whole school milieu and the approach of all personnel to the education of language minority students. When teachers, principals, and superintendents see what it takes to be proficient in a L2 and when they are shown the support that students need to attain that proficiency, they may be more willing to allocate the necessary resources to services for ESOL students.

Disseminating the Standards to Educators Beyond the Local School

Audience

Educators who work at a regional or state level should also be targeted as a potential audience for *ESL Standards*. Disseminating the standards to local, regional, or statewide educational committees serves as a crucial form of advocacy on behalf of ESOL students. Much work is being done currently on school improvement and standards attainment throughout the United States. Many state boards of education have formed task forces and committees to focus on curricular, assessment, and general policy topics. These groups typically do not have the welfare of language minority students as their primary concern, and even if they do, they are likely to lack awareness of specific issues concerning ESOL students. These committees typically are made up of mainstream educators who may not realize that some of the policies being established do not make sense in light of what can be normally expected of ESOL students. Members of these committees need to become aware of the principles of L2 development on which the standards are based as well as the goals and objectives ESOL students can attain at different levels. If, for example, graduation requirements are being determined at the district level, educators need to consider how those requirements apply to ESOL students who are entering school beyond the primary level with limited formal schooling. If a graduation test is being considered as a requirement, educators need to consider what the implications are for ESOL students who know the content area but lack the English language skills to demonstrate their knowledge.

How to Disseminate the Standards

The best way to get policy-making groups to become aware of the needs of ESOL students is to arrange to be invited or to volunteer to work on the committees that have been formed. This is not always easy, as the people who form these groups typically do not think of the education of language minority students as a primary concern. Lobbying state board members or the office of the district superintendent may be necessary to make a slot available to the "ESL representative" on these working groups.

Another strategy is to form a committee, parallel to the others that have already been formed, that focuses on ESL issues. The danger in doing this exclusively is that, once again, issues of language minority students are seen as the sole domain of the ESL specialists and not of the mainstream. If an ESL-specific task force or committee is formed, it is essential that representatives from the mainstream be invited to participate as core members of the group. Having these individuals on the committee not only ensures that they make the connection between the work that is being carried out in the mainstream, but also may mean that they become spokespersons and advocates for the rights of ESOL students.

Disseminating the Standards to Parents and Other Community Members

Audience

Parents of ESOL students, other parents in the district, and the community at large also need to be informed of the standards for and expectations of ESOL students. Each of these groups may have a slightly different interest in the standards. Parents of ESOL students should know the stages of language development that their children are likely to pass through as they gain proficiency in English, their children's likely rate of acquisition, and the various aspects of language that will emerge as their children learn ESL. They need to know when a school's expectations are not realistic and when to demand changes in the assessment, instruction, or curriculum. Other parents and the community at large need to know what constitutes fair expectations of ESOL students and what resources they need to develop their L2 skills as efficiently as possible.

The current sociopolitical atmosphere is leading many members of society to harbor negative attitudes toward linguistic minorities. Taking these attitudes into account when presenting to groups who may not be sympathetic to linguistic minorities will help teachers gauge how those groups will receive information on the ESL standards. Supportive evidence gathered from the various research centers and from the TESOL organization is crucial in changing individuals' attitudes.

How to Disseminate the Standards

Workshops can inform parents of the standards. Teachers should make sure that the ideas are presented in a way that is comprehensible to all parents—that is, in a language that they understand and that is free of jargon. Newsletters sent home from school can also effectively inform parents of developments in the curriculum or in assessment that reflect the ESL standards. When accompanied by illustrative students' work, information regarding language standards is even more effective and comprehensible to parents who may not have the theoretical context with which to interpret those standards.

TASK 1

Identify different sections of *ESL Standards for Pre-K-12 Students* and indicate the primary audience(s) who would benefit most from learning about that particular section of the documents. List the reason for your choice of primary audience. For example, for "Myths About Second Language Learning," the primary audience might be mainstream classroom teachers because they are least likely to know about second language acquisition and may jump to the wrong conclusion regarding expectations of students.

■ Evaluating the Dissemination Plan

Formulating an effective and cost-efficient dissemination plan is a difficult task. Information often does not reach the people it is intended for, and sometimes the people that it reaches turn a deaf ear to it. The following checklist may help ensure that a plan for disseminating the ESL standards is well organized and that it addresses the essential components of education and advocacy.

Checklist for a Dissemination Plan

Organizational Considerations

- Have you identified the reason for dissemination?

- Have you identified the audience?

- Have you determined the methods of dissemination?

Educational Considerations

- Are you comfortably familiar with the content of the standards?

- Do you know how the standards will be used in the given context?

- Do you understand the context in which the standards are to be applied?

- Do you know the people who will be using the standards?

Advocacy Considerations

- Are you fully aware of the changes that would result from the application of the standards?

- Do you understand the implications of those changes for the existing educational system?

- Do you understand the general social, political, economic, and cultural climate in which the changes resulting from the use of standards would occur?

- Do you know the stakeholders who will be affected by the changes resulting from the use of standards?

- Do you know the stakeholders' attitudes, feelings, or predispositions with respect to the changes resulting from the use of the standards?

- Do you have evidence that will counteract any opposition and reassure reluctant and resistant stakeholders that the changes resulting from standards are desirable?

TASK 2

Choose one of the sections you identified in Task 1, and develop strategies/plans for using the information for educational and advocacy purposes.

TASK 3

Using the Checklist for a Dissemination Plan, evaluate the effectiveness of the strategies/plans you developed in Task 2.

■ Conclusion

Effective dissemination of the ESL standards involves the following steps:

1. Determine the purpose of disseminating the standards (to educate others or to advocate on behalf of ESOL students and their teachers). Using dissemination for advocacy fulfills a much-needed role in the provision of quality education for language minority students.

2. Determine the dissemination strategies to use based on the audience that will receive the information.

3. Evaluate the extent to which the educational or advocacy purposes have been achieved.

Practicing teachers and those who are still in training can play a central role in disseminating the ESL standards. Not only do teachers have strong links to all the people who are potential recipients of information about the standards, but they are also the students' best advocates.

■ Appendix A: Organizational Targets for Dissemination of the ESL Standards

Organizations for Language Teachers or Teachers of Language Minority Students

International Reading
  Association
800 Barksdale Road,
  PO Box 8139
Newark, DE 19714-8139
Telephone 302-731-1600
Fax 302-731-1057
http://www.ira.org/

National Association for
  Bilingual Education
1220 L Street NW, Suite 605
Washington, DC 20005-4018

Tel. 202-898-1829
Fax 202-789-2866
http://www.nabe.org/

National Council for Teachers
  of English
1111 West Kenyon Road
Urbana, IL 61801
Tel. 217-328-3870;
  800-369-6283
Fax 217-328-9645
http://www.ncte.org/

General Educational Organizations

American Association for
  Applied Linguistics
PO Box 21686
Eagan, MN 55121-0686
Tel. 612-953-0805
Fax 612-431-8404
http://www.aaal.org/

American Educational Research
  Association
1230 17th Street, NW
Washington, DC 20036-3078
Tel. 202-223-9485
Fax 202-775-1824
http://www.aera.net

Association for Supervision and
  Curriculum Development
1703 North Beauregard Street
Alexandria, VA 22311-1714
Tel. 703 578-9600;
  1-800-933-ASCD
Fax 703-575-5400
http://www.ascd.org/

The Council for Exceptional
  Children
1920 Association Drive
Reston, VA 20191-1589
Tel. 888-CEC-SPED
http://www.cec.sped.org/

Council of the Great City
  Schools
1301 Pennsylvania Avenue NW,
  Suite 702
Washington, DC 20004
Tel. 202-393-2427
Fax 202-393-2400
http://www.cgcs.org/

Sample Organizations for Teachers of Specific Academic Subjects

American Association of
  School Librarians
c/o American Library
  Association
50 E. Huron
Chicago, IL 60611
Tel. 800-545-2433
http://www.ala.org/aasl/

National Council for the
  Social Studies
3501 Newark Street NW
Washington, DC 20016
Tel. 202-966-7840
Fax 202-966-2061
http://www.ncss.org/

National Council of Teachers of
Mathematics
1906 Association Drive
Reston, VA 20191-1593
Tel. 703-620-9840
Fax 703-476-2970
http://www.nctm.org/

National Science Teachers
Association
1840 Wilson Boulevard
Arlington, VA 22201-3000
Tel. 703-243-7100
http://www.nsta.org/

Organizations for School, District-Level, and State-Level Administrators

American Association of School
Administrators
1801 North Moore Street
Arlington, VA 22209
Tel. 703-528-0700
Fax 703-841-1543
http://www.aasa.org/

Council of Chief State School
Officers
One Massachusetts Avenue
NW, Suite 700
Washington, DC 20001-1431
Tel. 202-408-5505
Fax 202-408-8072
http://www.ccsso.org/

National Association of
Elementary School Principals
1615 Duke Street
Alexandria, VA 22314
Tel. 800-38-NAESP;
800-39-NAESP
http://www.naesp.org/

National Association of
Secondary School Principals
1904 Association Drive
Reston, VA 20191
Tel. 703-860-0200
Fax 703-476-5432
http://www.nasp.org/

National Association of State
Boards of Education
1012 Cameron Street
Alexandria, VA 22314
Tel. 703-684-4000
http://www.nasbe.org/

National Middle School
Association
4151 Executive Parkway,
Suite 300
Westerville, OH 43081
Tel. 800-528-NMSA
http://www.nmsa.org/

National School Boards
Association
1680 Duke Street
Alexandria, VA 22314
Tel. 703-838-6722
Fax 703-683-7590
http://www.nsba.org/

National Centers of
Research in Education

Center for Research on
Education, Diversity, and
Excellence
University of California,
Santa Cruz
College Eight, Room 201
1156 High Street
Santa Cruz, CA 95064
Tel. 831-459-3500
Fax 831-459-3502
http://www.crede.ucsc.edu/

Center for Research on the
Education of Students Placed
at Risk
Johns Hopkins University
Center for Social Organization
of Schools
3505 North Charles Street
Baltimore, MD 21218
Tel. 410-516-8800
Fax 410-516-8890
http://www.scov.csos.jhu.edu/
crespar/

Center for Research on
Evaluation, Standards, and
Student Testing
301 GSE&IS, Box 951522
Los Angeles, CA 90095-1522
Tel. 310-206-1532
Fax 310-825-3883
http://www.cse.ucla.edu/

Center on English Learning and
Achievement
School of Education
State University of New York at
Albany
1400 Washington Avenue
Albany, NY 12222
Tel. 518-442-5026
Fax 518-442-5933
http://www.albany.edu/cela/

National Center on Educational
Outcomes
University of Minnesota
350 Elliott Hall
75 East River Road
Minneapolis, MN 55455
Tel. 612-626-1530
Fax 612-624-0879
http://www.coled.umn.edu/nceo/

Glossary

academic language: language used in the learning of academic subject matter in formal schooling contexts; aspects of language strongly associated with literacy and academic achievement, including specific academic terms or technical language, and speech registers related to each field of study

additive bilingualism: process by which individuals develop proficiency in a second language subsequent to or simultaneous with the development of proficiency in the primary language, without loss of the primary language; a bilingual situation in which the addition of a second language and culture is unlikely to replace or displace the first language and culture

alignment: the match among the ESL standards, curriculum, instruction, and/or assessment

alternative assessment: systematic collection, analysis, and reporting of information on students' performance from sources other than a standardized, norm-referenced test

assessment: systematic cycle of planning, collecting, analyzing, interpreting, and reporting information on students' performance, preferably based on different sources over time

assessment standards: statements that establish guidelines for evaluating student performance and attainment of content standards; often include philosophical statements of good assessment practice (see *performance standards*)

authentic language: real or natural language, as used by native speakers of a language in real-life contexts; language that is not artificial or contrived for purposes of learning grammatical forms or vocabulary

biculturalism: near-native knowledge of two cultures; includes the ability to respond effectively to the different demands of these two cultures

bilingual: using more than one language, without specification of the learners' proficiency in either language; a variety of additional labels are used to define the levels of proficiency (e.g., *balanced bilingual,* referring to more or less equal proficiency in both languages)

bilingual instruction: provision of instruction in school settings through the medium of two languages, usually a native and a second language; the proportion of the instructional day delivered in each language varies by the type of the bilingual education program in which instruction is offered and the goals of said program

body language: gestures and mannerisms by which a person communicates with others

checklist: form to document students' performance on assessment tasks to indicate whether a competency or skill has been attained or not

cloze test: reading test that also provides an indication of overall language ability; consists of passages from which words are omitted at regular intervals

code switching: bilingual person's ability to use two languages within the same speech act; may occur at the lexical, phrase, clause, sentence, and discourse level for a variety of reasons, both linguistic and social

communicative competence: ability to recognize and to produce authentic and appropriate language correctly and fluently in any situation; use of language in realistic, everyday settings; involves grammatical competence, sociolinguistic competence, discourse competence, and strategic competence

communicative functions: purposes for which language is used; includes three broad functions: communicative, integrative, and expressive; where language aids the transmission of information, aids affiliation and belonging to a particular social group, and allows the display of individual feelings, ideas, and personality

comprehensible input: construct developed to describe understandable and meaningful language directed at second language learners under optimal conditions; characterized as the language the learner already knows plus a range of new language that is made comprehensible by the use of certain planned strategies (e.g., the use of concrete referents)

content-based ESL: model of language education that integrates language and content instruction in the second language classroom; a second language learning approach in which second language teachers use instructional materials, learning tasks, and classroom techniques from academic content areas as the vehicle for developing second language, content, cognitive, and study skills

content standards: statements that define what one is expected to know and be able to do in a content area; the knowledge, skills, processes, and other understandings that schools should teach in order for students to attain high levels of competency in challenging subject matter; the subject-specific knowledge, processes, and skills that schools are expected to teach and students are expected to learn

cooperative/collaborative group: grouping arrangement in which positive interdependence and shared responsibility for task completion are established among group members; the type of organizational structure encouraging heterogeneous grouping, shared leadership, and social skills development

criterion-referenced assessment: assessment based on preset criteria or descriptions of language ability rather than on performances of other students

critical period hypothesis: proposition that language learning is accomplished most naturally, easily, and efficiently before the age of puberty and lateralization of the language function in the brain; originally supported by studies of brain-damaged children who were able to learn language

cross-cultural competence: ability to function according to the cultural rules of more than one cultural system; ability to respond in culturally sensitive and appropriate ways according to the cultural demands of a given situation

culture: sum total of the ways of life of a people; includes norms, learned behavior patterns, attitudes, and artifacts; also involves traditions, habits, or customs; how people behave, feel, and interact; the means by which they order and interpret the world; ways of perceiving, relating, and interpreting events based on established social norms; a system of standards for perceiving, believing, evaluating, and acting

descriptors: broad categories of discrete, representative behaviors that students exhibit when they meet a standard

dialect: regional or social variety of language distinguished by features of vocabulary, grammar, pronunciation, and discourse that differ from other varieties

dictation: guided writing test that also provides an indication of overall language ability; consists of a unified passage read with pauses at regular intervals as students write down what they hear

diglossia: bilingual individual's or community's separation of two languages by function; use of each language for distinct functions and purposes

ESL: field of English as a second language; courses, classes, and/or programs designed for students learning English as an additional language

ESOL: English to speakers of other languages; refers to learners who are identified as still in the process of acquiring English as an additional language; students who may not speak English at all or, at least, do not speak, understand, and write English with the same facility as their classmates because they did not grow up speaking English (but rather primarily spoke another language at home)

evaluation: interpretation of assessment data that have been scored and analyzed to make judgments or draw inferences about the quality or worth of students' performance in order to guide instruction and learning

formative evaluation: ongoing collection, analysis, and reporting of data on students' performance in order to guide instruction and learning

genre: category of literary composition characterized by a particular style, form, or content (e.g., a historical novel is one fictional genre); type of oral or written communication with understood form and functions (e.g., lab report, formal lecture)

holistic score: single, integrated score or level on a rubric with specified criteria, based on a students' performance

home language: language(s) spoken in the home by significant others (e.g., family members, caregivers) who reside in the child's home; sometimes used as a synonym for first language, primary language, or native language

interrater reliability: technical measure of the degree of agreement between two raters rating the same assessment item (e.g., a student writing sample) using the same scale

journal: thoughts, opinions, and reactions recorded on a regular basis; alternative assessment technique that determines students' content knowledge by asking them to respond to prompts

language minority student: student who comes from a home in which a language other than English is primarily spoken; the student may or may not speak English well

language proficiency: level of competence at which an individual is able to use language for both basic communicative tasks and academic purposes

language variety: variations of a language used by particular groups of people; includes regional dialects characterized by distinct vocabularies, speech patterns, grammatical features, and so forth; may also vary by social group (sociolect) or idiosyncratically for a particular individual (idiolect)

large-scale assessment: district- or statewide assessment program that includes all or most students; often used as an accountability tool to measure how well the system is doing its job of educating all students

learning strategies: mental activities or actions that assist in enhancing learning outcomes; may include metacognitive strategies (e.g., planning for learning, monitoring one's own comprehension and production, evaluating one's performance); cognitive strategies (e.g., mental or physical manipulation of the material), or social/affective strategies (e.g., interacting with another person to assist learning, using self-talk to persist at a difficult task until resolution)

limited English proficient (LEP): term used by the U.S. government for students identified as using a home language other than English and as needing English language instruction to participate fully in regular classes; often contrasted with *fluent English proficient* (FEP), used for students who use a language other than English but either test on entry as no longer needing additional English instruction or who were formerly LEP and have acquired sufficient English to enter mainstream classes; other labels, such as *English language learner* (ELL) or *English language development* (ELD), are becoming more popular

linguistic competence: broad term used to describe the totality of a given individual's language ability; the underlying language system believed to exist as inferred from an individual's language performance

matrix: rubric with separate cells containing specified criteria created by crossing the assessment category with the levels of attainment

multilingualism: ability to speak more than two languages; proficiency in many languages

multiple measures: variety of assessment types to determine students' performance; often used to make educational decisions so as not to rely on a single assessment

native language: primary or first language spoken by an individual

nonverbal communication: paralinguistic and nonlinguistic messages that can be transmitted in conjunction with language or without the aid of language; paralinguistic mechanisms include intonation, stress, rate of speech, and pauses or hesitations; nonlinguistic behaviors include gestures, facial expressions, and body language, among others

norm-referenced assessment: assessment in which scores are based on relative performances of other students performing the same task

performance-based assessment: task requiring students to construct a response, create a product, or demonstrate applications of knowledge; interpreted using preset criteria

performance standards: statements that refer to how well students are meeting a content standard; specify the quality and effect of student performance at various levels of competency (benchmarks) in the subject matter; specify how students must demonstrate their knowledge and skills and can show student progress toward meeting a standard

portfolio assessment: systematic collection of processes and products of students' original work and associated documentation that is determined in part by the student based on defined targets with clear-cut criteria and a specified purpose

primary language: first or native language spoken by an individual

proficiency-based assessment: assessment based on a person's overall language proficiency

progress indicators: assessable, observable activities that students may perform to show progress toward meeting the standard; organized by grade-level clusters

pull-out instruction: in the case of ESL pull-out instruction, when students are withdrawn from their regular classrooms for one or more periods a week for special classes of ESL instruction in small groups

rating scale: form for documenting students' performance on assessment tasks that indicates the range (e.g., low to high) on which a competency or skill has been attained; also called *Likert scale*

register: usage of different varieties of language, depending on the setting, the relationship among the individuals involved in the communication, and the function of the interaction; form of a language that is appropriate to the social or functional context

regular class: as used in this document, a class with or without ESOL students that does not systematically accommodate the language learning needs of ESOL students; may be a regular elementary class or a subject-area class at a secondary level in which all instruction is delivered and materials are provided almost exclusively in English; sometimes referred to as a *mainstream class*

reliability: technical measure to determine an assessment's ability to produce consistent results

rubric: scale with descriptive criteria at each score point or level; used to document students' performance

scenario: hypothetical instructional or assessment situation

self-assessment: students' reflection on and analysis of their own work, including the processes and strategies used in creating the product, either at one point in time or over time

self-contained ESL class: typically an ESL class with only ESOL students; all subject matter taught to ESOL students by their ESL classroom teacher with no pull-out ESL instruction used

sheltered instruction: an approach in which students develop knowledge in specific subject areas through the medium of English, their second language; teachers adjust the language demands of the lesson in many ways, such as modifying speech rate and tone, using context clues and models extensively, relating instruction to student experience, adapting the language of texts or tasks, and using certain methods familiar to language teachers (e.g., demonstrations, visuals, graphic organizers, or cooperative work) to make academic instruction more accessible to students of different English proficiency levels; also involves teaching language learning strategies

social functions: use of language to accomplish various purposes, such as asking for or giving information, describing past actions, expressing feelings, and expressing regret

social language: aspects of language proficiency strongly associated with basic fluency in face-to-face-interaction; natural speech in social interactions, including those that occur in a classroom

sociocultural competence: ability to function effectively in a particular social or cultural context according to the rules or expectancies for behavior held by members of that social or cultural group

sociolinguistic competence: related to communicative competence; the extent to which language is appropriately understood and used in a given situation (e.g., the ability to make apologies, give compliments, and politely refuse requests)

stakeholder: someone involved in the assessment process and concerned about assessment results (e.g., student, parent, teacher, the community)

subtractive bilingualism: the learning of a majority language at the expense of the first; refers to cases in which the first language and culture have low status and in which because of this, learners are encouraged to divest themselves of their first language and culture and to replace them with the second language and culture; primary language attrition or loss and cultural anomie (uncertainty, alienation) often result from a subtractive bilingual situation

standards-based assessment: the systematic planning, gathering, analyzing, and reporting of students' performance according to the ESL standards

summative evaluation: collection, analysis, and reporting of information at the culmination of a marking period, semester, academic year, or other set time frame

task: instructional or assessment activity that invites a varied response to a question, issue, or problem

two-way bilingual immersion program: program in which monolingual English-speaking children study the regular school curriculum alongside children who are native speakers of the target, or second, language; a portion of the instructional day is taught in English and another portion is in the target language; aims for additive bilingualism and biculturalism for all the students involved

validity: technical measure of an assessment's match between the information collected by the items and its specified purposes

vernacular: language or dialect native to a region or country; normal spoken form of a language; includes nonstandard dialects

vignette: description of an instructional sequence drawn from the real-life experiences of teachers

■ Sources of Definitions Used in Glossary

Baker, C. (1993). *Foundations of bilingual education and bilingualism.* Clevedon, England: Multilingual Matters.

Bilingual Education Office, California State Department of Education. (1994). *Schooling and language minority students: A theoretical framework* (2nd ed.). Los Angeles: California State University, Evaluation, Dissemination and Assessment Center.

Canale, M., & Swain, M. (1980). Theoretical bases of communicative approaches to second language teaching and testing. *Applied Linguistics, 1,* 1–47.

Chamot, A. U., & O'Malley, J. M. (1994). *The CALLA handbook: Implementing the cognitive academic language learning approach*. Reading, MA: Addison-Wesley.

Crandall, J. (1994). *Content-centered language learning* (ERIC Digest). Washington, DC: ERIC Clearinghouse on Languages and Linguistics, Center for Applied Linguistics.

Lessow-Hurley, J. (1990). *The foundations of dual language instruction*. White Plains, NY: Longman.

Prince, C. D., & Forgione, P. D. (1993). Raising standards and measuring performance equitably: Challenges for the National Education Goals Panel and state assessment systems. In G. Burkart (Ed.), *Goal three: The issues of language and culture* (pp. 11–22). Washington, DC: Center for Applied Linguistics.

Scarcella, R. (1990). *Teaching language minority students in the multicultural classroom*. Englewood Cliffs, NJ: Prentice Hall.

Schumann, J. (1978). *The pidginization process: A model for second language acquisition*. Rowley, MA: Newbury House.

Snow, M. A., Met, M., & Genesee, F. (1989). A conceptual framework for the integration of language and content in second/foreign language instruction. *TESOL Quarterly, 23*, 201–217.

Struggling for standards. (1995, April 12). *Education Week*, p. 8.

Watson, D. L., Northcutt, L., & Rydell, L. (1989). Teaching bilingual students successfully. *Educational Leadership, 46*, 59–61.

Webster's ninth new collegiate dictionary. (1988). Springfield, MA: Merriam-Webster.

Zehler, A. M. (1994). *Working with English language learners: Strategies for elementary and middle school teachers* (Program Information Guide No. 19). Washington, DC: National Clearinghouse for Bilingual Education.

References

ACCESS ERIC. (1995). *All about ERIC*. Washington, DC: U.S. Department of Education, Office of Educational Research and Improvement, National Library of Education, Educational Resources Information Center. Retrieved July 19, 1999, from the World Wide Web: http://www.accesseric.org/resources/allabout/.

Adger, C. T. (1996, October). *Language minority students in school reform: The role of collaboration* (ERIC Digest EDO-FL-97-01). Washington, DC: ERIC Clearinghouse on Languages and Linguistics. (ERIC Document Reproduction Service No. ED 400 681)

Alberta Education. (1997). *English as a second language*. Edmonton, Canada: Author.

Ali, S. (1994). The reader-response approach: An alternative for teaching literature in a second language. *Journal of Reading, 37*, 288–296.

Allexsaht-Snider, M. (1991). Family literacy in a Spanish speaking context: Joint construction of meaning. *Quarterly Newsletter of Comparative Human Cognition, 13*(1), 15–21.

American Council on the Teaching of Foreign Languages. (1996). *Standards for foreign language learning*. Yonkers, NY: Author.

American Federation of Teachers. (1997, February 22). *AFT President Albert Shanker dies* [Press release]. Washington, DC: Author.

Au, K. H. (1980). Participation structures in a reading lesson with Hawaiian children: Analysis of a culturally-appropriate instructional event. *Anthropology and Education Quarterly, 11*, 91–115.

Au, K. H. (1993). *Literacy instruction in multicultural settings*. Fort Worth, TX: Harcourt Brace Jovanovich.

Bachman, L. F. (1990). *Fundamental considerations in language testing*. New York: Oxford University Press.

Bachman, L. F., & Palmer, A. S. (1996). *Language testing in practice*. New York: Oxford University Press.

Baghban, M. (1984). *Our daughter learns to read and write.* Newark, DE: International Reading Association.

Bailey, D. B., & Palsha, S. A. (1992). Qualities of the Stages of Concern Questionnaire and implications for educational innovations. *Journal of Educational Research, 85,* 226–232.

Baker, C. (1996). *Foundations of bilingual education and bilingualism* (2nd ed.). Clevedon, England: Multilingual Matters.

Barnes, D. R. (1976). *From communication to curriculum.* Middlesex, England: Penguin Books.

Barnes, D. R., Britton, J. N., & Torbe, M. (1969). *Language, the learner and the school.* Middlesex, England: Penguin Books.

Barnwell, D. P. (1996). *A history of foreign language testing in the United States.* Tempe, AZ: Bilingual Press.

Beebe, R. M., & Leonard, K. (1994, January). *Second language learning in a social context* (ERIC Digest EDO-FL-94-05). Washington, DC: ERIC Clearinghouse on Languages and Linguistics. (ERIC Document Reproduction Service No. ED 367 143)

Bellugi, U., & Brown, R. (Eds.). (1964). *The acquisition of language.* Lafayette, IN: Society for Research in Child Development.

Berkman, M. (1996). No problem. We can speak with the hands: Group work in a sheltered high school classroom. In National Writing Project (Ed.), *Cityscapes: Eight views from the urban classroom* (pp. 25–56). Berkeley, CA: National Writing Project.

Berko-Gleason, J. (Ed.). (1989). *The development of language.* Columbus, OH: Merrill.

Berman, P., Chambers, J., Gandara, P., McLaughlin, B., Minicucci, C., Nelson, B., Olsen, L., & Parrish, T. (1992). *Meeting the challenge of language diversity.* Berkeley, CA: B&W Associates.

Bernhardt, E. (1992). Life in immersion classrooms. Clevedon, England: Multilingual Matters.

Bertrand, J. E. (1991). Student assessment and evaluation. In B. Harp (Ed.), *Assessment and evaluation in whole language programs* (pp. 17–33). Norwood, MA: Christopher-Gordon.

Bialystok, E. (1987). Influences of bilingualism on metalinguistic development. *Second Language Research, 3,* 154–166.

Bialystok, E. (Ed.). (1991). *Language processing in bilingual children.* Cambridge: Cambridge University Press.

Bialystok, E., & Hakuta, K. (1994). *In other words: The science and psychology of second language acquisition.* New York: Basic Books.

Blake, B. E. (1992). Talk in non-native and native English speakers' peer writing conferences: What's the difference? *Language Arts, 69,* 604–610.

Boswood, T. (Ed.). (1997). *New ways of using computers in language teaching.* Alexandria, VA: TESOL.

Bradley, A. (1996, September 18). Teaching focus called the key in reform push. *Education Week.* Retrieved July 15, 1999, from the World Wide Web: http://www.edweek.org/ew/vol-16/03teach.h16.

Brinton, D. M., & Master, P. (Eds.). (1997). *New ways in content-based instruction.* Alexandria, VA: TESOL.

Britton, J. N. (1973). *Language and learning.* Coral Gables, FL: University of Miami Press.

Brown, A. (1995). The effect of rater variables in the development of an occupation-specific language performance test. *Language Testing, 12,* 1–15.

Brown, J. D. (Ed.). (1998). *New ways of classroom assessment.* Alexandria, VA: TESOL.

Brown, J. D., & Hudson, T. (1998). The alternatives in language assessment. *TESOL Quarterly, 32,* 653–675.

Brown, R. (1973). *A first language: The early stages.* Cambridge, MA: Harvard University Press.

Bruner, J. S. (1983). *Child's talk: Learning to use language.* New York: Norton.

Bullock, A. (Ed.). (1975). *A language for life: Report of the committee of inquiry appointed by the secretary of state for education and science.* London: Her Majesty's Stationery Office.

Bullough, R. V., Jr., & Gitlin, A. (1995). *Becoming a student of teaching.* New York: Garland Press.

Butler, F. A., & Stevens, R. (1997, October). *Accommodation strategies for English language learners on large-scale assessments: Student characteristics and other considerations* (CSE Technical Report No. 448). Los Angeles: University of California, Center for Research and Evaluation, Standards, and Student Testing.

California State Department of Education. (1984). *Studies on immersion education: A collection for U.S. educators.* Sacramento, CA: Author.

California State Department of Education. (1987). *Home language survey (English version).* Sacramento, CA: Author.

California State Department of Education, Educational Demographics Unit. (1998). *Language census.* Sacramento, CA: Author.

Calkins, L. M. (1983). *Lessons from a child: On the teaching and learning of writing.* Exeter, NH: Heinemann.

Calkins, L. M. (1992). *Living between the lines.* Exeter, NH: Heinemann.

Calkins, L. M. (1994). *The art of teaching writing* (2nd ed.). Portsmouth, NH: Heinemann.

Canale, M., & Swain, M. (1980). Theoretical bases of communicative approaches to second language teaching and testing. *Applied Linguistics, 1,* 1–47.

Cancino, H., Rosansky, E. J., & Schumann, J. (1975). The acquisition of the English auxiliary by native Spanish speakers. *TESOL Quarterly, 9,* 421–430.

Carger, C. (1993). Louie comes to life: Pretend reading with second language emergent readers. *Language Arts, 70,* 542–547.

Carlson, L. M. (Ed.). (1994). *Cool salsa: Bilingual poems on growing up Latino in the United States.* New York: Fawcett Juniper Press.

Carrell, P. L. (1981). Culture-specific schemata in L2 comprehension. In R. A. Orem & J. F. Haskell (Eds.), *Selected papers from the Ninth Illinois TESOL/BE Annual Convention and the First Midwest TESOL Conference* (pp. 123–132). Chicago: Illinois TESOL/BE.

Carrell, P. L., & Eisterhold, J. C. (1983). Schema theory and ESL reading pedagogy. *TESOL Quarterly, 17,* 553–573.

Cazden, C. B. (1972). *Child language and education.* New York: Holt, Rinehart, & Winston.

Cazden, C. B. (1988). *Classroom discourse: The language of teaching and learning.* Portsmouth, NH: Heinemann.

Cazden, C. B. (1994). Vygotsky and ESL literacy teaching. *TESOL Quarterly, 28,* 172–176.

Cazden, C. B., John, V., & Hymes, D. (Eds.). (1972). *Functions of language in the classroom.* New York: Teachers College Press.

Center for Applied Linguistics. (n.d.). *ESL standards implementation database.* Retrieved July 20, 1999, from the World Wide Web: http://www2.cal.org /eslstds/.

Center for Resource Management. (1997). *Curriculum planner.* Unpublished handout. (Available from Center for Resource Management, 2 Highland Road, South Hampton, NH 03827)

Chamot, A. U., & O'Malley, J. M. (1986). *A cognitive academic language learning approach: An ESL content-based curriculum.* Washington, DC: National Clearinghouse for Bilingual Education.

Chamot, A. U., & O'Malley, J. M. (1987). The cognitive academic language learning approach: A bridge to the mainstream. *TESOL Quarterly, 21,* 227–249.

Chomsky, C. (1971). Write first, read later. *Childhood Education, 47,* 296–301.

Chomsky, N. (1957). *Syntactic structures.* The Hague: Mouton de Gruyter.

Chomsky, N. (1965). *Aspects of the theory of syntax.* Cambridge, MA: MIT Press.

Christian, D. (1996). Two-way immersion education: Students learning through two languages. *The Modern Language Journal, 80,* 66–76.

Christian, D., Montone, C., Lindholm, K., & Carranza, I. (1997). *Profiles in two-way immersion education.* McHenry, IL: Center for Applied Linguistics/Delta Systems.

Clark, E. V. (1973). What's in a word? On the child's acquisition of semantics in his first language. In T. Moore (Ed.), *Cognitive development and the acquisition of language* (pp. 65–109). New York: Academic Press.

Clark, H. H. (1970). The primitive nature of children's relational concepts. In J. Hayes (Ed.), *Cognition and the development of language* (pp. 269–278). New York: Wiley.

Clark, H. H., & Clark, E. V. (1977). *Psychology and language: An introduction to psycholinguistics.* New York: Harcourt Brace Jovanovich.

Clay, M. M. (1975). *What did I write?* Auckland, New Zealand: Heinemann.

Cloud, N., Genesee, F., & Hamayan, E. (in press). *Enriched basic education.* Boston: Heinle & Heinle.

Collier, V. P. (1995). Acquiring a second language for school. *Directions in Language and Education, 1*(4), 1–12.

Corder, P. (1967). The significance of learners' errors. *International Review of Applied Linguistics, 4,* 161–169.

Crandall, J. A. (1994, January). *Content-centered language learning* (ERIC Digest EDO-FL-94-06). Washington, DC: ERIC Clearinghouse on Languages and Linguistics. (ERIC Document Reproduction Service No. ED 367 142)

Crawford, J. (1997). *Best evidence: Research evidence of the Bilingual Education Act.* Washington, DC: National Clearinghouse on Bilingual Education.

Cummins, J. (1976). The influence of bilingualism on cognitive growth: A synthesis of research findings and explanatory hypotheses. *Working Papers on Bilingualism, 9,* 1–43.

Cummins, J. (1992). Language proficiency, bilingualism, and academic achievement. In P. A. Richard-Amato & M. A. Snow (Eds.), *The multicultural classroom: Readings for content-area teachers* (pp. 16–26). White Plains, NY: Addison-Wesley.

Darling-Hammond, L. (1997, November). *Reforming pre-service education.* Paper presented at the National Commission on Teaching and America's Future/Consortium for Policy Research in Education conference, Washington, DC.

Delgado-Gaitán, C., & Trueba, H. T. (1991). *Crossing cultural borders: Education for immigrant families in America.* London: Falmer Press.

Delpit, L. D. (1995). *Other people's children: Cultural conflict in the classroom.* New York: Norton.

Díaz-Rico, L. T., & Weed, K. Z. (1995). *The crosscultural, language and academic development handbook.* Needham Heights, MA: Allyn & Bacon.

Doake, D. (1985). Reading-like behavior: Its role in learning to read. In A. Jaggar & M. T. Smith-Burke (Eds.), *Observing the language learner* (pp. 82–98). Newark, DE: International Reading Association.

Donly, B., Henderson, A., & Strang, W. (1995). *Summary of bilingual education state educational agency program survey of states' LEP persons and available educational services 1993–94.* Arlington, VA: Development Associates.

Dulay, H. C., & Burt, M. K. (1973). Should we teach children syntax? *Language Learning, 23,* 245–258.

Dulay, H. C., & Burt, M. K. (1974). Natural sequences in child second language acquisition, *Language Learning, 24,* 37–54.

Dyson, A. H. (1989). *Multiple worlds of child writers: Friends learning to write.* New York: Teachers College Press.

Dyson, A. H. (1993). *The social worlds of children learning to write in an urban primary school.* New York: Teachers College Press.

Edelsky, C. (1982). Writing in a bilingual program: The relation of L1 and L2 texts. *TESOL Quarterly, 16,* 211–228.

Edelsky, C. (1986). *Había una vez: Writing in a bilingual program.* Norwood, NJ: Ablex.

Edelsky, C. (1994). Education for democracy. *Language Arts, 71,* 252–257.

Edelsky, C. (1996). *With literacy and justice for all* (2nd ed). Philadelphia: Falmer Press.

Edelsky, C. (Ed.). (in press). *Making justice their project: Teachers working toward critical whole language practice.* Urbana, IL: National Council of Teachers of English.

Edelsky, C., & Hudelson, S. (1980). Second language acquisition of a marked language. *National Association for Bilingual Education Journal, 5,* 1–15.

Education Week. (1995, April 12). *Struggling for standards.* Washington, DC: Author. (Available from Education Week, Suite 100, 6935 Arlington Rd., Bethesda, MD 20814-5233; telephone 800-346-1834, 301-280-3100; http://www.edweek.org/)

Ellis, R. (1984). *Understanding second language acquisition.* Oxford: Oxford University Press.

Ellis, R. (1997). *Second language acquisition.* Oxford: Oxford University Press.

Enright, D. S. (1986). Use everything you have to teach English: Providing useful input to second language learners. In P. Rigg & D. S. Enright (Eds.), *Children and ESL: Integrating perspectives* (pp. 113–162). Washington, DC: TESOL.

Enright, D. S., & McCloskey, M. (1988). *Integrating English: Developing English language and literacy in the multilingual classroom.* Reading, MA: Addison-Wesley.

Faltis, C. J., & Hudelson, S. J. (1998). *Bilingual education in elementary and secondary school communities: Toward understanding and caring.* Needham Heights, MA: Allyn & Bacon.

Family Research Council. (1999). *Out of their own mouths: Selected quotations on the significance of Goals 2000.* Retrieved August 14, 1999, from the World Wide Web: http://www.frc.org/infocus/if95d2ed.html.

Fantini, A. E. (Ed.). (1997). *New ways in teaching culture.* Alexandria, VA: TESOL.

Farr, B. P., & Trumbull, E. (1997). *Assessment alternatives for diverse classrooms.* Norwood, MA: Christopher-Gordon.

Fassler, R. (1998). "Let's do it again!" Peer collaboration in an ESL kindergarten. *Language Arts, 75,* 202–210.

Ferreiro, E., Pontecorvo, C., Moreira, N. R., & Hidalgo, I. G. (1996). *Caperucita roja aprende a escribir: Estudios psicolinguísticos comparativos en tres idiomas* [Little Red Riding Hood learns to write: Comparative psycholinguistic studies in three languages]. Barcelona, Spain: Gedisa Editorial.

Ferreiro, E., & Teberosky, A. (1982). *Literacy before schooling*. Portsmouth, NH: Heinemann.

Fishman, J. A. (1964). Language maintenance and language shift as a field of inquiry. *Linguistics, 9*, 32–70.

Fishman, J. A. (1972). *The sociology of language*. Rowley, MA: Newbury House.

Fitzgerald, N. B. (1995). *ESL instruction in adult education: Findings from a national evaluation*. Washington, DC: National Clearinghouse for ESL Literacy Education. (ERIC Document Reproduction Service No. ED 385 171)

Fleischman, H. L., Arterburn, S., & Wiens, E. M. (1995). *State certification requirements for teachers of limited-English-proficient students*. Arlington, VA: Development Associates.

Fleischman, H. L., & Hopstock, P. J. (1993). *Descriptive study of services to limited English proficient students*. Arlington, VA: Development Associates.

Florida Department of Education, Division of Public Schools and Community Education, Bureau of School Reform, Improvement and Accountability, Office of Multicultural Student Language Education. (1999). *Language arts through ESOL: A guide for Florida teachers and administrators*. Tallahassee, FL: Author.

Fosnot, C. T. (1993). Preface. In J. G. Brooks & M. G. Brooks, *The case for constructivist classrooms* (pp. vii–viii). Alexandria, VA: Association for Supervision and Curriculum Development.

Freeman, D., with Cornwell, S. (Eds.). (1993). *New ways in teacher education*. Alexandria, VA: TESOL.

Freeman, D. (1998). *Doing teacher research: From inquiry to understanding*. Boston: Heinle & Heinle.

Freeman, Y., & Freeman, D. (1994). Whole language learning and teaching for second language learners. In C. Weaver (Ed.), *Reading process and practice: From socio-psycholinguistics to whole language* (2nd ed., pp. 558–628). Portsmouth, NH: Heinemann.

Freeman, Y., & Freeman, D. (1998). *Teaching reading and writing in Spanish in the bilingual classroom*. Portsmouth, NH: Heinemann.

Freire, P. (1970). *Pedagogy of the oppressed* (M. B. Ramos, Trans.). New York: Herder & Herder.

Freire, P., & Macedo, D. (1987). *Literacy: Reading the word and the world*. South Hadley, MA: Bergin & Garvey.

Fries, C. C. (1952). *The structure of English*. New York: Harcourt Brace Jovanovich.

Fries, C. C. (1964). *Linguistic study*. New York: Holt, Rinehart, & Winston.

Fu, D. (1995). *"My trouble is my English": Asian students and the American dream*. Portsmouth, NH: Boynton/Cook.

Fu, D., & Townsend, J. (1998). A Chinese boy's joyful initiation into American literacy. *Language Arts, 75*, 193–201.

Galloway, A. (1993, June). *Communicative language teaching: An introduction and sample activities* (ERIC Digest EDO-FL-93-05). Washington, DC: ERIC Clearinghouse on Languages and Linguistics. (ERIC Document Reproduction Service No. ED 357 642)

García, G. E., & Pearson, P. D. (1993). Assessment and diversity. In L. Darling-Hammond (Ed.), *Review of research in education* (Vol. 20, pp. 337–391). Washington, DC: American Educational Research Association.

Gardner, H. (1991). Assessment in context: The alternative to standardized testing. In B. R. Gifford & M. C. O'Connor (Eds.), *Changing assessments: Alternative views of aptitude, achievement and instruction* (pp. 239–252). Boston: Kluwer.

Gardner, R. C. (1979). Social psychology aspects of second language acquisition. In H. Giles & R. St. Clair (Eds.), *Language and social psychology* (pp. 193–219). Oxford: Blackwell.

Gardner, R. C., & Lambert, W. E. (1972). *Attitudes and motivation in second language learning.* Rowley, MA: Newbury House.

Gass, S. M. (1988). Integrating research areas: A framework for second language studies. *Applied Linguistics, 9,* 198–217.

Gee, J. P. (1989). Language, discourse, and linguistics: Introduction. *Journal of Education, 171,* 5–18.

Gee, J. P. (1992). *The social mind: Language, ideology and social practice.* New York: Bergin & Garvey.

Gee, R. (1996). Reading/writing workshops for the ESL classroom. *TESOL Journal, 5*(3), 4–10.

Genesee, F. (1976). The role of intelligence in second language learning. *Language Learning, 26,* 267–280.

Genesee, F. (1978). Second language learning and attitudes. *Working Papers on Bilingualism, 16,* 19–42.

Genesee, F. (1987). *Learning through two languages: Studies in immersion and bilingual education.* New York: Newbury House.

Genesee, F. (1994a). *Integrating language and content: Lessons from immersion.* Santa Cruz, CA: National Center for Research on Cultural Diversity and Second Language Learning.

Genesee, F. (1994b, October/November). President's message: Assessment alternatives. *TESOL Matters,* p. 3.

Genesee, F. (Ed.). (1999). *Program alternatives for linguistically diverse students.* Santa Cruz, CA: Center for Research on Education, Diversity & Excellence.

Genesee, F., & Upshur, J. A. (1996). *Classroom-based evaluation in second language education.* New York: Cambridge University Press.

Genishi, C., & Dyson, A. H. (1984). *Language assessment in the early years.* Norwood, NJ: Ablex.

Giles, H., & Byrne, J. L. (1982). An intergroup approach to second language acquisition. *Journal of Multilingual and Multicultural Development, 3,* 17–40.

Goals 2000: Educate America Act. (1994). Pub. L. No. 103-227.

Goals panel expresses concern for status of U.S. education. (1993, January). *Numbers and Needs, 3*(2), 2.

Gollnick, D. M., & Chinn, P. C. (1997). *Multicultural education in a pluralistic society* (5th ed.). Englewood Cliffs, NJ: Prentice Hall.

Gómez, E. L., Montiel, V., & Rosenberg, M. (1998, June/July). Montgomery County, Maryland, revises its ESOL curriculum using the *ESL Standards. TESOL Matters*, p. 23.

González, N. (1995). The funds of knowledge for teaching project. *Practicing Anthropology, 17,* 2–6.

González, N., Moll, L., Floyd-Tenery, M., Rivera, A., Rendon, P., González, R., & Amanti, C. (1993). *Teacher research on funds of knowledge: Learning from households.* Santa Cruz, CA: National Center for Research on Cultural Diversity and Second Language Learning.

Goodman, K. S. (1967). Reading: A psycholinguistic guessing game. *Journal of the Reading Specialist, 4,* 126–135.

Goodman, K. S. (1996). *On reading: A commonsense look at the nature of science and the science of reading.* Portsmouth, NH: Heinemann.

Goodman, K. S., & Goodman, Y. M. (1978). *Reading of American children whose language is a stable rural dialect of English or a language other than English* (NIE-C-00-3-0087). Washington, DC: U.S. Department of Health, Education and Welfare.

Goodman, Y. M. (Ed.). (1991). *How children construct literacy: Piagetian perspectives.* Newark, DE: International Reading Association.

Gottlieb, M. (1995). Nurturing student learning through portfolios. *TESOL Journal, 5*(1), 12–14.

Gottlieb, M. (1997). A peek into portfolio practices. In A. Huhta, V. Kohonen, L. Kurki-Suonio, & S. Luoma (Eds.), *Current developments and alternatives in language assessment: Proceedings of LTRC 96* (pp. 23–36). Jyväskylä, Finland: University of Jyväskylä.

Gottlieb, M. (1999). *The language proficiency handbook: A practitioner's guide to instructional assessment.* Springfield: Illinois State Board of Education.

Gould, S. J. (1981). *The mismeasure of man.* New York: Norton.

Graves, D. H. (1983). *Writing: Teachers and children at work.* Exeter, NH: Heinemann.

Grosjean, F. (1982). *Life with two languages: An introduction to bilingualism.* Cambridge, MA: Harvard University Press.

Guskey, T. R. (Ed.). (1994). *High stakes performance assessment: Perspectives on Kentucky's educational reform.* Thousand Oaks, CA: Corwin.

Hakuta, K. (1975). Learning to speak a second language: What exactly does the child learn? In D. P. Dato (Ed.), *Georgetown University Round Table on Languages and Linguistics: Developmental psycholinguistics: Theory and applications* (pp. 110–134). Washington, DC: Georgetown University Press.

Hakuta, K. (1986). *Mirror of language: The debate on bilingualism.* New York: Basic Books.

Hakuta, K., & Cancino, H. (1977). Trends in second language acquisition research. *Harvard Educational Review, 47,* 294–316.

Hall, G. E., & Loucks, S. (1978). Teacher concerns as a basis for facilitating and personalizing staff development. *Teachers College Record, 80*(1), 36–53.

Halliday, M. A. K. (1973). *Explorations in the functions of language.* London: Edward Arnold.

Halliday, M. A. K. (1977). *Learning how to mean: Explorations in the development of language.* New York: Elsevier.

Hancock, C. R. (1994, July). *Alternative assessment and second language study: What and why?* (ERIC Digest). College Park, MD: ERIC Clearinghouse on Assessment and Evaluation. (ERIC Document Reproduction Service No. ED 376 695)

Hanson-Smith, E. (1997). *Technology in the classroom: Practice and promise in the 21st century* (TESOL Professional Papers 2). Alexandria, VA: TESOL.

Harste, J. C., Woodward, V. A., & Burke, C. L. (1984). *Language stories and literacy lessons.* Portsmouth, NH: Heinemann.

Hartmann, P., Watson, J., & Brickman, R. G. (1997).*Course of study: English as a second language handbook and guidelines (draft).* Lyndhurst, OH: South Euclid–Lyndhurst City School District.

Hatch, E. M. (Ed.). (1978). *Second language acquisition: A book of readings.* Rowley, MA: Newbury House.

Hatch, E. M., Peck, S., & Wagner-Gough, J. (1979). A look at process in child second language acquisition. In E. Ochs & B. Schieffelin (Eds.), *Developmental pragmatics* (pp. 269–280). New York: Academic Press.

Heath, S. B. (1983). *Ways with words: Language, life, and work in communities and classrooms.* Cambridge: Cambridge University Press.

Henderson, A., Abbott, C., & Strang, W. (1993). *Summary of the bilingual education state educational agency program survey of states' limited English proficient persons and available educational services 1991–1992.* Arlington, VA: Development Associates.

Herman, J. L., Aschbacher, P. R., & Winters, L. (1992). *A practical guide to alternative assessment.* Alexandria, VA: Association for Supervision and Curriculum Development.

Hernandez-Chavez, E. (1984). The inadequacy of English immersion education as an educational approach for language minority students in the United States. In *Studies on immersion education: A collection for U.S. educators* (pp. 144–183). Sacramento: California State Department of Education.

Huang, J., & Hatch, E. M. (1978). A Chinese child's acquisition of English. In E. M. Hatch (Ed.), *Second language acquisition: A book of readings* (pp. 118–131). Rowley, MA: Newbury House.

Hudelson, S. (Ed.). (1981). *Learning to read in different languages.* Washington, DC: Center for Applied Linguistics.

Hudelson, S. (1981/1982). An introductory examination of children's invented spelling in Spanish. *National Association for Bilingual Education Journal, 6,* 53–68.

Hudelson, S. (1983). Beto at the sugar table: Codeswitching in a bilingual classroom. In T. Escobedo (Ed.), *Early childhood education: A bilingual perspective* (pp. 31–49). New York: Academic Press.

Hudelson, S. (1984). Kan yu ret an rayt en ingles: Children become literate in English as a second language. *TESOL Quarterly, 18,* 221–238.

Hudelson, S. (1987). The role of native language literacy in the education of language minority children. *Language Arts, 64,* 827–841.

Hudelson, S. (1989a). A tale of two children: Individual differences in second language writing. In D. M. Johnson & D. H. Roen (Eds.), *Richness in writing: Empowering ESL students* (pp. 84–99). New York: Longman.

Hudelson, S. (1989b). *Write on: Children writing in ESL.* Englewood Cliffs, NJ: Prentice Hall.

Hudelson, S. (1994). Literacy development for second language children. In F. Genesee (Ed.), *Educating second language children: The whole child, the whole curriculum, the whole community* (pp. 129–158). New York: Cambridge University Press.

Hudelson, S., & Serna, I. A. (1994). Beginning literacy in English in a whole language bilingual program. In A. S. Flurkey & R. J. Meyer (Eds.), *Under the whole language umbrella: Many cultures, many voices* (pp. 278–294). Urbana, IL: National Council of Teachers of English.

Hymes, D. H. (1974). *Foundations in sociolinguistics: An ethnographic approach.* Philadelphia: University of Pennsylvania Press.

Improving America's Schools Act of 1994. Pub. L. No. 103-382.

Individuals With Disabilities Education Act of 1997. Pub. L. No. 105-17.

Jacobson, R., & Faltis, C. (1990). *Language distribution issues in bilingual schooling.* Clevedon, England: Multilingual Matters.

Janzen, J. (1996). Teaching strategic reading. *TESOL Journal, 6*(1), 6–9.

Jiménez, R. T. (1997). The strategic reading abilities and potential of five low-literacy Latina/o readers in middle school. *Reading Research Quarterly, 32,* 224–243.

Johnson, D. M., & Chen, L. (1992). Researchers, teachers and inquiry. In D. M. Johnson (Ed.), *Approaches to research in second language learning* (pp. 212–231). New York: Longman.

Johnson, P. (1981). Effects on reading comprehension of language complexity and cultural background of a text. *TESOL Quarterly, 15,* 169–181.

Kaufman, D., & Brooks, J. G. (1996). Interdisciplinary collaboration in teacher education: A constructivist approach. *TESOL Quarterly, 30,* 231–251.

Klima, E., & Bellugi-Klima, U. (1966). Syntactic regularities in the speech of children. In A. Bar-Adon & W. Leopold (Eds.), *Child language: A book of readings* (pp. 152–178). Englewood Cliffs, NJ: Prentice Hall.

Krashen, S. D. (1981). *Second language acquisition and second language learning.* Oxford: Pergamon Press.

Krashen, S. D. (1982). *Principles and practice in second language acquisition.* New York: Pergamon Press.

Krashen, S. D. (1985). *The input hypothesis: Issues and implications.* London: Longman.

Krashen, S. (1993). *The power of reading: Insights from the research.* Englewood, CO: Libraries Unlimited.

Krashen, S. D., & Terrell, T. D. (1983). *The natural approach: Language acquisition in the classroom.* Oxford: Pergamon Press.

Kucer, S., & Silva, C. (1995). Guiding students "through" the literacy process. *Language Arts, 72,* 20–29.

Labov, W. (1972a). *Language in the inner city: Studies in the Black English vernacular.* Philadelphia: University of Pennsylvania Press.

Labov, W. (1972b). *Sociolinguistic patterns.* Philadelphia: University of Pennsylvania Press.

Lado, R. (1957). *Linguistics across cultures: Applied linguistics for language teachers.* Ann Arbor: University of Michigan Press.

Lado, R. (1964). *Language teaching: A scientific approach.* New York: McGraw-Hill.

Ladson-Billings, G. (1994). *The dreamkeepers: Successful teachers of African American children.* San Francisco: Jossey-Bass.

Lambert, W. E. (1984). An overview of issues in immersion education. In *Studies on immersion education: A collection for U.S. educators* (pp. 8–30). Sacramento: California State Department of Education.

Lambert, W. E., & Tucker, G. R. (1972). *The bilingual education of children: The St. Lambert experiment.* Rowley, MA: Newbury House.

Langer, G. M., & Colton, A. B. (1994). Reflective decision making: The cornerstone of school reform. *Journal of Staff Development, 15,* 2–7.

Lemke, J. L. (1990). *Talking science: Language, learning and values.* New York: Ablex.

Lenneberg, E. (1967). *Biological foundations of language.* New York: Wiley.

Leone, B. (1997, August/September). Paterson develops a new K–8 ESL curriculum using the *ESL Standards. TESOL Matters,* p. 6.

Lindfors, J. W. (1987). *Children's language and learning* (2nd ed.). Englewood Cliffs, NJ: Prentice Hall.

Long, M. H. (1981). Input, interaction, and second language acquisition. In H. Winitz (Ed.), *Native language and foreign language acquisition: Annals of the New York Academy of Science, 379,* 259–278.

Loucks, S., & Pratt, H. (1979). A concerns-based approach to curriculum change. *Educational Leadership, 37,* 212–215.

Macdonald, M. B. (1997, June). *Unveiling standards for students and standards for teachers.* Paper presented at the Second Annual Title VII Bilingual/ESL Summer Institute, Bronx, NY.

Maryland State Department of Education. (1996). *Maryland high school core learning goals skills for success.* Baltimore: Author.

Marzano, R. J., & Kendall, J. S. (1996). *A comprehensive guide to designing standards-based districts, schools, and classrooms.* Aurora, CO: Mid-Continent Regional Educational Laboratory.

McGee, L., & Purcell-Gates, V. (1997). Conversations: So what's going on in research in emergent literacy? *Reading Research Quarterly, 32,* 310–320.

McLaughlin, B. (1978). The monitor model: Some methodological considerations. *Language Learning, 28,* 309–332.

McLaughlin, B. (1984). *Second language acquisition in childhood: Vol. 1. Preschool children* (2nd ed.). Hillsdale, NJ: Erlbaum.

McLaughlin, B. (1992, December). *Myths and misconceptions about second language learning: What every teacher needs to unlearn* (ERIC Digest EDO-FL-91-10). College Park, MD: ERIC Clearinghouse on Assessment and Evaluation. (ERIC Document Reproduction Service No. ED 352 806)

McLaughlin, B., Rossman, T., & McLeod, B. (1983). Second language learning: An information processing perspective. *Language Learning, 3,* 135–158.

McNeill, D. (1970). *The acquisition of language.* New York: Harper & Row.

Michaels, S. (1981). "Sharing time": Children's narrative styles and differential access to literacy. *Language in Society, 10,* 423–432.

Moll, L. C. (Ed.). (1995). *Vygotsky and education: Instructional implications and applications of sociohistorical psychology* (5th ed.). New York: Cambridge University Press.

Montgomery County Public Schools, Office of Instruction and Program Development, Department of Academic Programs, Division of ESOL/Bilingual Programs. (1999). *Middle school ESOL/bilingual curriculum. Intermediate level instructional guide.* Rockville, MD: Author.

Montiel, Y. (1992). *Spanish-speaking children's emergent literacy during first and second grades: Three case studies.* Unpublished doctoral dissertation, Arizona State University, Tempe.

Moss, M., & Puma, M. (1995). *Prospects: The congressionally mandated study of educational growth and opportunity.* Washington, DC: U.S. Department of Education.

National Association for the Education of Young Children. (1996). Responding to linguistic and cultural diversity: Recommendations for effective early childhood education. *Young Children, 51,* 4–12. Retrieved July 19, 1999, from the World Wide Web: http://www.naeyc.org/about/position/psdiv98.htm.

National Board for Professional Teaching Standards. (1998). *English as a new language standards for national board certification.* Southfield, MI: Author.

National Clearinghouse for ESL Literacy Education. (1996). The waiting game. *NCLE Notes, 6*(1), 1–2.

National Commission on Excellence in Education. (1983). *A nation at risk:*

The imperative for educational reform. Washington, DC: U.S. Government Printing Office.

National Commission on Teaching and America's Future. (1996). *What matters most: Teaching for America's future.* Kutztown, PA: Kutztown Publishing. Retrieved July 19, 1999, from the World Wide Web: http://www.tc.columbia.edu/~teachcomm/what.htm.

National Commission on Teaching and America's Future. (1997). *Doing what matters most: Investing in quality teaching.* New York: Author. Retrieved July 20, 1999, from the World Wide Web: http://www.tc.columbia.edu/~teachcomm/dwhat.htm.

National Council for Accreditation of Teacher Education. (1995). *Standards, procedures and policies for the accreditation of professional education units.* Washington, DC: Author.

National Council of Teachers of English/International Reading Association. (1996). *Standards for the English language arts.* Urbana, IL: National Council of Teachers of English.

National Council of Teachers of Mathematics. (1989). *Curriculum and evaluation standards for school mathematics.* Reston, VA: Author.

National Education Goals Panel. (1991). *The national education goals report: Building a nation of learners.* Washington, DC: U.S. Government Printing Office.

National Languages and Literacy Institute of Australia. (1993). *ESL development: Language and literacy in schools: Vol. 1. Teachers' volume.* Canberra, Australia: Author.

National Research Council. (1996). *National science education standards.* Washington, DC: National Academy Press.

National Study of School Evaluation. (1997). *Indicators of schools of quality: Vol. 1. Schoolwide indicators of quality.* Schaumburg, IL: Author.

Navarrete, C. J. (1990). Reaching out: Using portfolios to combine formal and informal assessments. *EAC-West News, 4*(1), 1, 8–9.

Navarrete, C. J., & Gustkee, C. (1996). *A guide to performance assessment for linguistically diverse students.* Albuquerque, NM: Evaluation Assistance Center—West.

New K–12 accreditation process features TESOL standards. (1998, February/March). *TESOL Matters,* p. 5.

Noffke, S. (1997). Professional, personal, and political dimensions of action research. In M. W. Apple (Ed.), *Review of Research in Education, 22,* 305–343.

North Carolina Department of Public Instruction. (1999). *Guide to the standard course of study for LEP students.* Raleigh, NC: Author.

Nunan, D. (1990). Action research in the language classroom. In J. C. Richards & D. Nunan (Eds.), *Second language teacher education* (pp. 62–81). New York: Cambridge University Press.

Nunan, D. (1992). *Research methods in language learning.* Cambridge: Cambridge University Press.

Ochs, E. (1988). *Culture and language development: Language acquisition and language socialization in a Samoan village.* Cambridge: Cambridge University Press.

Ochs, E., & Schieffelin, B. B. (1983). *Acquiring conversational competence.* London: Routledge & Kegan Paul.

Office of Language and Cultural Education. (1998). *English as a second language goals and standards pre-K through Grade 12: Field test.* Chicago: Chicago Public Schools.

Olsen, L. (1988). *Crossing the schoolhouse border: Immigrant students in the California Public Schools.* San Francisco: California Tomorrow.

Olson, J. F., & Goldstein, A. A. (1997, July). *The inclusion of students with disabilities and limited English proficient students in large-scale assessments: A summary of recent progress* (National Center for Educational Statistics Research and Development Report). Washington, DC: U.S. Department of Education, Office of Educational Research and Improvement.

O'Malley, J. M., & Chamot, A. U. (1990). *Learning strategies in second language acquisition.* Cambridge: Cambridge University Press.

O'Malley, J. M., & Valdez Pierce, L. (1996). *Authentic assessment for English language learners: Practical approaches for teachers.* New York: Addison-Wesley.

Ovando, C. J., & Collier, V. P. (1998). *Bilingual and ESL classrooms: Teaching in multicultural contexts* (2nd ed.). Boston: McGraw-Hill.

Paris, S. G., & Ayers, L. R. (1994). *Becoming reflective students and teachers with portfolios and authentic assessment.* Washington, DC: American Psychological Association.

Paterson Public Schools. (1997). *The ESL Pre-K–8 language and content curriculum: DRAFT.* Paterson, NJ: Author.

Pease-Alvarez, L., & Vásquez, O. A. (1994). Language socialization in ethnic minority communities. In F. Genesee (Ed.), *Educating second language children: The whole child, the whole curriculum, the whole community* (pp. 82–102). New York: Cambridge University Press.

Peck, S. (1978). Child-child discourse in second language acquisition. In E. M. Hatch (Ed.), *Second language acquisition: A book of readings* (pp. 383–400). Rowley, MA: Newbury House.

Penfield, W., & Roberts, L. (1959). *Speech and brain mechanisms.* New York: Atheneum Press.

Peterson, B. (1991). Teaching how to read the world and change it: Critical pedagogy in the intermediate grades. In C. Walsh (Ed.), *Literacy as praxis: Culture, language and pedagogy* (pp. 156–182). Norwood, NJ: Ablex.

Pevalin Associates Inc. (1991). *A revised analysis of the supply of bilingual and ESL teachers: An analysis of schools and staffing survey data.* Washington, DC: U.S. Department of Education.

Peyton, J. K. (1990). Profiles of individual student writers. In J. K. Peyton & L. Reed (Eds.), *Dialogue journal writing with nonnative English speakers: A handbook for teachers* (pp. 81–100). Alexandria, VA: TESOL.

Peyton, J. K., Jones, C., Vincent, A., & Greenblatt, L. (1994). Implementing writing workshop with ESL students: Visions and realities. *TESOL Quarterly, 28,* 469–488.

Peyton, J. K., & Staton, J. (Eds.). (1993). *Dialogue journals in the multilingual classroom: Building language fluency and writing skills through written interaction.* Norwood, NJ: Ablex.

Philips, S. U. (1983). *The invisible culture: Communication in classroom and community on the Warm Springs Indian Reservation.* New York: Longman.

Pinnell, G. (1975). Language in primary classrooms. *Theory Into Practice, 14,* 318–332.

Putnam Valley Central Schools. (1999a). *Developing educational standards.* Retrieved July 19, 1999, from the World Wide Web: http://putwest.boces.org/standards.html.

Putnam Valley Central Schools. (1999b). *Educational standards and curriculum frameworks for foreign language/ESL.* Retrieved July 19, 1999, from the World Wide Web: http://putwest.boces.org/StSu/Flang.html.

Ramírez, J. D. (1992). Executive summary. *Bilingual Research Journal, 16,* 1–62.

Ramírez, J. D., Yuen, S. D., Ramey, D. R., & Pasta, D. J. (1991). *Final report: Longitudinal study of structured English immersion strategy, early-exit and late-exit transitional bilingual education programs for language-minority children* (Vols. 1, 2). San Mateo, CA: Aguirre International.

Read, C. (1975). *Children's categorization of speech sounds in English.* Urbana, IL: National Council of Teachers of English.

Recruiting New Teachers. (1998). The bilingual ed debate heats up—as the need for qualified teachers continues to rise. *Future Teacher, 5*(2), 1–2.

Recruiting New Teachers. (n.d.). *Facts about the teaching profession.* Retrieved July 20, 1999, from the World Wide Web: http://www/rnt.org/mtfacts.html.

Richards, J. C. (Ed.). (1998). *Teaching in action: Case studies from second language classrooms.* Alexandria, VA: TESOL.

Richards, J. C., & Lockhart, C. (Eds.). (1994). *Reflective teaching in second language classrooms.* New York: Cambridge University Press.

Richards, J. C., & Nunan, D. (Eds.). (1990). *Second language teacher education.* New York: Cambridge University Press.

Rigg, P. (1986). Reading in ESL: Learning from kids. In P. Rigg & D. S. Enright (Eds.), *Children and ESL: Integrating perspectives* (pp. 55–92). Washington, DC: TESOL.

Riis, J. A. (1971). *How the other half lives: Studies among the tenements of New York.* Cambridge, MA: Harvard University Press. (Original work published 1890)

Rivera, C., & Vincent, C. (1998). High school graduation testing: Policies and practices in the assessment of English language learners. *Educational Assessment, 4,* 335–355.

Rosebery, A. S., Warren, B., & Conant, F. (1992). *Appropriating scientific discourse: Findings from language minority classrooms.* Santa Cruz, CA: National Center for Research on Cultural Diversity and Second Language Learning.

Rosen, H., & Rosen, C. (1973). *The language of primary school children.* London: Penguin Books.

Rosenblatt, L. M. (1983). *Literature as exploration.* New York: Modern Language Association. (Original work published 1938)

Samway, K. D. (1987). *The writing processes of non-native English speaking children in the elementary grades.* Unpublished doctoral dissertation, University of Rochester, New York.

Samway, K. D., & Taylor, D. (1993). Inviting children to make connections between reading and writing. *TESOL Journal, 2*(3), 7–11.

Samway, K. D., & Whang, G. (1995). *Literature study circles in a multicultural classroom.* York, ME: Stenhouse.

Schieffelin, B. B., & Cochran-Smith, M. (1984). Learning to read culturally: Literacy before schooling. In H. Goelman, A. Oberg, & F. Smith (Eds.), *Awakening to literacy* (pp. 3–23). Exeter, NH: Heinemann.

Schifini, A. (1994). Language, literacy, and content instruction: Strategies for teachers. In K. Spangenberg-Urbschat & R. Pritchard (Eds.), *Kids come in all languages: Reading instruction for ESL students* (pp. 158–179). Newark, DE: International Reading Association.

Schinke-Llano, L. & Rauff, R. (Eds.). (1996). *New ways in teaching young children.* Alexandria, VA: TESOL.

School District of Philadelphia, Office of Curriculum Support. (1997). *Academic content standards, benchmarks, and performance examples.* Philadelphia: Author.

Schumann, J. H. (1978). *The pidginization process: A model for second language acquisition.* Rowley, MA: Newbury House.

Seawell, R. P. M. (1985). *A micro-ethnographic study of a Spanish/English bilingual kindergarten in which literature and puppet play were used as a method of enhancing language growth.* Unpublished doctoral dissertation, University of Texas at Austin.

Serna, I., & Hudelson, S. (1993a). Becoming writers in Spanish and English. *Quarterly of the National Writing Project, 15,* 1–22.

Serna, I., & Hudelson, S. (1993b). Emergent Spanish literacy in a whole language bilingual program. In R. Donmoyer & R. Kos (Eds.), *At-risk students: Portraits, programs, and practices* (pp. 291–322). Albany: State University of New York Press.

Serna, I., & Hudelson, S. (1997). Special feature in chapter 7: Alicia's biliteracy development in first and second grade. In J. Christie, B. Enz, & C. Vukelich (Eds.), *Teaching language and literacy: Preschool through the elementary grades* (pp. 255–264). New York: Longman.

Shanker, A. (1996, November 20). *Statement by Albert Shanker, president, American Federation of Teachers, on the Third International Math and Science Study (TIMSS)* [Press release]. Washington, DC: American Federation of Teachers.

Short, D. J. (1993). *Integrating language and culture in middle school American history classes.* Santa Cruz, CA: National Center for Research on Cultural Diversity and Second Language Learning.

Short, D. J. (1997a, October/November). Local districts develop curricula with TESOL's *ESL Standards. TESOL Matters,* p. 19.

Short, D. J. (1997b). Reading and 'riting and . . . social studies: Research on integrated language and content in secondary classrooms. In M. A. Snow & D. M. Brinton (Eds.), *The content-based classroom: Perspectives on integrating language and content* (pp. 213–232). White Plains, NY: Longman.

Short, D. J., Gómez, E. L., Cloud, N., Katz, A., Gottlieb, M., Malone, M., with Hamayan, E., Hudelson, S., & Ramírez, J. (2000). *Training others to use the ESL standards: A professional development manual.* Alexandria, VA: TESOL.

Short, K., & Burke, C. (1996). Examining our beliefs and practices through inquiry. *Language Arts, 73,* 97–104.

Skinner, B. F. (1957). *Verbal behavior.* Englewood Cliffs. NJ: Prentice Hall.

Skutnabb-Kangas, T., & Toukomaa, P. (1976). *Teaching migrant children mother tongue and learning the language of the host country in the context of the sociocultural situation of the migrant family.* Tampere, Finland: Tukimuksia Research Reports.

Slobin, D. I. (1966). Comments on developmental psycholinguistics. In F. Smith & G. A. Miller (Eds.), *The genesis of language: A psycholinguistic approach* (pp. 129–148). Cambridge, MA: MIT Press.

Snow, C. (1994). Beginning from baby talk: Twenty years of research on input in interaction. In C. Gallaway & B. Richards (Eds.), *Input and interaction in language acquisition* (pp. 3–13). Cambridge: Cambridge University Press.

Snow, C., & Ferguson, C. (Eds.). (1977). *Talking to children: Language input and acquisition.* Cambridge: Cambridge University Press.

Snow, M. A., & Brinton, D. M. (Eds.). (1997). *The content-based classroom: Perspectives on integrating language and content.* White Plains, NY: Longman.

Snow, M. A., Met, M., & Genesee, F. (1989). A conceptual framework for the integration of language and content in second/foreign language instruction. *TESOL Quarterly, 23,* 201–217.

Solomon, J., & Rhodes, N. C. (1995). *Conceptualizing academic language.* Washington, DC: Center for Applied Linguistics; Santa Cruz, CA: National

Center for Research on Cultural Diversity and Second Language Learning.

Sperling, D. (1997). *The Internet guide for English language teachers*. Englewood Cliffs, NJ: Prentice Hall Regents.

Stocking, B., & García, E. (1998, August 17). An influx of Latinos. *San Jose Mercury News*, pp. 1A, 8A, 9A.

Swain, M. (1985). Communicative competence: Some roles of comprehensible input and comprehensible output in its development. In S. M. Gass & C. G. Madden (Eds.), *Input in second language acquisition* (pp. 235–253). Rowley, MA: Newbury House.

Swain, M., & Lapkin, S. (1982). *Evaluating bilingual education: A Canadian case study*. Clevedon, England: Multilingual Matters.

Taylor, D. (1983). *Family literacy: Young children learn to read and write*. Exeter, NH: Heinemann.

Taylor, D. (1990). Writing and reading literature in a second language. In N. Atwell (Ed.), *Workshop 2: Beyond the basal* (pp. 105–116). Portsmouth, NH: Heinemann.

Taylor, D. (Ed.). (1997). *Many families, many literacies*. Portsmouth, NH: Heinemann.

Taylor, D., & Dorsey-Gaines, C. (1988). *Growing up literate: Learning from inner-city families*. Portsmouth, NH: Heinemann.

Teale, W. H., & Sulzby, E. (1986). Emergent literacy as a perspective for examining how young children become readers and writers. In W. H. Teale & E. Sulzby (Eds.), *Emergent literacy: Writing and reading* (pp. vii–xxv). Norwood, NJ: Ablex.

Teale, W. H., & Sulzby, E. (1989). Emergent literacy: New perspectives on young children's reading and writing. In D. S. Strickland & L. M. Morrow (Eds.), *Emerging literacy: Young children learn to read and write* (pp. 1–15). Newark, DE: International Reading Association.

TESOL. (1993). *Access brochure*. Alexandria, VA: Author.

TESOL. (1996). *Promising futures: ESL standards for pre-K–12 students* (TESOL Professional Papers 1). Alexandria, VA: Author.

TESOL. (1997). *ESL standards for pre-K–12 students*. Alexandria, VA: Author.

TESOL. (1998). *Managing the assessment process: A framework for measuring student attainment of the ESL standards* (TESOL Professional Papers 5). Alexandria, VA: Author.

TESOL. (in press). *Scenarios for ESL standards-based assessment*. Alexandria, VA: Author.

TESOL. (n.d.). *TESOL resource packet*. Alexandria, VA: Author. (No longer available)

Tharp, R. G. (1997). *From at-risk to excellence: Research, theory, and principles for practice*. Santa Cruz, CA: Center for Research on Education, Diversity & Excellence.

Thomas, W., & Collier, V. P. (1995). *Language minority student achievement and program effectiveness.* Washington, DC: National Clearinghouse for Bilingual Education.

Tough, J. (1977). *Talking and learning.* London: Ward Lock Educational.

Tough, J. (1985). *Talk two: Children using English as a second language.* London: Onyx.

Trueba, H. T., Guthrie, G. P., & Au, K. H. (Eds.). (1981). *Culture and the bilingual classroom: Studies in classroom ethnography.* New York: Newbury House.

Two-way immersion portfolio assessment. (n.d.). Unpublished manuscript, Los Angeles Unified School District, Los Angeles County Office of Education, ABC Unified School District, and Santa Monica–Malibu Unified School District. (Available from Los Angeles County Office of Education, Division of Curriculum, Instruction, and Assessment)

Urzúa, C. (1987). "You stopped too soon": Second language children composing and revising. *TESOL Quarterly, 21,* 279–305.

U.S. Department of Education. (1978). *The student oral language observation matrix.* Washington, DC: Author.

Valdés, G. (1996). *Con respeto: Bridging the distances between culturally diverse families and schools: An ethnographic study.* New York: Teachers College Press.

Valdez Pierce, L., & O'Malley, J. M. (1992). *Performance and portfolio assessment for language minority students.* Washington, DC: National Clearinghouse for Bilingual Education.

Valencia, S. W. (1991). Portfolios: Panacea or Pandora's box? In F. L. Finch (Ed.), *Educational performance assessment* (pp. 33–46). Chicago: Riverside.

Vásquez, O. A. (1991). Reading the world in a multicultural setting: A Mexicano perspective. *Quarterly Newsletter of the Laboratory of Comparative Human Cognition, 13,* 13–15.

Vásquez, O. A., Pease-Alvarez, L., & Shannon, S. M. (1994). *Pushing boundaries: Literacy and culture in a Mexicano community.* Cambridge: Cambridge University Press.

Vygotsky, L. S. (1978). *Mind in society: The development of higher psychological processes* (M. Cole, V. John-Steiner, S. Scribner, & E. Souberman, Eds. & Trans.). Cambridge, MA: Harvard University Press. (Original work published 1955)

Wagner-Gough, J., & Hatch, E. M. (1975). The importance of input data in second language acquisition studies. *Language Learning, 25,* 297–308.

Walsh, C. E. (Ed.). (1996). *Education reform and social change: Multicultural voices, struggles, and visions.* Mahwah, NJ: Erlbaum.

Walton, P. (in press). *CREDE directory of teacher preparation programs with a focus on linguistic and cultural diversity.* Santa Cruz, CA: Center for Research on Education, Diversity & Excellence.

Wardhaugh, R. (1970). The "contrastive analysis" hypothesis. *TESOL Quarterly, 4,* 123–30.

Warschauer, M. (1995). *E-mail for English teaching: Bringing the Internet and computer learning networks into the language classroom.* Alexandria, VA: TESOL.

Weaver, C. (1994). *Reading process and practice: From socio-psycholinguistics to whole language* (2nd ed). Portsmouth, NH: Heinemann.

Wolf, D., Bixby, J., Glenn, J., III, & Gardner, H. (1991). To use their minds well: Investigating new forms of student assessment. In G. Grant (Ed.), *Review of research in education* (Vol. 17, pp. 31–74). Washington, DC: American Educational Research Association.

Wolfe, P. (1996). Literacy bargains: Toward critical literacy in a multilingual classroom. *TESOL Journal, 5*(4), 22–26.

Wong Fillmore, L. (1976). *The second time around: Cognitive and social strategies in second language acquisition.* Unpublished doctoral dissertation, Stanford University, Stanford, CA.

Wong Fillmore, L. (1979). Individual differences in second language acquisition. In C. J. Fillmore, D. Kempler, & W. S. Wang (Eds.), *Individual difference in language ability and language behavior* (pp. 271–289). New York: Academic Press.

Wong Fillmore, L. (1982). Instructional language as linguistic input: Second language learning in classrooms. In L. C. Wilkinson (Ed.), *Communicating in the classroom* (pp. 283–296). New York: Academic Press.

Wong Fillmore, L. (1989). Teachability and second language acquisition. In R. Schiefelbusch & M. Rice (Eds.), *The teachability of language* (pp. 311–332). Baltimore: Brookes.

Wong Fillmore, L. (1991). Second language learning in children: A model of learning in social context. In E. Bialystok (Ed.), *Language processing in bilingual children* (pp. 49–69). Cambridge: Cambridge University Press.

Wormuth, D. R., & Hughey, J. B. (1988). *The English composition profile.* College Station, TX: Writing Evaluation Systems.

Wrigley, H. P. (1993). *Adult ESL literacy findings from a national study.* Washington, DC: National Clearinghouse for ESL Literacy Education. (ERIC Document Reproduction Service No. ED 365 169)

Contributors

■ Editor

Marguerite Ann Snow is professor at California State University, Los Angeles where she teaches in the TESOL MA program. She is coauthor of *Content-Based Second Language Instruction* (Newbury House, 1989), and coeditor of *The Multicultural Classroom: Readings for Content-Area Teachers* (Longman, 1992) and *The Content-Based Classroom: Perspectives on Integrating Language and Content* (Longman, 1997). She directed Project LEAP (Learning English for Academic Purposes), a Fund for the Improvement of Postsecondary Education grant. She has published in *TESOL Quarterly*, *The Modern Language Journal*, and *Applied Linguistics*. She taught in Hong Kong on a Fulbright fellowship and has trained EFL teachers in Argentina, Brazil, the Czech Republic, Hungary, Italy, Japan, Latvia, Russia, Spain, Morocco, and Pakistan.

■ Authors

Nancy Cloud is on the faculty of the Feinstein School of Education and Human Development of Rhode Island College in the Department of Special Education. She coordinated the MS TESL and bilingual education teacher preparation programs at Hofstra University and worked as a staff developer at the Institute for Urban and Minority Education at Teachers College, Columbia University, and at the Illinois Resource Center. A former bilingual/ESL classroom teacher and program coordinator, she was a member of TESOL's ESL Standards and Assessment Project.

Bridget Fitzgerald Gersten is regional English teaching officer for the United States Information Agency for North Africa and the Mideast Gulf. She has worked as an ESL and EFL teacher trainer, materials developer, and instructor for 15 years. Her research interests include bilingualism, second language education, and second language writing development.

Emily Lynch Gómez, a researcher and teacher trainer at the Center for Applied Linguistics, has been involved in the development of national ESL standards and related companion documents. She has provided technical assistance to numerous districts and states in the development and design of standards-based ESL curricula. Having taught ESL and content-based courses at the middle and high school levels, including ESL language arts, ESL mathematics, and ESL social studies, she has extensive experience in language minority education. In addition to her secondary teaching experience, she has expertise in curriculum development, content-based language instruction, and professional development. She recently completed research on the use of portfolio assessment with English language learners.

Margo Gottlieb is director of assessment and evaluation at the Illinois Resource Center in Des Plaines. Having served as chair of TESOL's Elementary Education Interest Section in 1998, she is currently a member of the ESL Standards and Assessment Project, the Elementary and Secondary Education Act Reauthorization Task Force, and the *TESOL Journal* Editorial Advisory Board. Her latest publication is *Standards-Based Alternate Assessment for Limited English Proficient Students: A Guide for Wisconsin Educators* (Wisconsin Department of Public Instruction, in press).

Else V. Hamayan is director of the Illinois Resource Center in Des Plaines. At McGill University in Montreal, she conducted research on patterns of second language acquisition and individual learner characteristics that contribute to the attainment of proficiency in a second language. She has subsequently taught EFL in Lebanon and has trained ESL, bilingual, and EFL teachers internationally on issues of language and culture education. She has coedited a book on assessment of bilingual students with special needs and has written on topics of literacy, second language acquisition, and holistic teaching approaches. Chair of TESOL's Task Force on Policy and Standards for Pre-K–12 Students from 1994 to 1995, she is currently a member of the resulting ESL Standards and Assessment Project.

Sarah Hudelson is a former elementary school teacher who taught in migrant education and bilingual education programs in Texas and Michigan. She has been a teacher educator in Arizona, Florida, and Texas, and she is currently professor in the Division of Curriculum and Instruction of the College of Education at Arizona State University. She teaches courses in bilingual children's spoken and written first and second language development and carries out research in the same areas. Her publications have appeared in *NABE Journal, TESOL Quarterly, TESOL Journal, Language Arts, The Reading Teacher,* and other journals.

Anne Katz is a senior research associate at ARC Associates in Oakland, California. For over 20 years, she has been involved in second language education in the United States and Brazil, focusing on literacy and assessment issues. She has worked on TESOL's ESL Standards and Assessment Project since 1994.

Natalie Kuhlman is professor of education in the Policy Studies in Language and Cross Cultural Education Department at San Diego State University, in California. She served on the TESOL Board of Directors as affiliate representative (1996–1999) and is a past president of California TESOL (1993–1994). Her research and teaching focus on language policy, assessment, and biliteracy. She serves on a variety of state and national advisory panels related to English language development and to ESL content and teacher standards.

Margaret E. Malone is a language testing specialist for Peace Corps–Worldwide. She has an extensive background in language testing and evaluation, including test development, program evaluation, and classroom-based assessment. She has taught graduate-level courses in language testing and teaching methodology and has worked with TESOL's ESL Standards and Assessment Project since 1995.

Denise E. Murray is professor and chair of the Department of Linguistics and Language Development at San José State University, in California. She has been an ESL teacher and teacher educator for 30 years in Australia, England, Thailand, and the United States. She has been involved in numerous standards projects for both learners and educators, including TESOL's ESL Standards and Assessment Project and the National Council for Accreditation of Teacher Education.

Deborah Short is a division director at the Center for Applied Linguistics in Washington, DC. She has directed the ESL Standards and Assessment Project for TESOL since 1995. Her primary research interest is the integration of language and content in classrooms with English language learners. She also provides professional development and designs curricular and instructional materials.

Index

Bilingualism, 41, 78, 91, 227–28
    additive, 41, 82, 227
    early social approaches to, 91
    in second language acquisition,
        75–76
    subtractive, 41, 233
Bilingual/multicultural program, 46
Bilingual program, 45
Bilingual teacher certification,
    models for, in United States, 43–
    46
Binet, Alfred, 140
Bixby, J., 140, 141
Blake, B. E., 95
Body language, 228
Boswood, T., 8
Bradley, A., 1
Brickman, R. G., 128
Brinton, D. M., 8, 88
Britton, J. N., 86, 87
Brooks, J. G., 7
Brown, A., 143
Brown, J. D., 8, 144
Brown, R., 78–79, 79
Bruner, J. S., 85
Bullock's Report, 87
Bullough, R. V., Jr., 31
Burke, C. L., 88, 96
Burt, M. K., 81
Bush, George, 52
Butler, F. A., 172
Byrne, J. L., 81

C

Calkins, L. M., 94
Canale, M., 142
Cancino, H., 81
Candidate examinations, 26
Carger, C., 97
Carlson, L. M., 11, 12
Carranza, I., 41
Carrell, P. L., 93
Cazden, C. B., 85, 86, 87, 89, 90
Center for Applied Linguistics, 10,
    59
Center for Equity and Excellence in
    Education Test Database, 30

Center for Research on Education,
    Diversity, and Excellence, 44,
    226
Center for Research on Evaluation,
    Standards, and Student Testing,
    226
Center for Research on the Educa-
    tion of Students Placed at Risk,
    226
Center on English Learning and
    Achievement, 226
Chambers, J., 40
Chamot, A. U., 88
Checklists, 157, 160
    for aligning standards and
        assessments, 152
    in application of *ESL Standards*
        during field experiences, 25
    defined, 228
    peer critique, 202, 206
    for reviewing assessment tools,
        30
    for selecting language profi-
        ciency instruments, 30
    in student assessment, 190
Chen, L., 32
Chicago Public Schools, standards
    in, 177
Child-child interaction at school,
    90–91
Children's writing development, 94–
    95
Chinn, P. C., 46
Chomsky, C., 96
Chomsky, Noam, 77–78, 86
Christian, D., 41
Clarity, 164
Clark, E. V., 79
Clark, H. H., 79
Classroom-based assessment, 138.
    See also Assessment
    approaches to, 188–91
    sample application of, 191–208
    using standards for, 187–210
Classrooms
    action research in, 31
    role of social interactions in
        learning in, 100–102

ESL *(continued)*
    use of language by students,
        90–91
English as a second language (ESL)
    Standards Project, 57–63
        basic interpersonal communi-
            cation skills (BICS), 57–58
        cognitive academic language
            proficiency (CALP), 58
        future of, 67
English as a second language
    program, 45
English language arts standards, 55
English language development and
    multicultural program, 45
English language development
    (ELD), 231
English language learner (ELL),
    231
English language proficiency levels,
    defining, 58
English to speakers of other
    languages (ESOL), 229
English to speakers of other
    languages (ESOL) students
        defined, 34–35
        diversity of, and program
            models, 37–42
        educational backgrounds of,
            37
        numbers of, 35–36
        preparing teachers to meet
            needs of, 42–43
        standards-based, large-scale
            assessment of, 167–86
                language proficiency and
                    academic achievement
                    in, 168–70
                options for participation
                    in, 173–74
Enrichment models, forms of, 40–41
Enright, D. S., 87
ERIC, 28
    research using, 30–31
*ERIC Clearinghouse on Assessment and
    Evaluation*, 29
ERIC Digests, 16

ESL standards-based assessment,
    233
        of English to speakers of other
            languages (ESOL) students,
            167–86
        using portfolios for, 182–85
ESL Standards for Pre-K–12 Students,
    v–vi, 25
        action research related to, 31–
            32
        applying, during field experi-
            ence, 22–24
        background of, v–vi
        for classroom-based assess-
            ment, 187–210
        creating, 137
        creating linkages between
            assessment and, in assess-
            ment planning, 152
        in culminating projects and
            research, 26–32
        for curriculum development,
            103–36
        database research on, 30–31
        disseminating, 211–26
            evaluating, 221–23
            framework for, 213–21
            purposes of, 211–13
        goals for second language (L2)
            learners in, v–vi
        history of, 49–74
        impact of, 64–66
        implementation of
            on *ESLSTDS*, 67
            selecting framework for,
                175–77
            success in, 4
            through teacher educa-
                tion, vi
        incorporating, into teacher
            education programs, 1–32
        for in-service teacher, vii–viii
        integrating
            into instructional method-
                ology and assessment
                courses, 18–22
            into specific program
                components, 7–32

Multiple measures, 145, 231

Murray, Denise, 57

"Myths About Second Language Learning," 8

N

National Assessment of Educational Progress (NAEP), 60

National Association for Bilingual Education (NABE), 54, 65, 223

National Association for the Education of Young Children, 14

National Association of Elementary School Principals, 225

National Association of Secondary School Principals, 225

National Association of State Boards of Education, 225

National Board for Professional Teaching Standards (NBPTS), 2, 3–4

English as a New Language Standards for National Board Certification, standards in, 4

National Center for History in the Schools, development of science standards by, 53

National Center on Educational Outcomes, 226

National Centers of Research in Education, 226

National Clearinghouse for Bilingual Education, 16

National Commission on Excellence in Education, 49

National Commission on Teaching and America's Future (NCTAF), 1, 2

What Matters Most: Teaching for America's Future, 42

National Council for Accreditation of Teacher Education (NCATE) standards, 2–3, 15
  on field experiences, 22
  purpose of, 2
  and teacher education programs, 2–4

National Council for Geographic Education, development of geography standards, 55

National Council for Teachers of English, 223

National Council for the Social Studies, 61, 224

National Council of Teachers of English (NCTE), development of science standards by, 53

National Council of Teachers of English (NCTE)-International Reading Association (IRA) English language arts standards, 61

National Council of Teachers of Mathematics (NCTM), 66, 225
  development of math standards by, 50, 53
  development of standards by, 52

National education goals, 69
  defining, 52

The National Education Goals Report: Building a Nation of Learners, 52

National Geography Society, development of geography standards, 55

National Governors' Association Education Summit, 52

National Languages and Literacy Institute, 56

National Middle School Association, 225

National Research Council, development of science standards by, 53

National School Boards Association, 225

National Science Education Standards, 53

National Science Teachers Association, 217, 225

National Study of School Evaluation (NSSE), 11
  Indicators of Schools of Quality, Volume I: Schoolwide Indicators of Quality, 66

Also Available from TESOL

ESL Standards for Pre-K–12 Students
TESOL

New Ways in Content-Based Instruction
Donna M. Brinton and Peter Master, Editors

New Ways in English for Specific Purposes
Peter Master and Donna M. Brinton, Editors

New Ways in Teaching Adults
Marilyn Lewis, Editor

New Ways in Teaching English at the Secondary Level
Deborah J. Short, Editor

New Ways in Using Authentic Materials in the Classroom
Ruth E. Larimer and Leigh Schleicher, Editors

New Ways in Using Communicative Games in Language Teaching
Nikhat Shameem and Makhan Tickoo, Editors

New Ways of Classroom Assessment
James Dean Brown, Editor

Reading and Writing in More Than One Language: Lessons for Teachers
Elizabeth Franklin, Editor

■ 277

Teacher Education
Karen E. Johnson, Editor

Teaching in Action: Case Studies From Second Language Classrooms
Jack C. Richards, Editor

Training Others to Use the ESL Standards:
A Professional Development Manual
Deborah J. Short, Emily L. Gómez, Nancy Cloud,
Anne Katz, Margo Gottlieb, Margaret Malone

For more information, contact
Teachers of English to Speakers of Other Languages, Inc.
700 South Washington Street, Suite 200
Alexandria, Virginia 22314 USA
Tel 703-836-0774 • Fax 703-836-6447
publ@tesol.edu • http://www.tesol.edu/

Founded 1966